Australia's Grand Slam
Tennis Champions

John Coomer

© John Coomer

The moral rights of the author have been asserted. All rights reserved. No part of this publication may be reproduced, stored in or introduced into a retrieval system or transmitted in any form or by any means (electronic, mechanical, photocopying, recording or otherwise) without the prior written permission of the copyright owner of this book.

First published in 2023 and updated at the end of each calendar year.

Publisher: JC Editorial (www.jceditorial.com)
For all enquiries: info@jceditorial.com

A catalogue record for this book is available from the National Library of Australia

Licensed cover images (from left to right, see credits at the back of the book):
Norman Brookes, Jack Crawford, Nancy Wynne (Bolton), Frank Sedgman, Ken Rosewall, Mervyn Rose, Lew Hoad, Ashley Cooper, Neale Fraser, Rod Laver, Roy Emerson, Margaret Smith (Court), Lesley Turner (Bowrey), Fred Stolle, John Newcombe, Evonne Goolagong (Cawley), Pat Cash, Pat Rafter, Mark Woodforde, Todd Woodbridge, Lleyton Hewitt, Sam Stosur, Dylan Alcott, Ash Barty.

Contents

Part 1 — Singles in the Amateur Era (pre-April 1968) — 1

Chapter 1 — The Majors and the Aussie Male Pioneers (1905–1952) — 3
  The Australasian/Australian Championships — 3
    Multiple Aussie Champions — Australasian/Australian Men's Singles Championships: 1905–1952 — 4
      Jack Crawford (4 titles) — 4
      James Anderson (3 titles) — 5
      Adrian Quist (3 titles) — 5
      Rodney Heath (2 titles) — 6
      Pat O'Hara Wood (2 titles) — 6
      John Bromwich (2 titles) — 7
      Frank Sedgman (2 titles) — 8
    All Aussie Champions — Australasian/Australian Men's Singles Championships: 1905–1952 — 9
    Multiple Aussie Runners-Up — Australasian/Australian Men's Singles Championships: 1905–1952 — 9
      Harry Hopman — 10
      Horace Rice — 10
      Gerald Patterson — 11
      Richard Schlesinger — 11
      Ken McGregor — 11
    All Aussie Runners-Up — Australasian/Australian Men's Singles Championships: 1905–1952 — 12
  Pioneering Aussie Men at the French Championships (1905–1952) — 13
    Jack Crawford — 13
    Frank Sedgman — 14
  Pioneering Aussie Men at Wimbledon (1905–1952) — 14

Norman Brookes	*15*
Gerald Patterson (2 titles)	*16*
Jack Crawford	*16*
Frank Sedgman	*17*
Geoff Brown	*17*
John Bromwich	*18*
Ken McGregor	*18*

Pioneering Aussie Men at the US Championships (1905–1952) — 19
Jack Crawford — *19*
Frank Sedgman (2 titles) — *20*

Chapter 2 — The Majors and the Aussie Female Pioneers (1922–1959) — 21
Multiple Aussie Champions
Australasian/Australian Women's Singles Championships: 1922–1959 — 21

Nancye Wynne (Bolton) – 6 titles	*22*
Daphne Akhurst (Cozens) – 5 titles	*23*
Joan Hartigan (Bathurst) – (3 titles)	*23*
Margaret Mutch (Molesworth) – 2 titles	*24*
Coral McInnes (Buttsworth) – 2 titles	*24*
Thelma Coyne (Long) – 2 titles	*24*
Mary Carter (Reitano) – 2 titles	*25*

All Aussie Champions — Australasian/Australian Women's Singles Championships: 1922–1959 — 26
Multiple Aussie Runners-Up — Australasian/Australian Women's Singles Championships: 1922–1959 — 26

Esna Boyd (Robertson) — *27*
Sylvia Lance (Harper) — *27*
Nell Hall (Hopman) — *28*

All Aussie Runners-Up — Australasian/Australian Women's Singles Championships: 1922–1959 — 29

The French Championships, Wimbledon and the US Championships — 29
Nancye Wynne (Bolton) — *30*

Chapter 3 — Aussie Men at the Majors (1953–January 1968) — 31
Multiple Aussie Champions — Australian Men's Singles Championships: 1953–January 1968 — 31

Roy Emerson (6 titles) — *32*
Ken Rosewall (2 titles) — *33*
Rod Laver (2 titles) — *33*

Contents

Ashley Cooper (2 titles)	*34*
All Aussie Australian Champions Australian Men's Singles Championships: 1953–January 1968	35
Multiple Aussie Runners-Up — Australian Men's Singles Championships: 1953–January 1968	**35**
Neale Fraser	*35*
Fred Stolle	*36*
All Aussie Runners-Up — Australian Men's Singles Championships: 1953–January 1968	37
All Aussie French Champions — French Championships: 1953–1967	**38**
Roy Emerson (2 titles)	*39*
Ken Rosewall	*39*
Rod Laver	*40*
Lew Hoad	*41*
Mervyn Rose	*41*
Fred Stolle	*42*
Tony Roche	*42*
All Aussie Wimbledon Champions (1953–1967)	**43**
Rod Laver (2 titles)	*44*
Lew Hoad (2 titles)	*44*
Roy Emerson (2 titles)	*45*
Ashley Cooper	*46*
Neale Fraser	*46*
John Newcombe	*47*
All Aussie Wimbledon Runners-Up (1953–1967)	**47**
Ken Rosewall	*48*
Fred Stolle	*48*
Marty Mulligan	*49*
All Aussie US Champions — US Championships: 1953–1967	**50**
Neale Fraser (2 titles)	*51*
Roy Emerson (2 titles)	*51*
Ken Rosewall	*52*
Rod Laver	*53*
John Newcombe	*54*
Mal Anderson	*54*
Ashley Cooper	*55*
Fred Stolle	*55*
All Aussie US Championship Runners-Up (1953–1967)	**56**

Rex Hartwig	*57*
Lew Hoad	*57*
The Aussie Pro Pioneers	**58**

Chapter 4 — Aussie Women at the Majors (1960–January 1968) — 61

The Australian Championships (1960–January 1968) — 61
Margaret Smith (Court) – 7 titles — *62*
Jan Lehane (O'Neill) — *63*
Lesley Turner (Bowrey) — *63*

The French Championships (1960–1967) — 64
Margaret Smith (Court) – 2 titles — *64*
Lesley Turner (Bowrey) – 2 titles — *65*

Wimbledon (1960–1967) — 66
Margaret Smith (Court) – 2 titles — *66*

The US Championships (1960–1967) — 68
Margaret Smith (Court) – 2 titles — *68*

Part 2 — Singles in the Open Era (April 1968 onwards) — 71

Chapter 5 — Aussie Men at the Majors (April 1968–1986) — 73

The French Open (1968–1986) — 74
Ken Rosewall — *75*
Rod Laver — *75*

Wimbledon (1968–1986) — 76
Rod Laver — *77*
John Newcombe — *77*
Tony Roche — *79*
Ken Rosewall — *79*

The US Open (1968–1986) — 80
Rod Laver — *80*
Ken Rosewall — *82*
John Newcombe — *83*
Tony Roche — *83*

The Australian Open (1969–1986) — 83
Ken Rosewall (2 titles) — *85*
John Newcombe (2 titles) — *85*
Rod Laver — *86*
Mark Edmondson — *87*

Chapter 6 — Aussie Women at the Majors (April 1968–1986) — 89
The French Open (1968–1986) — 90
- *Margaret Smith (Court) – 2 titles* — 90
- *Evonne Goolagong (Cawley)* — 91
- *Helen Gourlay (Cawley)* — 92
- *Wendy Turnbull* — 93

Wimbledon (1968–1986) — 93
- *Evonne Goolagong (Cawley) – 2 titles* — 93
- *Margaret Smith (Court)* — 95
- *Judy Tegart (Dalton)* — 96

The US Open (1968–1986) — 97
- *Margaret Smith (Court) – 3 titles* — 97
- *Evonne Goolagong (Cawley)* — 99
- *Kerry Melville (Reid)* — 100
- *Wendy Turnbull* — 100

The Australian Open (1969–1986) — 101
- *Margaret Smith (Court) – 4 titles* — 102
- *Evonne Goolagong (Cawley) – 4 titles* — 103
- *Kerry Melville (Reid)* — 104
- *Chris O'Neil* — 104

Chapter 7 — Aussie Men and Women at the Majors (1987–Present Day) — 107
The Australian Open (1987–Present Day) — 107
- *Ash Barty* — 108
- *Pat Cash* — 109
- *Lleyton Hewitt* — 110

The French Open (1987–Present Day) — 111
- *Ash Barty* — 111
- *Sam Stosur* — 112

Wimbledon (1987–Present Day) — 113
- *Pat Cash* — 113
- *Lleyton Hewitt* — 114
- *Ash Barty* — 115
- *Pat Rafter* — 116
- *Mark Philippoussis* — 118
- *Nick Kyrgios* — 118

The US Open (1987–Present Day) — 119
- *Pat Rafter (2 titles)* — 120
- *Lleyton Hewitt* — 121

Sam Stosur	*122*
Mark Philippoussis	*124*

Aussie Wheelchair and Quad Tennis Pioneers at the Majors (2002–Present Day) — **124**

David Hall – Wheelchair Tennis	*125*
Dylan Alcott – Wheelchair Quad Tennis	*126*
Danni Di Toro – Wheelchair Tennis	*128*
Heath Davidson – Wheelchair Quad Tennis	*129*

Top All-Time Aussie Grand Slam Singles Winners (Men and Women)* — **129**
Aussie Winners of at least 2 of the 4 Grand Slam Singles Titles* — **132**
Top Aussie Australian Open Singles Winners (Men and Women)* — **133**
Top Aussie French Open Singles Winners (Men and Women)* — **134**
Top Aussie Wimbledon Singles Winners (Men and Women)* — **135**
Top Aussie US Open Singles Winners (Men and Women)* — **136**

Part 3 — Doubles in the Amateur Era (pre-April 1968) — 139

Chapter 8 — Aussies in Grand Slam Men's Doubles (Amateur Era) — 141

Multiple Aussie Men's Doubles Champions
Australasian/Australian Championships: 1905–1968 — **141**

Adrian Quist (10 titles) and John Bromwich (8 titles)	*142*
Gerald Patterson (5 titles) and John Hawkes (3 titles)	*143*
Pat O'Hara Wood (4 titles) and Ron Thomas (2 titles)	*143*
Jack Crawford (4 titles) and Harry Hopman (2 titles)	*144*
Lew Hoad (3 titles) and Ken Rosewall (2 titles)	*144*
Neale Fraser (3 titles)	*145*
Rod Laver and Bob Mark (3 titles)	*146*
Fred Stolle (3 titles) and Bob Hewitt (2 titles)	*146*
Rodney Heath (2 titles)	*147*
Ernie Parker (2 titles)	*147*
Ashley Campbell (2 titles) and Horace Rice (2 titles)	*147*
Frank Sedgman and Ken McGregor (2 titles)	*148*
Roy Emerson (2 titles)	*148*
John Newcombe and Tony Roche (2 titles)	*149*

All Aussie Men's Doubles Champions — Australasian/Australian Championships: 1905–1968 — **150**
Aussie Men's Doubles Runners-Up — Australasian/Australian Championships: 1905–1968 — **151**

Contents

Aussie Men's Doubles Champions — French Championships: Amateur Era pre-1968 — *152*
    Roy Emerson (6 titles) — *153*
    Neale Fraser (3 titles) — *153*
    Frank Sedgman and Ken McGregor (2 titles) — *154*
    Ashley Cooper (2 titles) — *154*
    Jack Crawford and Adrian Quist — *155*
    Ken Rosewall and Lew Hoad — *155*
    Don Candy — *156*
    Mal Anderson — *156*
    Rod Laver — *157*
    Ken Fletcher — *157*
    Fred Stolle — *157*
    John Newcombe and Tony Roche — *158*
  Aussie Men's Doubles Runners-Up — French Championships: Amateur Era pre-1968 — *158*

Aussie Men's Doubles Champions — Wimbledon: Amateur Era pre-1968 — *159*
    Frank Sedgman (3 titles) and Ken McGregor (2 titles) — *160*
    Lew Hoad (3 titles) and Ken Rosewall (2 titles) — *161*
    Norman Brookes (2 titles) — *161*
    Adrian Quist (2 titles) — *162*
    John Bromwich (2 titles) — *162*
    Rex Hartwig (2 titles) — *163*
    Roy Emerson and Neale Fraser (2 titles) — *163*
    Fred Stolle and Bob Hewitt* (2 titles) — *164*
    John Newcombe (2 titles) and Tony Roche (1 title) — *165*
    Pat O'Hara Wood and Ron Thomas — *165*
    James Anderson — *166*
    Jack Crawford — *166*
    Mervyn Rose — *166*
    Ken Fletcher — *167*
  Aussie Men's Doubles Runners-Up — Wimbledon: Amateur Era pre-1968 — *167*

Aussie Men's Doubles Champions — US Championships: Amateur Era pre-1968 — *168*
    Roy Emerson (4 titles) — *168*
    John Bromwich (3 titles) — *169*
    Neale Fraser (3 titles) — *169*
    Frank Sedgman (2 titles) and Ken McGregor (1 title) — *170*

    Mervyn Rose (2 titles)   171
    Fred Stolle (2 titles)   171
    Gerald Patterson and Norman Brookes   172
    Adrian Quist   172
    Bill Sidwell   173
    Rex Hartwig   173
    Ken Rosewall and Lew Hoad   174
    Ashley Cooper   174
    John Newcombe and Tony Roche   175
  Aussie Men's Doubles Runners-Up — US Championships: Amateur Era pre–1968   175

Chapter 9 — Aussies in Grand Slam Women's Doubles (Amateur Era)   177
  Multiple Aussie Women's Doubles Champions — Australasian/Australian Championships: 1922–1968   177
    Thelma Coyne (Long) – 12 titles and Nancye Wynne (Bolton) – 10 titles   178
    Mary Bevis (Hawton) – 5 titles   179
    Esna Boyd (Robertson) – 4 titles   179
    Daphne Akhurst (Cozens) – 4 titles   180
    Margaret Smith (Court) – 4 titles   180
    Louie Bickerton (Cozens) – 3 titles   181
    Margaret Mutch (Molesworth) and Emily Hood (Westacott) – 3 titles   181
    Lesley Turner (Bowrey) – 3 titles and Judy Tegart (Dalton) – 2 titles   181
    Sylvia Lance (Harper) – 2 titles   182
    Meryl Waxman (O'Hara Wood) – 2 titles   182
    Beryl Penrose (Collier) – 2 titles   182
    Robyn Ebbern (Vincenzi) – 2 titles   183
    Judy Tegart (Dalton) – 2 titles   183
  All Aussie Women's Doubles Champions — Australasian/Australian Championships: 1905–1968   183
  Aussie Women's Doubles Runners-Up — Australasian/Australian Championships: 1922–1968   185

Aussie Women's Doubles Champions — French Championships: Amateur Era pre–1968   187
    Margaret Smith (Court) – 3 titles and Lesley Turner (Bowrey) – 2 titles   187
    Nell Hall (Hopman)   188
    Judy Tegart (Dalton)   188
  Aussie Women's Doubles Runners-Up — French Championships: Amateur Era pre–1968   189

Contents

Aussie Women's Doubles Champions — Wimbledon: Amateur Era pre-1968   **189**
    Margaret Smith (Court) and Lesley Turner (Bowrey)   *190*
  Aussie Women's Doubles Runners-Up — Wimbledon: Amateur Era pre-1968   191
Aussie Women's Doubles Champions — US Championships: Amateur Era pre-1968   **191**
    Lesley Turner (Bowrey)   *191*
    Margaret Smith (Court) and Robyn Ebbern (Vincenzi)   *192*
  Aussie Women's Doubles Runners-Up — US Championships: Amateur Era pre-1968   192

Chapter 10 — Aussies in Grand Slam Mixed Doubles (Amateur Era)   **193**
  Multiple Aussie Mixed Champions — Australasian/Australian Championships: 1922–1968   193
    Daphne Akhurst (Cozens) – 4 titles   *194*
    Nell Hall (Hopman) and Harry Hopman (4 titles)   *194*
    Nancye Wynne (Bolton) and Colin Long (4 titles)   *195*
    Thelma Coyne (Long) – 4 titles and George Worthington (3 titles)   *195*
    Esna Boyd (Robertson) and John Hawkes (3 titles)   *196*
    Marjorie Cox (Crawford) and Jack Crawford (3 titles)   *196*
    Margaret Smith (Court) – 3 titles and Ken Fletcher (2 titles)   *197*
    Jim Willard (2 titles)   *197*
    Edgar Moon (2 titles)   *198*
    Frank Sedgman (2 titles)   *198*
    Rex Hartwig (2 titles)   *199*
    Jan Lehane (O'Neill) – 2 titles   *199*
    Lesley Turner (Bowrey) – 2 titles   *199*
    Owen Davidson (2 titles)   *200*
  All Aussie Mixed Doubles Champions — Australasian/Australian Championships: 1922–1968   200
  Aussie Mixed Doubles Runners-Up — Australasian/Australian Championships: 1922–1968   202
Aussie Mixed Doubles Champions — French Championships: Amateur Era pre-1968   **204**
    Margaret Smith (Court) and Ken Fletcher (3 titles)   *204*
    Frank Sedgman (2 titles)   *205*
    Bob Howe (2 titles)   *205*
    Jack Crawford   *206*
    Lew Hoad   *206*
    Thelma Coyne (Long)   *206*

Rod Laver	*207*
Owen Davidson	*207*
Aussie Mixed Doubles Runners-Up — French Championships: Amateur Era pre–1968	207

Aussie Mixed Doubles Champions — Wimbledon: Amateur Era pre-1968 — **208**

Margaret Smith (Court) and Ken Fletcher (3 titles)	*209*
John Bromwich (2 titles)	*210*
Frank Sedgman (2 titles)	*210*
Rod Laver (2 titles)	*211*
Lesley Turner (Bowrey) and Fred Stolle (2 titles)	*211*
Gerald Patterson	*212*
Pat O'Hara Wood	*212*
Jack Crawford	*212*
Mervyn Rose	*212*
Lorraine Coghlan (Robinson) and Bob Howe	*213*
Neale Fraser	*213*
Owen Davidson	*213*
Aussie Mixed Doubles Runners-Up — Wimbledon: Amateur Era pre–1968	214

Aussie Mixed Doubles Champions — US Championships: Amateur Era pre-1968 — **215**

Margaret Smith (Court) – 5 titles	*215*
Neale Fraser (3 titles)	*216*
John Hawkes (2 titles)	*216*
Frank Sedgman (2 titles)	*217*
Fred Stolle (2 titles)	*217*
Owen Davidson (2 titles)	*217*
Edward Dewhurst	*218*
Harry Hopman	*218*
John Bromwich	*219*
Ken McGregor	*219*
Ken Rosewall	*219*
Bob Mark	*220*
Ken Fletcher	*220*
John Newcombe	*220*
Aussie Mixed Doubles Runners-Up — US Championships: Amateur Era pre–1968	221

Contents

Part 4 — Doubles in the Open Era (April 1968 onwards) — 223

Chapter 11 — Aussies in Grand Slam Men's Doubles (Open Era) — 225
Aussie Men's Doubles Champions — French Open: 1968–Present Day — 225
- John Newcombe (2 titles) and Tony Roche — 226
- John Fitzgerald (2 titles) — 226
- Ken Rosewall and Fred Stolle — 227
- Dick Crealy — 227
- Mark Edmondson and Kim Warwick — 227
- Todd Woodbridge and Mark Woodforde — 228

Aussie Men's Doubles Runners-Up — French Open: 1968–Present Day — 228

Aussie Men's Doubles Champions — Wimbledon: 1968–Present Day — 229
- Todd Woodbridge (9 titles) and Mark Woodforde (6 titles) — 230
- John Newcombe and Tony Roche (4 titles) — 231
- Peter McNamara and Paul McNamee (2 titles) — 231
- John Fitzgerald (2 titles) — 231
- Roy Emerson and Rod Laver — 232
- Geoff Masters and Ross Case — 232
- Stephen Huss — 232
- Matthew Ebden and Max Purcell — 233

Aussie Men's Doubles Runners-Up — Wimbledon: 1968–Present Day — 234

Aussie Men's Doubles Champions — US Open: 1968–Present Day — 234
- Todd Woodbridge (3 titles) and Mark Woodforde (3 titles) — 235
- John Newcombe (2 titles) — 235
- John Fitzgerald (2 titles) — 236
- Ken Rosewall and Fred Stolle — 236
- Owen Davidson — 237
- Sandon Stolle — 237
- Lleyton Hewitt — 237
- Max Purcell and Jordan Thompson — 238

Aussie Men's Doubles Runners-Up — US Open: 1968–Present Day — 238

Multiple Aussie Men's Doubles Champions — Australian Open: 1968–Present Day — 239
- Mark Edmondson (4 titles) and Kim Warwick (3 titles) — 239
- John Newcombe (3 titles) and Tony Roche (3 titles) — 240
- Todd Woodbridge (3 titles) and Mark Woodforde (2 titles) — 241
- John Alexander (2 titles) — 241
- Paul McNamee (2 titles) — 241

All Aussie Men's Doubles Champions	
Australian Open: 1969–Present Day	242
Aussie Men's Doubles Runners-Up	
Australian Open: 1969–Present Day	243

Aussie Men's Wheelchair and Quad Doubles at the Majors (2004–Present Day) — 244

Dylan Alcott (8 titles) and Heath Davidson (4 titles) — 245

Top All-Time Aussie Men's Grand Slam Doubles Winners* — 246

Top All-Time All-Aussie Men's Grand Slam Doubles Teams* — 248

Aussie Winners of at least 2 of the 4 Grand Slam Men's Doubles Titles* — 249

Top All-Time Aussie Australian Men's Doubles Winners* — 250

Top All-Time Aussie French Men's Doubles Winners* — 252

Top All-Time Aussie Wimbledon Men's Doubles Winners* — 253

Top All-Time Aussie US Men's Doubles Winners* — 254

Chapter 12 — Aussies in Grand Slam Women's Doubles (Open Era) — 257

Aussie Women's Doubles Champions — French Open: 1968–Present Day — 257

Margaret Smith (Court) — 257
Wendy Turnbull — 258
Sam Stosur — 258
Alicia Molik — 258

Aussie Women's Doubles Runners-Up — French Open: 1968–Present Day — 259

Aussie Women's Doubles Champions — Wimbledon: 1968–Present Day — 260

Rennae Stubbs (2 titles) — 260
Margaret Smith (Court) and Judy Tegart (Dalton) — 261
Evonne Goolagong (Cawley) — 261
Helen Gourlay (Cawley) — 261
Kerry Melville (Reid) and Wendy Turnbull — 262
Liz Sayers (Smylie) — 262

Aussie Women's Doubles Runners-Up — Wimbledon: 1968–Present Day — 263

Aussie Women's Doubles Champions — US Open: 1968–Present Day — 264

Margaret Smith (Court) – 4 titles — 264
Judy Tegart (Dalton) – 2 titles — 265
Wendy Turnbull – 2 titles — 265
Sam Stosur – 2 titles — 265
Rennae Stubbs — 266
Ash Barty — 266

Aussie Women's Doubles Runners-Up — US Open: 1968–Present Day — 266

Contents

Multiple Aussie Women's Doubles Champions — Australian Open: 1968–Present Day   **268**
- *Evonne Goolagong (Cawley) – 5 titles*   268
- *Margaret Smith (Court) – 4 titles and Judy Tegart (Dalton) – 2 titles*   269
- *Helen Gourlay (Cawley) – 4 titles*   269

All Aussie Women's Doubles Champions — Australian Open: 1969–Present Day   270

Aussie Women's Doubles Runners-Up — Australian Open: 1969–Present Day   271

Aussie Women's Wheelchair Doubles at the Majors (2004–Present Day)   **272**
- *Danni Di Toro – Wheelchair Tennis*   272

Top All-Time Aussie Women's Grand Slam Doubles Winners*   **273**

Top All-Time All-Aussie Women's Grand Slam Doubles Teams*   **274**

Aussie Winners of at least 2 of the 4 Grand Slam Women's Doubles Titles*   **274**

Top All-Time Aussie Australian Women's Doubles Winners*   **275**

Top All-Time Aussie French Women's Doubles Winners*   **276**

Top All-Time Aussie Wimbledon Women's Doubles Winners*   **276**

Top All-Time Aussie US Women's Doubles Winners*   **277**

Chapter 13 — Aussies in Grand Slam Mixed Doubles (Open Era)   **279**

Aussie Mixed Doubles Champions — French Open: 1968–Present Day   **279**
- *Kim Warwick (2 titles)*   279
- *Wendy Turnbull (2 titles)*   280
- *Margaret Smith (Court)*   280
- *Evonne Goolagong (Cawley)*   280
- *Todd Woodbridge*   281
- *Mark Woodforde*   281
- *Casey Dellacqua*   282

Aussie Mixed Doubles Runners-Up — French Open: 1968–Present Day   282

Aussie Mixed Doubles Champions — Wimbledon: 1968–Present Day   **282**
- *Margaret Smith (Court) – (2 titles) and Ken Fletcher*   283
- *Wendy Turnbull (2 titles)*   284
- *Sam Stosur (2 titles)*   284
- *Fred Stolle*   284
- *Owen Davidson*   285
- *Tony Roche*   285
- *Paul McNamee*   285
- *Liz Sayers (Smylie) and John Fitzgerald*   286
- *Mark Woodforde*   286

Todd Woodbridge	*286*
Aussie Mixed Doubles Runners-Up — Wimbledon: 1968–Present Day	287
Aussie Mixed Doubles Champions — US Open: 1968–Present Day	**288**
Margaret Smith (Court) – 3 titles	*288*
Todd Woodbridge (3 titles)	*289*
Owen Davidson (2 titles)	*289*
Liz Sayers (Smylie) – 2 titles and John Fitzgerald	*289*
Geoff Masters	*290*
Phil Dent	*290*
Wendy Turnbull	*291*
Nicole Provis (Bradtke) and Mark Woodforde	*291*
Rennae Stubbs	*291*
Storm Sanders (Hunter) and John Peers	*292*
Aussie Mixed Doubles Runners-Up — US Open: 1968–Present Day	292
Multiple Aussie Mixed Doubles Champions — Australian Open: 1968–Present Day	**293**
Mark Woodforde – 2 titles	*293*
All Aussie Mixed Doubles Champions Australian Open: 1969–Present Day	294
Aussie Mixed Doubles Runners-Up Australian Open: 1969–Present Day	294
Top All-Time Aussie Grand Slam Mixed Doubles Winners*	**295**
Top All-Time All-Aussie Grand Slam Mixed Doubles Teams*	**296**
Aussie Winners of at least 2 of the 4 Grand Slam Mixed Doubles Titles*	**296**
Top All-Time Aussie Australian Mixed Doubles Winners*	**297**
Top All-Time Aussie French Mixed Doubles Winners*	**298**
Top All-Time Aussie Wimbledon Mixed Doubles Winners*	**299**
Top All-Time Aussie US Mixed Doubles Winners*	**299**
Chapter 14 — The Greatest Aussie Grand Slam Winners of All Time	**301**
Image Credits	**305**
Endnotes	**307**

Part 1
Singles in the Amateur Era
(pre-April 1968)

Chapter 1
The Majors and the Aussie Male Pioneers
(1905–1952)

Wimbledon, and the US, French and Australian Opens are the major Grand Slam tournaments in world tennis. They have captured the imaginations of tennis players and fans for generations. Winning any one of these "majors" is a career highlight for any player, whether it be in singles or doubles. These tournaments are where all the best players dream of playing and winning almost as soon as they pick up a racquet.

Here's a brief look at the history of each major in turn, along with the Aussie pioneers at each one. They blazed a trail for future generations of players all over the world to follow.

The Australasian/Australian Championships

What we now know as the Australian Open began as the Australasian Championships in 1905, just 4 years after Federation in Australia. Traditionally played on grass courts (and in different cities in the early years in both Australia and New Zealand), the event was officially sanctioned as a tennis major in 1924 by the International Lawn Tennis Federation. It was renamed the Australian Championships in 1927, and the Australian Open in 1969.[1]

Not surprisingly (given our geographic isolation and the travel limitations of the early 20th century), our Aussie tennis pioneers dominated the early decades of our local major. Aussie players won 29 of the 38 singles tournaments played between 1905 and 1952. The annual event was suspended during both World War I and World War II.

Multiple Aussie Champions
Australasian/Australian Men's Singles Championships: 1905–1952

Multiple Aussie winners of our premier tennis tournament for men during the 1905–1952 era were:

- Jack Crawford (4)
- James Anderson (3)
- Adrian Quist (3)
- Rodney Heath (2)
- Pat O'Hara Wood (2)
- John Bromwich (2)
- Frank Sedgman (2).[2]

Both Adrian Quist and John Bromwich won the tournament either side of World War II, so would likely have won more but for the global conflict.

Victorian Rodney Heath won the first ever event in 1905 when 17 players competed in an unseeded tournament.[3] He was just 21 years old at the time.

New South Welshman James Anderson won in 1924 when the then Australasian Championships was first designated as a major. He was the top seed and there were 40 competitors.[4]

Jack Crawford (4 titles)

New South Welshman Jack Crawford had an incredible 6-year stretch at the Australian Championships (as it was then known) in the 1930s.

He won the singles event 3 times in a row from 1931-33, then lost the 1934 final, before bouncing back to win his fourth crown in 1935. He was runner-up again in 1936, and once more in 1940 in the last year before the tournament was suspended for World War II.

As you'll see later in this chapter, Jack Crawford also made an impact at Wimbledon and the French and US Championships in the 1930s. He narrowly missed becoming the first player in the world to achieve the Grand Slam of winning all 4 majors in a calendar year in 1933 when he was ranked as the world's number 1 male singles player.

Jack Crawford was a true Australian pioneer on the world tennis stage.[5]

James Anderson (3 titles)

James Anderson made 3 finals of the Australasian Championships (as it was known in the 1920s) in a 4-year period, and won all 3 (1922, 1924 and 1925).

None of his finals' victories came easily. He was taken to 5 sets twice, and 4 sets once.

Tall, lean and fast, Anderson's nickname was "The Greyhound", and his strong forehand was a feature of his game.[6]

Adrian Quist (3 titles)

Three-time champion Adrian Quist was a South Australian who had the distinction of beating Jack Crawford in two of his finals' victories, and two-time champion John Bromwich in the other.

Both players took him to 5 sets – Crawford in 1936 and Bromwich in 1948. Quist was 35 years old in his 1948 victory and Bromwich was nearly 6 years younger. Bromwich had defeated him in the 1939 final in straight sets.

Arguably his career-best performance though was his 1940 straight sets victory over Crawford. He was 27 at the time and in his prime, but World War II forced the cancellation of the Australian Championships for the next 5 years.

As you'll see in Chapter 8 of this book, Quist also had a lot of success at the majors as a doubles player, especially with fellow Aussie pioneer John Bromwich.[7]

Rodney Heath (2 titles)

The inaugural winner of the then Australasian Championships in 1905, Rodney Heath defeated New South Welshman Albert Curtis in 4 sets in the final in his home city of Melbourne.

Being the Australasian Championships back then, the second ever tournament was held in New Zealand the next year. Heath was the only Australian to cross the ditch and enter in an attempt to defend his title, but he was beaten in 5 sets in the first round in an 8-man draw.[8]

He didn't compete in the tournament again until 1910, when we won his second title in a 14-man draw. The 1910 event was held at the Adelaide Oval.[9]

Pat O'Hara Wood (2 titles)

Pat O'Hara Wood was the younger brother of 1914 Australasian Championship winner Arthur O'Hara Wood (who was tragically killed in World War I in 1918 aged 28).[10]

Pat also served in World War I[11] but survived and returned to win the Australasian Championship final in 1920 in 5 sets. He won the title for the second time with a straight sets victory in the final in 1923. Who knows how many titles the Victorian brothers may have won between them but for World War I.

John Bromwich (2 titles)

New South Welshman John Bromwich won the first of his 2 Australian Championships in 1939 when he was just twenty years old. He beat Adrian Quist in straight sets in the final, and he didn't drop a set in the entire tournament.

His victory came on the back of him losing the 2 previous Australian Championship finals in 1937 and 1938, including a 5-setter in 1937 when he was just 18. The 1938 final pitted him against top-seeded American Don Budge, who beat him in straight sets on his way to becoming the first player in history to win a calendar year Grand Slam.[12]

Bromwich had an unusual style, serving right-handed but having a left-handed forehand. He was also one of the first players to use a double-handed backhand.[13]

His second singles title came in 1946 when the tournament resumed after World War II. He won the final in 5 sets. But for World War II, John Bromwich would have likely won many more singles finals at the Australian Championships.

He also lost a further 3 consecutive finals in 1947, 1948 and 1949, coming agonisingly close to winning his third Australian title in both 1947 and 1948. He lost the final in 5 sets in both years.

In Chapter 8, you'll find out all about John Bromwich's incredible doubles success at the majors, especially with fellow Aussie Adrian Quist.

Frank Sedgman (2 titles)

Victorian Frank Sedgman won 2 Australian Championships in a row in 1949 and 1950 in the early years of his tennis career. He helped to usher in a golden age for Australian tennis on the world stage in the 1950s, as you'll see in Chapter 3.

However, his opportunity to win more majors was taken away when he opted to turn professional in his prime at the age of 25 in 1953. He was subsequently banned from competing in all 4 of the then amateur majors. Professionals weren't allowed to compete in them until 1968.

Frank Sedgman would have no doubt won many more majors had he stayed an amateur, but he was a pioneer of pro tennis globally, as well as Australian tennis.

Sedgman was also one of the pioneers of the serve and volley style.[14] His first Australian Championship final came in 1949 when he was just 21 and the fourth seed at the event. He beat top seed John Bromwich in straight sets. He went back-to-back as the fifth seed a year later in the singles final against the man who became his long-term men's doubles partner, fellow Aussie Ken McGregor, who was unseeded.

And as you'll see in Chapters 8 and 10, he won both calendar year and career Grand Slams in men's doubles, and career Grand Slams in mixed doubles.

Chapter 1 – The Majors and the Aussie Male Pioneers (1905–1952)

All Aussie Champions
Australasian/Australian Men's Singles Championships: 1905–1952

The following table lists all of the Aussie men's singles winners at the Australasian or Australian Championships (as the Australian Open was called in the pioneering years (1905–1952). No Australians competed at the 1912 event held in New Zealand.[15]

Year	Winner	Year	Winner
1905	Rodney Heath	1930	Edgar Moon
1907	Horace Rice	1931	Jack Crawford
1910	Rodney Heath	1932	Jack Crawford
1911	Norman Brookes	1933	Jack Crawford
1913	Ernie Parker	1935	Jack Crawford
1914	Arthur O'Hara Wood	1936	Adrian Quist
1920	Pat O'Hara Wood	1937	Vivian McGrath
1921	Rhys Gemmel	1939	John Bromwich
1922	James Anderson	1940	Adrian Quist
1923	Pat O'Hara Wood	1946	John Bromwich
1924	James Anderson	1947	Dinny Pails
1925	James Anderson	1948	Adrian Quist
1926	John Hawkes	1949	Frank Sedgman
1927	Gerald Patterson	1950	Frank Sedgman
		1952	Ken McGregor

Multiple Aussie Runners-Up
Australasian/Australian Men's Singles Championships: 1905–1952

Multiple Aussie runners-up in our premier tennis tournament for men during the 1905–1952 era were:

- John Bromwich (5, including 3 years in a row)
- Harry Hopman (3 years in a row)
- Jack Crawford (3)
- Horace Rice (3)
- Gerald Patterson (3)

- Richard Schlesinger (2)
- Ken McGregor.[16]

Harry Hopman and Richard Schlesinger unfortunately never won our major in their careers, unlike fellow multiple runners-up John Bromwich, Jack Crawford, Horace Rice, Gerald Patterson and Ken McGregor. Still, making the final of the tournament in any era is an outstanding achievement, especially making it multiple times.

Harry Hopman

New South Welshman Harry Hopman was the runner-up in the Australian Championship final 3 years in a row (1930, 1931 and 1932). He was beaten twice by the legendary Jack Crawford (pushing him to 5 sets in 1932).

However, as you'll see in Chapters 8 and 10, he did have success in doubles at the majors, including 4 mixed titles with his first wife, Nell Hall.

Hopman also went on to become a legendary coach who was a hard task master, helping to guide Australia to 15 Davis Cup victories. He also coached many of Australia's best players in the 1950s and 1960s at various stages of their careers.[17]

Horace Rice

Horace Rice was a left hander from New South Wales who was known for wearing distinctive knickerbockers and black socks while playing.

Although he was a three-time runner-up in the Australasian Championships (in 1910, 1911 and 1915), he won the tournament in 1907 in Brisbane just prior to turning 35 years of age. That means he was in his late thirties and early forties when he lost his 3 Australasian Championship finals!

Two of his losses were to two-time winner Rodney Heath, while the other was to Norman Brookes (who you'll discover later in this chapter was one of our Aussie pioneers at Wimbledon).[18]

Gerald Patterson

Victorian Gerald Patterson was a runner-up in 3 Australasian Championships either side of World War I (in 1914, 1922 and 1925). The War interrupted his career, but he was awarded a Military Cross for bravery for his service in World War I.[19]

Two of his Australasian Championship final losses were to three-time winner James Anderson. He finally broke through to win the tournament in 1927 (the year the event was renamed the Australian Championships). He was 31 years old at the time. The 1927 final was a 5-set marathon against fellow Aussie John Hawkes. Down 2 sets to 1 and facing a fourth final defeat, he saved 5 match points and won the fourth set 18-16, before going on to clinch the fifth set and the match.

Richard Schlesinger

Richard Schlesinger was a Victorian and two-time runner-up. His first loss was in 1924 to three-time champion James Anderson. He won the first 2 sets before Anderson came back to win in 5. In 1929, he lost to Englishman John Gregory.[20]

Ken McGregor

Tall South Australian Ken McGregor lost the 1950 and 1951 Australian Championship finals, before breaking through to win in 1952 in his home city of Adelaide.

In 1950, he lost to his long-time doubles partner Frank Sedgman in 4 sets, while in 1951 he was also beaten in 4 by American Dick Savitt.

But he turned the tables on Sedgman in 1952, beating him in 4 sets, including a 12-10 second-set marathon. McGregor briefly joined the fledgling pro tennis tour along with Sedgman in 1953, before retiring from tennis at the age of 25 and going on to play Aussie Rules football in South Australia for the West Adelaide club.[21]

All Aussie Runners-Up
Australasian/Australian Men's Singles Championships: 1905–1952

The following table lists all of the Aussie runners-up in the Australian Open men's singles (its Australasian or Australian Championship predecessors) in the pioneering years (1905–1952).

Year	Runner-Up
1905	Albert Curtis
1908	Alfred Dunlop
1909	Ernie Parker
1910	Horace Rice
1911	Horace Rice
1913	Ernie Parker
1914	Gerald Patterson
1915	Horace Rice
1919	Eric Pockley
1920	Ronald Thomas
1921	Alf Hedeman
1922	Gerald Patterson
1923	Bert St. John
1924	Richard Schlesinger
1925	Gerald Patterson
1926	James Willard
1927	John Hawkes
1928	Jack Cummings
1929	Richard Schlesinger
1930	Harry Hopman
1931	Harry Hopman
1932	Harry Hopman
1934	Jack Crawford
1936	Jack Crawford
1937	John Bromwich
1938	John Bromwich
1939	Adrian Quist

Chapter 1 – The Majors and the Aussie Male Pioneers (1905–1952)

Year	Runner-Up
1940	Jack Crawford
1946	Dinny Pails
1947	John Bromwich
1948	John Bromwich
1949	John Bromwich
1950	Ken McGregor
1951	Ken McGregor
1952	Frank Sedgman

Pioneering Aussie Men at the French Championships (1905–1952)

The men's French Championships (as the French Open was called in the Amateur Era prior to 1968) began in 1891. The tournament was only open to French players or international players who were members of French tennis clubs until 1924. That restriction was lifted in 1925 when it was sanctioned as a major by the International Lawn Tennis Federation. The event has been played on clay at the famous Stade Roland Garros in Paris since 1928. It was suspended twice in the first half of the 20th century for World War I and World War II.

French players still dominated the entries after the event was opened up to international competitors in 1925, winning every final until 1933 when an Aussie broke through.[22]

Jack Crawford

Jack Crawford had already won the Australian Championships earlier in 1933 when he ventured to Paris as the second seed behind local favourite Henri Cochet. The Frenchman had already won his national tournament 5 times (including 4 since it had been opened up to international competition in 1925) and he was the defending champion. Both of the top seeds made it through to the 1933 French Championships final, but Crawford prevailed in straight sets.[23]

Crawford returned to Roland Garros in 1934 to

> defend his title. Once again, he was the second seed, but this time he was behind Englishman Fred Perry. Perry was knocked out in the quarter-finals, but Crawford won through to his second consecutive final where he faced German Gottfried von Cramm. After going 2 sets to 1 up, he was beaten in 5.[24]

Frank Sedgman

Frank Sedgman went to Roland Garros in 1952 as the second seed behind Czech-born Egyptian citizen Jaroslav Drobný, who was the defending champion.

Sedgman didn't drop a set on the way to the final, but he ended up losing in 4 to Drobný.[25]

Pioneering Aussie Men at Wimbledon (1905–1952)

Wimbledon was first played as a men's event in 1877 after the rules of lawn tennis were patented 3 years earlier by Welsh-born London resident Walter Clopton Wingfield in 1874.[26] The tournament has always been a major and played on grass at the All England Lawn Tennis and Croquet Club in Wimbledon in south-west London.[27] It was suspended twice in the 20th century for World War I and World War II.

Up until 1921, the defending Wimbledon champion was automatically in the final of the following year's event if they chose to enter it. If not, it was a normal knockout tournament with each player having to win in each round to progress through to the final. British players won every men's singles event held between 1877 and 1906, until Aussie pioneer Norman Brookes arrived in 1907.

Norman Brookes

Nicknamed 'the wizard', left-handed Victorian Norman Brookes was a trailblazer who became Australia's first player to win an international major when he won Wimbledon in 1907 at the age of 29. He was also the first non-British player to win the prestigious tournament when he beat veteran Englishman Arthur Gore in straight sets in the 1907 final.

Brookes' win meant that he could have returned to Wimbledon in 1908 and gone straight into the final but work and family commitments in Australia prevented him from competing.[28] Given that the man he easily beat in 1907 (Arthur Gore) went on to win the next 2 Wimbledon finals, there's a very good chance Brookes would have done the same.

Brookes was also the first non-British player to make the final when he won through to the last match of the 1905 tournament, but he was beaten by England's defending champion Laurence Doherty in straight sets. Doherty won Wimbledon 5 times during his career.

Brookes didn't return to Wimbledon after his 1907 win until 1914 at 36 years of age. He won the tournament for a second time by defeating defending New Zealand champion (and his long-time doubles partner) Anthony Wilding in straight sets in the final.

At the time, Wilding was attempting to win his fifth consecutive Wimbledon singles title. Given that he beat Wilding in straight sets at Wimbledon in 1914, there's a good chance that Brookes would have won the 4 previous titles that Wilding won had he competed in the tournament in those years.

Sadly, Wimbledon was suspended from 1915 through to 1918 due to World War I. Brookes served in the Australian Red Cross in Egypt during the War.[29]

When the event resumed in 1919, Brookes was nearly 42 when he was given automatic entry into the final as the reigning champion. He was defeated in straight sets by fellow Aussie Gerald Patterson.

Brookes also won the Australasian Championships during his career (in

1911). He was knighted in 1939, and the modern day Australian Open men's singles trophy is named the Norman Brookes Challenge Cup in his honour.[30]

Gerald Patterson (2 titles)

Gerald Patterson won 2 Wimbledon singles titles. At 24, he beat an ageing Norman Brookes in the 1919 final. That win made him an automatic finalist when he entered the 1920 event, but he was beaten in 4 sets by American "Big Bill" Tilden.

He returned to Wimbledon in 1922 and won his second title against England's Randolph Lycett in straight sets. This was the first year that the tradition of the winner gaining automatic entry into the final of the next year's event was abolished. Patterson didn't return to Wimbledon until 1928, when he was past his prime.[31]

Jack Crawford

Jack Crawford had already won the Australian Championships and the French Championships in 1933 when he arrived at Wimbledon that same year, but he was the second seed for the tournament behind American Ellsworth Vines, the defending champion.

Both top seeds won their way through the final, but it was Crawford who came out on top over 5 tough sets, including an 11-9 marathon in the second.

He returned to Wimbledon as the defending champion and top seed in 1934 where he won through to the final again. This time though, he was beaten by England's second seed Fred Perry in straight sets.[32]

Frank Sedgman

Frank Sedgman won Wimbledon in 1952, the year before he turned pro and was banned from competing in major tournaments.

Sixty years after his Wimbledon triumph, he said: *"You always wanted to win the Wimbledon title, and I had offers to turn professional before I won Wimbledon and I had put it off because I thought, gee, I wanted to win the Wimbledon title to cap your career, really, as an amateur."*[33]

Sedgman had previously lost the 1950 Wimbledon final as the top seed to fifth-seeded American Edward "Budge" Patty in 4 sets, but he achieved his dream in the 1952 final against Czech-born Egyptian Jaroslav Drobný. The second-seeded Drobný had beaten him on clay in the French Championships final at Roland Garros just months earlier, but the top-seeded Sedgman had his revenge on grass at Wimbledon, winning in 4 sets.

Geoff Brown

New South Welshman Geoff Brown came agonisingly close to winning the first Wimbledon tournament held after the end of World War II, losing the 1946 final in 5 sets to Frenchman Yvon Petra. He won the first 2 sets. Brown was just 22 years old and entered the tournament as the third seed, while Petra was seeded fifth.

It was to be Brown's only career appearance in a singles final at one of the majors. Amazingly, he also reached both the men's and mixed doubles finals at Wimbledon that same year. Unfortunately though, he and fellow Aussie Dinny Pails finished as runners-up in the men's double final, and he and his American partner Dorothy Cheney did the same in the mixed doubles.[34]

John Bromwich

John Bromwich had already finished as the runner-up in the Australian Championships in 1948 when he arrived at Wimbledon that year as the second seed. Unfortunately, the same runner-up fate awaited him. This time though, he was beaten by seventh-seeded American (Bob Falkenburg) rather than a fellow Aussie (Adrian Quist). Like Geoff Brown in 1946, Bromwich came agonisingly close to winning, pushing Falkenburg to 5 sets.

Like Geoff Brown, Bromwich also made both the men's and mixed doubles finals at Wimbledon in the same year. He and his Aussie partner Frank Sedgman lifted the doubles trophy after a 4-set victory, and he and his American partner Louise Brough won the doubles in 3 sets. As the old saying goes, 2 out of 3 ain't bad![35]

Ken McGregor

Like John Bromwich, Ken McGregor finished runner-up at Wimbledon in singles in the same year that he was runner-up in singles at the Australian Championships as well. It was 1951, and the seventh-seeded McGregor was beaten in the Wimbledon final in straight sets by sixth-seeded American Dick Savitt.

He and Frank Sedgman did win the men's doubles that year though to cushion the blow.[36]

Chapter 1 – The Majors and the Aussie Male Pioneers (1905–1952)

Pioneering Aussie Men at the US Championships (1905–1952)

The first US Championships for men (as the US Open was known during the Amateur Era prior to 1968) were held in 1881. The annual event was a grass court championship up until the end of 1974, before switching to clay for 3 years and then hard court ever since. It was declared a major by the International Lawn Tennis Federation in 1924. Unlike the other 3 majors, the US Grand Slam event has been played every year since the tournament began. There were no suspensions of the event during World War I or World War II.[37]

Americans dominated the first 7 decades of the men's singles event, winning 63 of the 72 tournaments held in the pioneering era between 1881 and 1952.[38] Two Aussies featured in US Championship finals during that time, and their names are familiar.

Jack Crawford

Jack Crawford went to the US Championships in New York City in 1933 having already won the singles at the Australian Championships, the French Championships and Wimbledon that year. He had a chance to become the first man to win the Grand Slam of all 4 singles majors and entered the tournament as the top-seeded international player. The number 2 seed was England's Fred Perry and they both won through to the final.

Crawford dropped the first set but fought back to take a marathon second set 13-11, before winning the third as well to go 2-1 up. However, Perry won the last 2 sets to take the match.[39]

Frank Sedgman (2 titles)

Frank Sedgman became the first Aussie to lift the men's singles trophy at the US Championships when he beat American Vic Seixas in straight sets in New York City. Sedgman was the top-seeded international player for the event.

At the time, 8 US and 8 international players were seeded separately in the draw and the 2 groups didn't meet each other until the fourth round. Seixas was seeded seventh among the US players, so Sedgman entered the final as favourite.[40]

He backed up his 1951 win with another straight sets finals victory in the 1952 US Championships final against American Gardnar Mulloy, once again in New York City. Sedgman was again the top-seeded international player, and Mulloy was the sixth-seeded American. Sedgman didn't drop a set in the entire tournament.[41]

He was approaching the prime of his career in 1952 at age 25, having won Wimbledon and finished runner-up at both the Australian and French Championships earlier that year. It was to be his last major though, as he turned professional in 1953 and was banned from competing in the then-amateur Grand Slam events.

Chapter 2
The Majors and the Aussie Female Pioneers
(1922–1959)

The women's singles events at Wimbledon, and the US, French and Australian Championships all started a few years after the men's singles tournaments at each event. The Wimbledon women's singles began in 1884 (7 years after the men), the US women's in 1887 (6 years after the men), the French in 1897 (6 years after the men), and the Australasian (as the Australian event was then known) in 1922 (17 years after the men).[42] Here's a brief look at the Aussie pioneers at each one.

All female players throughout the book are listed with their maiden names first followed by their married name (if known and applicable) for consistency.

Multiple Aussie Champions
Australasian/Australian Women's Singles Championships: 1922–1959

Multiple Aussie winners of our premier tennis tournament for women during the 1922–1959 era were:

- Nancye Wynne (Bolton) (6)
- Daphne Akhurst (Cozens) (5)
- Joan Hartigan (Bathurst) (3)
- Margaret Mutch (Molesworth) (2)
- Coral McInnes (Buttsworth) (2)
- Thelma Coyne (Long) (2)
- Mary Carter (Reitano) (2).[43]

Victorian Nancye Wynne (Bolton) won the tournament either side of World War II, so would likely have won even more than her incredible 6 titles but for the global conflict.

Queenslander Margaret Mutch (Molesworth) won the first ever event in 1922 when 14 players competed in an unseeded tournament in Sydney.[44]

Nancye Wynne (Bolton) – 6 titles

Nancye Wynne (Bolton)'s 6 singles wins in the Australian Championships (as the Australian Open was called in her era) is remarkable in its own right. It's incredible when you consider that she lost the peak years of her career during World War II. Tragically, she also lost her husband in the War. He was an RAAF pilot and killed in action.

Bolton was just 20 when she won her first title in 1937 as the second seed, and her second in 1940 just before the tournament was suspended for 5 years due to the War. She didn't drop a set in the entire tournament in winning the first 3 titles after the War ended (1946–1948), and also kept a clean slate when she won her sixth and final crown in 1951 at the age of 34. Two of her 6 wins in the singles final came against fellow Aussie pioneer Thelma Coyne (Long). She was a tall player for her era, standing at 5-foot-10.

And as you'll see in Chapter 9 of this book, Bolton also had a lot of success at the Australian Championships as a doubles player with Thelma Coyne (Long) in the women's event, and Colin Long in the mixed doubles.

Wynne Bolton was also runner-up twice in the women's singles event at the Australian Championships. The first time was in 1936 before she ever won the tournament. She was only 19 at the time and went down to three-time winner Joan Hartigan (Bathurst) in the last of her victories.

Her only other runner-up performance came 13 years later when she had already won 5 of her 6 singles titles.[45]

Daphne Akhurst (Cozens) – 5 titles

New South Wales' Daphne Akhurst (Cozens) won her 5 singles titles in Australia's premier tennis event during a golden 6-year period between 1925 and 1930.

The only year she didn't win during that time was 1927 when illness forced her to withdraw from her scheduled second round match. She won her first Australian Championship singles title as the second seed in 1925 at the age of 21.

Akhurst retired from tennis in 1931, but tragically died at just 29 less than 2 years later due to complications from an ectopic pregnancy. Since 1934, the Australian Open women's singles trophy has been named the Daphne Akhurst Memorial Cup in her honour.[46]

Joan Hartigan (Bathurst) – (3 titles)

New South Wales' Joan Hartigan (Bathurst) won the Australian Championship 3 times in 4 years between 1933 and 1936, picking up the scalps of fellow Aussie pioneers Coral McInnes (Buttsworth), Margaret Mutch (Molesworth) and Nancye Wynne (Bolton) in her straight sets finals' victories along the way.

She was just 20 when she won her first title and was a tennis fashion trailblazer, becoming one of the early female players to take the court without wearing stockings. She later served in the Australian Army during World War II.[47]

Margaret Mutch (Molesworth) – 2 titles

Margaret Mutch (Molesworth), affectionately known as "Mall", won the first 2 women's Australasian Championships (as the event was then called) ever contested in 1922 and 1923.

In the pre-tie-break era, she won the 1922 final in straight sets after a marathon 10-8 second set against fellow Australian Esna Boyd (Robertson). Mutch (Molesworth) was 28 years old at the time and known for her power hitting and range of shots.[48]

Had the women's event at the Australasian Championships started at the same time as the men's (1905), who knows how many titles she may have won. Incredibly, she still managed to reach the final in 1934 at the age of 39, going down to three-time winner Joan Hartigan (Bathurst).[49]

Coral McInnes (Buttsworth) – 2 titles

New South Wales' Coral McInnes (Buttsworth) made 3 consecutive Australian Championship singles finals, winning in 1931 and 1932 before going down to Joan Hartigan (Bathurst) in 1933.

She was 30 years old and seeded fourth when she won her first title, and was known for her speed around the court, her chopping style and regular use of the drop shot.[50]

Thelma Coyne (Long) – 2 titles

Another female tennis pioneer from New South Wales, Thelma Coyne (Long) had a long and successful career, despite it being interrupted by the Australian Championship's 5-year hiatus during World War II. She served in the Australian Women's Army Service during the War.[51]

Chapter 2 – The Majors and the Aussie Female Pioneers (1922–1959)

First reaching the singles final as a 21-year-old in 1940, she had to wait until 1952 to win the first of her 2 singles titles. Her second win came in 1954. At the time, she was the oldest woman to win the singles final at the Australian Championships at 35 years and 8 months.

Fellow Aussie pioneer Nancye Wynne (Bolton) denied her a victory in the 1940 final, but it obviously didn't harm their friendship. As you'll see in Chapter 9, Coyne (Long) and Wynne (Bolton) combined to win an incredible 10 doubles finals at Australia's premier tennis event.

Coyne (Long) also finished runner-up 4 times in the singles final of the Australian Championships, including twice to Nancye Wynne (Bolton). There was a 16-year gap between her first and last singles finals at the Australian Championships. She was 37 years old when she was runner-up for the last time in 1956.[52]

Mary Carter (Reitano) – 2 titles

Mary Carter (Reitano) won 2 Australian Championships singles titles. The first was an epic 3-setter against fellow pioneer Thelma Coyne (Long) in 1956 when she clinched the final set 9-7. The second was in 1959.

She was a pioneer for women's tennis in more ways than one. In 1956, she and fellow Aussie Daphne Seeney (Fancutt) refused to take the court for their semi-final match when it was rescheduled for an outside court because a men's show court match was dragging through 5 sets. She recalled the incident when being inducted into the Australian Tennis Hall of Fame in 2021: *"We decided to sit in the dressing room and wait until the men finished. Eventually we got our way and they set down the schedule for us to play on a show court the next morning. So that was a win for us."*[53]

All Aussie Champions
Australasian/Australian Women's Singles Championships: 1922–1959

Like the pioneering men, our Aussie female tennis pioneers dominated the early decades of our local major. Aussie players won 26 of the 33 singles tournaments played between 1922 and 1959. The following table lists all of the Aussie winners of the Australian Open women's singles (its Australasian or Australian Championship predecessors) in the pioneering years (1922–1959).

Year	Winner
1922	Margaret Mutch (Molesworth)
1923	Margaret Mutch (Molesworth)
1924	Sylvia Lance (Harper)
1925	Daphne Akhurst (Cozens)
1926	Daphne Akhurst (Cozens)
1927	Esna Boyd (Robertson)
1928	Daphne Akhurst (Cozens)
1929	Daphne Akhurst (Cozens)
1930	Daphne Akhurst (Cozens)
1931	Coral McInnes (Buttsworth)
1932	Coral McInnes (Buttsworth)
1933	Joan Hartigan (Bathurst)
1934	Joan Hartigan (Bathurst)
1936	Joan Hartigan (Bathurst)
1937	Nancye Wynne (Bolton)
1939	Emily Hood (Westacott)
1940	Nancye Wynne (Bolton)
1946	Nancye Wynne (Bolton)
1947	Nancye Wynne (Bolton)
1948	Nancye Wynne (Bolton)
1951	Nancye Wynne (Bolton)
1952	Thelma Coyne (Long)
1954	Thelma Coyne (Long)
1955	Beryl Penrose (Collier)
1956	Mary Carter (Reitano)
1959	Mary Carter (Reitano)

Multiple Aussie Runners-Up
Australasian/Australian Women's Singles Championships: 1922–1959

Multiple Aussie runners-up of our premier tennis tournament for women during the 1922–1959 era were:

- Esna Boyd (Robertson) (6, including 5 years in a row)
- Thelma Coyne (Long) (4)
- Sylvia Lance (Harper) (2)
- Nancye Wynne (Bolton) (2)
- Nell Hall (Hopman) (2).[54]

Chapter 2 – The Majors and the Aussie Female Pioneers (1922–1959)

Nell Hall (Hopman) unfortunately never won our singles major in her career, unlike fellow multiple runners-up Esna Boyd (Robertson), Thelma Coyne (Long), Sylvia Lance (Harper) and Nancye Wynne (Bolton). Still, making the final of the tournament in any era is an outstanding achievement, especially making it twice.

Esna Boyd (Robertson)

The incredibly consistent Victorian Esna Boyd (Robertson) reached the first 7 women's singles finals in Australia's premier tennis tournament, losing 6 of them. Fittingly, she won the 1927 event in 3 sets to finally get her name on the winner's trophy after her first 5 runners-up performances.

3 of her 6 finals' losses were against the formidable Daphne Akhurst (Cozens), and 2 against Margaret Mutch (Molesworth). But as you'll see in Chapters 8 and 10, she had far more finals' success in doubles than singles at the Australian Championships.[55]

Sylvia Lance (Harper)

Sylvia Lance (Harper) was a New South Wales tennis pioneer who made 3 singles finals at the tournament, finishing runner-up twice.

Her win in 1924 at the age of 28 was a tough 3-setter against perennial runner-up Esna Boyd (Robertson), though Boyd (Robertson) turned the tables on her in 3 sets in 1927 to record her only singles victory at the Australian Championships.

In 1930, Lance Harper pushed Daphne Akhurst (Cozens) all the way in a hard-fought final, losing the first set 10-8 in the pre-tie-break era before winning the second 6-2 and losing the decider 7-5. It was Akhurst's third straight singles final victory at the event, and the fifth and final one of her career.[56]

Nell Hall (Hopman)

Sydney-born Nell Hall (Hopman) finished runner-up in 2 Australian Championships either side of World War II (1939 and 1947). The second loss was against the legendary Nancye Wynne (Bolton).

Had it not been for World War II intervening and the event not being played between 1941 and 1945, who knows if

Hall Hopman would have broken through for a singles final victory during her career. She ended up marrying Australian men's tennis pioneer Harry Hopman. As you'll see in Chapter 10, they had considerable success as a mixed doubles pairing at the Australian Championships.[57]

Chapter 2 – The Majors and the Aussie Female Pioneers (1922–1959)

All Aussie Runners-Up
Australasian/Australian Women's Singles Championships: 1922–1959

The following table lists all of the Aussie female runners-up in the Australian Open singles (its Australasian or Australian Championship predecessors) in the pioneering years (1922–1959).

Year	Runner-Up
1922	Esna Boyd (Robertson)
1923	Esna Boyd (Robertson)
1924	Esna Boyd (Robertson)
1925	Esna Boyd (Robertson)
1926	Esna Boyd (Robertson)
1927	Sylvia Lance (Harper)
1928	Esna Boyd (Robertson)
1929	Louie Bickerton (Cozens)
1930	Sylvia Lance (Harper)
1931	Marjorie Cox (Crawford)
1932	Kathleen Le Messurier
1933	Coral McInnes (Buttsworth)
1934	Margaret Mutch (Molesworth)
1936	Nancye Wynne (Bolton)
1937	Emily Hood (Westacott)
1938	Dorothy Stevenson (Waddell)
1939	Nell Hall (Hopman)
1940	Thelma Coyne (Long)
1946	Joyce Fitch (Rymer)
1947	Nell Hall (Hopman)
1948	Marie Toomey
1949	Nancye Wynne (Bolton)
1951	Thelma Coyne (Long)
1952	Helen Angwin (Polkinghorne)
1954	Jenny Staley (Hoad)
1955	Thelma Coyne (Long)
1956	Thelma Coyne (Long)
1958	Lorraine Coghlan (Robinson)

The French Championships, Wimbledon and the US Championships

Only one Australian woman won through to a final of an international Grand Slam event during the pioneering era between 1922 and 1959 – Nancye Wynne (Bolton). However, fewer Australian female tennis pioneers ventured overseas to compete than men during that time.

Nancye Wynne (Bolton)

Nancye Wynne (Bolton) became the first Australian woman to reach an international Grand Slam final in 1938 at the US Championships (as the US Open was then called). She was only 21 years old at the time and had won the first of her 6 Australian Championships a year earlier in 1937.

International players were seeded separately to US players at the tournament in that era, and Wynne was the top-seeded Australian and the fourth-seeded international player overall in the 1938 US Grand Slam event. She won through to the final but was defeated by US second seed Alice Marble in straight sets.[58]

Chapter 3
Aussie Men at the Majors
(1953–January 1968)

The 1950s ushered in a golden era for Australian men's tennis at all 4 Grand Slam events across the globe. Not only did Australian men continue to dominate the Australian Championships like they had in the first half of the 20th century, but they also won the majority of the French, Wimbledon and US Championships held during the next 2 decades.

Chapter 1 outlined that Frank Sedgman led the Australian men's tennis charge into the 1950s before he turned professional. He was banned from competing at Grand Slam events for fifteen years from 1953 until April 1968 when the Open (professional) Era started.[59]

As you'll see in this chapter, plenty were ready to follow in his footsteps. There was seemingly a production line of male Australian tennis greats in the 1950s and 1960s that will never be repeated.

Multiple Aussie Champions
Australian Men's Singles Championships: 1953–January 1968

Aussies who won the men's singles at Australia's premier tennis tournament multiple times during the golden Amateur Era between 1953 and January 1968 were:

- Roy Emerson (6)
- Ken Rosewall (2, and he won another 2 in the Open Era – see Chapter 5)
- Rod Laver (2, and he won another in the Open Era – see Chapter 5)
- Ashley Cooper (2).[60]

Roy Emerson (6 titles)

Queenslander Roy Emerson had a golden run at the Australian Championships (as it was known pre-1969 in his era), winning the men's singles event 6 times in a 7-year period between 1961 and 1967 (including 5 in a row from 1963). His record of 6 wins was unbroken until Novak Djokovic won his seventh Australian Open title in 2019.

Emerson's first win came in 1961 against defending champion Rod Laver. "Emmo" (as he was known) was 24 years old at the time and the second seed behind Laver. He won the final in 4 sets after dropping the first.[61] A 6-foot-tall right hander, he was known for his serve-volley game and his high fitness level. He didn't drop a single set on his way to winning the men's singles at the 1964 Australian Championships.

Emerson resisted the temptation to turn professional for many years, once famously declaring that "he couldn't afford to take the pay cut". Despite being an amateur, it was rumoured that he was being paid between $1,000 and $1,500 per week by Tennis Australia during the 1960s. If it's true, that was incredible money at the time.[62]

As you will see later in this chapter, Emerson's Grand Slam success in singles wasn't confined to Australia. He earned a career Grand Slam by winning all 4 majors, and he became the first male player in history to win 12 Grand Slam singles titles. This record wasn't broken until Pete Sampras won his 13th Grand Slam title at Wimbledon in 2000.

And as you will see in Chapter 8, Emmo also had a lot of success in Grand Slam doubles events.[63]

Ken Rosewall (2 titles)

Jokingly known as "Muscles", the slightly built, 5-foot-7 New South Welshman was renowned for his backhand, volley, deft shot placement, and court speed. Rosewall won 2 Australian Championships as an amateur. The first was in 1953 when he was just 18 years old and the third seed against fellow Aussie and top seed Mervyn Rose.

The second was in 1955 against another Lew Hoad, yet another Aussie who was a good friend and his doubles partner. Hoad later turned the tables on Rosewall in the 1956 singles final at the Australian Championships.

At the end of 1956, Rosewall turned pro and was banned from competing at Australia's premier tennis event until 1969 (when pros were first allowed to compete at the renamed Australian Open). We'll never know how many more Grand Slam titles he would have won during the prime years of his career if not for the ban.

And as you'll see in Chapter 5, Rosewall also won 2 Australian Open singles titles as a pro in the 1970s, despite being in his mid-to-late thirties.[64]

Rod Laver (2 titles)

Left-handed Queenslander "Rocket" Rod Laver won 2 Australian Championships as an amateur – 1960 and 1962, including a win over defending champion Roy Emerson in 1962. He turned pro in December 1962 and was banned from competing in Australia's premier tennis event again until 1969. He won his third and final title at the renamed Australian Open that year.

Unfortunately, we'll never know how the Laver/Emerson rivalry would have played out had they both been allowed to compete at Grand Slam events between 1963 and April 1968 when the pro ban was lifted in time for the renamed French Open that year. Both players were in the prime years of their career during Laver's ban. They met in 2 singles finals at the amateur Australian Championships, winning one each.

As you'll see later in this chapter, Laver had a lot of success as an amateur at Grand Slam events across the globe, culminating in him being only the second male player in tennis history to win a calendar year Grand Slam in 1962, just before turning pro. Only 5-foot-8 and with a slight build, he was known for the top spin he put on his ground strokes, his speed around the court, and for his will to win. The Australian Open today is played at the Rod Laver Arena in Melbourne.[65]

Ashley Cooper (2 titles)

The Melbourne-born, Queensland-raised Cooper won back-to-back Australian Championships in 1957 and 1958 in his early twenties. He beat fellow Aussies both times (Mal Anderson and Neale Fraser).

Cooper was known for his powerful serve-volley game and he turned pro in 1959 when he was ranked as the number one singles player in the world.

As you'll see later in this chapter, he also had plenty of success at other Grand Slam singles events around the world before turning pro and being barred.

And as you'll see in Chapter 8, Cooper had plenty of success at Grand Slam doubles events as well.[66]

Chapter 3 – Aussie Men at the Majors (1953–January 1968)

All Aussie Australian Champions
Australian Men's Singles Championships: 1953-January 1968

Remarkably, Aussie men won 16 of the 17 singles events played in the Australian Grand Slam event between 1953 and January 1968. The following table lists all of our men's singles winners during that period.

Year	Winner		Year	Winner
1953	Ken Rosewall		1961	Roy Emerson
1954	Mervyn Rose		1962	Rod Laver
1955	Ken Rosewall		1963	Roy Emerson
1956	Lew Hoad		1964	Roy Emerson
1957	Ashley Cooper		1965	Roy Emerson
1958	Ashley Cooper		1966	Roy Emerson
1960	Rod Laver		1967	Roy Emerson
			1968	Bill Bowrey

Multiple Aussie Runners-Up
Australian Men's Singles Championships: 1953–January 1968

Two Aussies were multiple runners-up in the men's singles between 1953 and January 1968 – Neale Fraser (3 times) and Fred Stolle (twice). Unfortunately, neither managed to win an elusive singles title in their home country's major, but multiple runner-up finishes is still a remarkable achievement during this golden era for Australian tennis.[67]

And as you'll see in Chapter 5, Mal Anderson was a runner-up in this Amateur Era as well as the Open Era, making him a multiple runner-up.

Neale Fraser

Victorian left-hander Neale Fraser was a three-time singles finalist at the Australian Championships (1957, 1959 and 1960). In 1957, he lost to fellow Aussie Ashley Cooper in 4 sets. He was 2 sets up and held a match point in the 1960 final against the legendary Rod Laver, before "Rocket" came back to win an intense 5-set marathon.

Although Fraser never won the singles event at his home major, you'll see later in this chapter that he had more success at international Grand Slam singles events. Fraser was known for having a big serve and strong forehand. And you'll see in Chapters 8 and 10 that he had plenty of success at all 4 Grand Slam events in doubles, including in Australia with fellow Aussies Lew Hoad, Ashley Cooper and Roy Emerson.

After retiring from his own playing career, Fraser became a long-time non-playing Davis Cup captain for the Australian team.[68]

Fred Stolle

New South Welshman Fred Stolle was runner-up in back-to-back singles finals at the Australian Championships in 1964 and 1965. Both times he was beaten by the great Roy Emerson. In 1965, Stolle won the first 2 sets in the singles final at the Australian Championships before "Emmo" stormed back to win in 5.

However, despite failing to win the singles title at his home major, you'll see later in this chapter that Stolle had more singles success at the international Grand Slams (just like Neale Fraser did). Stolle was 6-foot-3 and known for his powerful serve and volley game. And as you'll see in Chapter 8, he had plenty of success at Grand Slam events in doubles with fellow Aussies Roy Emerson, Bob Hewitt (no relation to Lleyton) and Ken Rosewall.[69]

Chapter 3 – Aussie Men at the Majors (1953–January 1968)

All Aussie Runners-Up
Australian Men's Singles Championships: 1953–January 1968

Not surprisingly, Aussie men also dominate the entire runners-up list in the men's singles during this golden period. Usually the final was an Aussie against a fellow Aussie.

Year	Runner-Up
1953	Mervyn Rose
1954	Rex Hartwig
1955	Lew Hoad
1956	Ken Rosewall
1957	Neale Fraser
1958	Mal Anderson
1959	Neale Fraser
1960	Neale Fraser
1961	Rod Laver
1962	Roy Emerson
1963	Ken Fletcher
1964	Fred Stolle
1965	Fred Stolle

All Aussie French Champions
French Championships: 1953–1967

Seven Aussies won the men's singles event 8 times at the French Championships (as the French Open was called during the Amateur Era) in the fifteen-year period between 1953 and 1967. No other country provided more than 2 winners during this time, as the following graph shows.

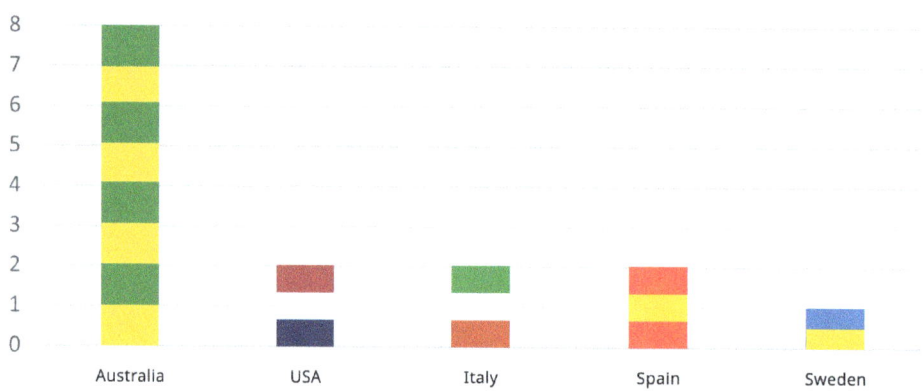

All of our Aussie men's singles winners at Roland Garros from this era were:

- Roy Emerson (2)
- Ken Rosewall (1, and he won another in the Open Era – see Chapter 5)
- Rod Laver (1, and he won another in the Open Era – see Chapter 5)
- Lew Hoad (1)
- Mervyn Rose (1)
- Fred Stolle (1)
- Tony Roche (1).

Two Aussies also finished as runners-up between 1953 and 1967 – Tony Roche (twice) and Roy Emerson (once).

The French Championships were renamed as the French Open in 1968. That tournament was the first time that professional players were allowed to compete at a Grand Slam event, and all of the majors subsequently followed suit.[70]

Roy Emerson (2 titles)

"Emmo" had already won his second Australian Championship in 1963 when he headed to the French Championships. He had also finished runner-up at the previous year's event, beaten by Rod Laver in a heart-breaking 5-setter after winning the first 2 sets.

With Laver having turned pro at the end of 1962, Emerson entered both events as the top seed. He beat third-seeded Frenchman and local favourite Pierre Darmon in 4 sets in the final.

Four years later in 1967 and on the back of his fifth consecutive singles victory at the Australian Championships (and his sixth in 7 years), he was the top seed at Roland Garros. Everything went according to plan and he beat the defending champion and fellow Aussie Tony Roche in 4 sets in the final. It was the twelfth and final Grand Slam singles title of his career, a men's tennis record that stood for the next 33 years until broken by Pete Sampras.[71]

Ken Rosewall

Ken Rosewall won the 1953 men's singles at the French Championships when he was still 18 years old. It came on the back of his singles win at the Australian Championships earlier the same year.

Like the Australian event, he entered the French tournament as the third seed, and won his way through to face US fifth seed Vic Seixas in the final. Rosewall beat him in 4 sets.

Rosewall turned pro in 1957 just after he'd turned 22. He was barred from the next 11 French Championships as a result. But as you'll see in Chapter 5, he returned to Roland Garros in 1968 and won the renamed French Open for a second time. That event was the first time that professionals were allowed to compete in a Grand Slam tournament.[72]

Rod Laver

Rod Laver won the 1962 French Championships in the men's singles as a 23-year-old. It followed his singles victory in the Australian Championships earlier that year.

He was the top seed in the French event, just as he had been in the Australian. And his opponent in the final of the French Championships was his fellow Aussie Roy Emerson, just as it had been at the Australian.

Emerson had pushed Laver to 4 sets in the Australian final, and looked to be set to turn the tables on his rival when he won the first 2 sets in the French final. But Laver came back to win in 5, including 9-7 in the fourth set. These were the days before tie-breakers were introduced. That didn't happen until the 1970 US Open.[73]

Laver didn't get the chance to defend his French title in 1963 when he turned pro. But as you'll see in Chapter 5, he returned to Roland Garros to win a second French title in 1969 after the ban on the pros had been lifted a year earlier.[74]

Lew Hoad

Lew Hoad was the top seed in the men's singles at the 1956 French Championships after beating good friend and doubles partner Ken Rosewall in the final of the Australian Championships earlier that year in 4 sets.

Hoad was still only 21 at the time, but he handled the pressure of being the top seed at both events, beating Swedish third seed Sven Davidson in straight sets in the French final. Strongly built, he was known for playing an aggressive brand of tennis and liked to win his points and matches as quickly as possible.[75]

Mervyn Rose

New South Welshman Mervyn Rose was a left hander known for his aggressive serve/volley game.

He was 28 when he entered the French Championships as the third seed in 1958, winning his way through to the final where he beat fifth-seeded Luis Ayala from Chile in straight sets.

It was his second and final Grand Slam singles title, after having won the Australian Championships 4 years earlier in 1954. Rose didn't get the chance to defend his French title in 1959 due to turning pro.

Long after he retired, Rose was described as the John McEnroe of his era. He once smashed 3 racquets in a match.[76]

Fred Stolle

Fred Stolle was the fourth seed at the 1965 French Championships and in good form after having finished runner-up to Roy Emerson at the Australian Championships earlier that year. Fellow Aussie and fourteenth seed Tony Roche upset second seed Emerson in the semi-finals, setting him for a showdown in the final with Stolle.

Stolle was the favourite for the final and got the job done, winning his first Grand Slam singles title in 4 sets. It was the sixth Grand Slam singles final of his career at that stage, and a welcome breakthrough after losing the first 5.[77]

Tony Roche

New South Wales left hander Tony Roche made 3 consecutive finals at Roland Garros between 1965 and 1967, winning in 1966 and losing to Stolle and Emerson in 1965 and 1967 respectively.[78]

Third-seeded Roche beat unseeded Hungarian István Gulyás in straight sets in the 1966 final. In an amazing display of sportsmanship, Gulyás agreed to let the final be delayed by a day to allow Roche more recovery time from an ankle injury that he suffered during the doubles semi-final at the event. The injury forced him to withdraw from that match and put him in huge doubt to play in the singles final. More than 50 years later, Roche described Gulyás as a *"wonderful human being... I couldn't imagine that happening today. That was a pretty big thing for him because at that stage he was 34 years of age, coming from the Iron Curtain, they hardly got out to play."*[79]

The 1966 French Championships was to be the only Grand Slam singles title of his career, but as you'll see in Chapters 8, he had a huge amount of success in Grand Slam doubles with fellow Aussie John Newcombe. After his retirement, Roche became a very successful coach.

All Aussie Wimbledon Champions (1953–1967)

Six Aussie men won a total of 9 Wimbledon singles titles in the fifteen-year amateur period between 1953 and 1967. This is more than double the tally of the next best-performing country (the United States), as the following graph shows.

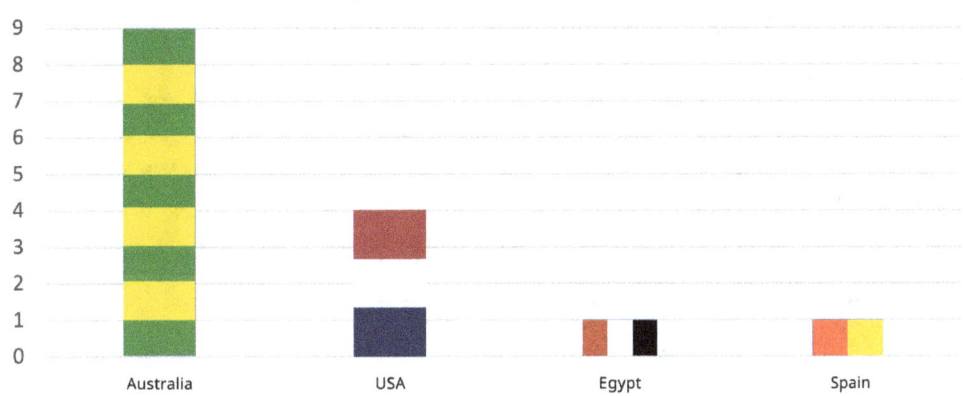

All of our Aussie men's Wimbledon singles winners from this era were:

- Rod Laver (2, and he won another 2 in the Open Era – see Chapter 5)
- Lew Hoad (2)
- Roy Emerson (2)
- Ashley Cooper (1)
- Neale Fraser (1)

- John Newcombe (1, and he won another 2 in the Open Era – see Chapter 5).

Professionals were invited to compete at Wimbledon for the first time in 1968.[80]

Rod Laver (2 titles)

Rod Laver won back-to-back Wimbledon titles in the Amateur Era in 1961 and 1962. They followed back-to-back losses in the 1959 and 1960 finals. His turning pro at the end of 1962 saw him banned from competing at Wimbledon again until 1968, and as you'll see in Chapter 5, he returned in triumph to win back-to-back titles in 1968 and 1969.

In 1962, he was 23 years old and had already won the men's singles at both the Australian and French Championships when he headed to Wimbledon as the number one seed. Laver beat unseeded fellow Aussie Marty Mulligan in straight sets in the final to give him a chance of becoming the first Australian (and only the second men's player in history) to win a calendar year Grand Slam. It would all come down to the US Championships in September of that year.[81]

Lew Hoad (2 titles)

Lew Hoad had already won the men's singles at the Australian and French Championships in 1956 when he arrived at Wimbledon as the number one seed.

He gave himself the opportunity to win a calendar year Grand Slam at the US Championships later that year by winning the third Wimbledon leg. He beat fellow Aussie, second seed, good friend and long-time doubles partner Ken Rosewall in the Wimbledon final in 4 sets. As you'll see later in this chapter, he came agonisingly close to winning his calendar

Chapter 3 – Aussie Men at the Majors (1953–January 1968)

year Grand Slam in the US.

Hoad defended his 1956 Wimbledon title in 1957 by beating fellow Aussie Ashley Cooper in straight sets. He turned pro immediately afterwards, so never had the chance for a "three-peat".[82]

Roy Emerson (2 titles)

"Emmo" won back-to-back Wimbledon titles in 1964 and 1965. Both times he was the top seed for the tournament after winning the Australian Championships on grass earlier in each year, and both times he beat fellow Aussie Fred Stolle in the final, just like he had at the Australian Championships in both years.

He won the Wimbledon final in 4 sets in 1964, and in straight sets in 1965. His 1964 win gave him a coveted career Grand Slam, having by that stage won the Australian Championships (1960, 1961, 1963 and 1964), the French Championship (1963), and as you'll see later in this chapter, the US Championships (1961). He wouldn't stop winning Grand Slams until 1967, winning 12 in total.[83]

Ashley Cooper

Ashley Cooper won the 1958 Wimbledon men's singles after finishing runner-up the year before as a 20-year-old to fellow Aussie Lew Hoad.

By the time he reached Wimbledon in 1958, he had already won the Australian Championships on grass earlier that year. That win in his home Grand Slam saw him become the top seed at Wimbledon. He beat fellow Aussie Neale Fraser in the final in both events.

Even though he was the top seed, he had to battle his way through an extraordinary 322 games to win his Wimbledon title. All but one of his matches were tough 4 and 5-set affairs, with many including marathon sets in the pre-tie-break era. In the Wimbledon final, fourth-seeded Fraser pushed him to 4 sets with Cooper winning the fourth 13-11.[84]

Neale Fraser

Neale Fraser was 26 and the top seed at the 1960 Wimbledon Championships, despite having finished runner-up to Rod Laver at the Australian Championships in 5 sets earlier that year. Laver was seeded third at Wimbledon in 1960.

Both won through to the final where it was a 4-set battle between the 2 left handers, but this time it was Fraser who came up trumps over the then 21-year-old. He had finished runner-up in 4 sets to fellow Aussie Ashley Cooper 2 years earlier.[85]

John Newcombe

Charismatic New South Welshman John Newcombe won the last Wimbledon men's singles final of the Amateur Era as a fresh-faced 23-year-old (minus his trademark moustache) in 1967. He was the third seed and beat unseeded West German Wilhelm Bungert in straight sets in the final.

Newcombe was known for his serve-volley game, powerful forehand, physical fitness and will to win. He later described his competitiveness like this: *"There was kind of a code that you had as an Australian that you never left the court losing unless you had blood all over you,"* Newcombe said. *"That's the sort of toughness you need to compete on the world stage. Sedge was the first one who caught my eye. He epitomized what an Australian player should be, someone who was extremely fit, fought to the end and behaved properly."*[86]

And as you'll see in Chapter 5, "Newk" (as he was affectionately known) won back-to-back Wimbledon titles in 1970 and 1971. In Chapter 8, you'll also see that he had success at all 4 Grand Slam events with his long-time double partner and fellow Aussie Tony Roche.

All Aussie Wimbledon Runners-Up (1953–1967)

Six Aussie men finished runner-up a total of ten times in the Wimbledon event in the fourteen-year amateur period between 1953 and 1967:

- Ken Rosewall (2, and he finished runner-up another 2 times in the Open Era – see Chapter 5)
- Fred Stolle (3)
- Rod Laver (2)
- Ashley Cooper (1)

- Neale Fraser (1)
- Marty Mulligan (1).

As you've just seen, Laver, Cooper and Fraser all tasted the ultimate Wimbledon success during their careers, but runner-up was the best finish for Rosewall, Stolle and Mulligan (including multiple times for both Rosewall and Stolle).

Ken Rosewall

Wimbledon was the only Grand Slam singles crown that eluded Ken Rosewall during his incredibly successful career over more than 2 decades, though he was barred from competing at all Grand Slam events for more than eleven years after turning pro in 1957.

He finished as the Wimbledon runner-up twice in the Amateur Era. In 1954 when he was just 19, he was the third seed and upset by the eleventh-seeded Czech-born Egyptian Jaroslav Drobný in 4 sets in the final. In 1956, he was beaten in 4 sets by fellow Aussie, good friend and doubles partner Ken Hoad.

And as you'll see in Chapter 5, he finished as runner-up twice more as a pro at Wimbledon when he was in his mid-to-late thirties.[87]

Fred Stolle

Fred Stolle finished runner-up at Wimbledon 3 years in a row from 1963 to 1965. In 1963, he was an unseeded 24-year-old. He beat fellow Aussie and third seed Ken Fletcher in 4 sets in the second round, and the second-seeded Spaniard Manual Santana in straight sets in the semi-final. Fourth-seeded American Chuck McKinley ended his giant-killing run in straight sets in the final.

His 1963 performance and a runner-up finish at the

Chapter 3 – Aussie Men at the Majors (1953–January 1968)

Australian Championships the following year earned him the sixth seeding at Wimbledon in 1964. He won his way through to the semi-final where he had his revenge on the second-seeded McKinley, beating him in 4 sets to set up a showdown in the final against fellow Aussie Roy Emerson. "Emmo" was the top seed and had beaten him in straight sets in the Australian final earlier in the year. Stolle pushed Emerson to 4 sets, but ultimately came up short.

In 1965, Stolle's lead-up to Wimbledon included a second consecutive runner-up finish on grass at the Australian Championships to Emerson, followed by victory at the French Championships on clay where he beat fellow Aussie Tony Roche in the final. Stolle entered Wimbledon as the second seed behind Emerson. Everything went according to script and the pair met in the final. Emerson proved too strong again, winning in straight sets.[88]

Marty Mulligan

Unseeded Marty Mulligan won his way through to the 1962 Wimbledon final against fellow Aussie and top seed Rod Laver. Mulligan was only 21 at the time.

His big break in the draw came in the fourth round against second-seeded Aussie Roy Emerson. "Emmo" was forced to retire injured with the match locked at one set all. Mulligan made the most of the opportunity, going on to beat eighth-seeded Aussie Bob Hewitt in 4 sets in the quarter-finals. He beat another unseeded Aussie (John Fraser, brother of Neale) in straight sets in the semis, setting up his meeting with Laver.

Laver had already won the Australian and French Championships earlier that year, and he added Wimbledon with a straight sets victory over Mulligan to set him up for a potential calendar year Grand Slam at the US Championships later that year.[89]

All Aussie US Champions
US Championships: 1953–1967

Eight Aussies won the men's singles event at the US Championships (as the US Open was called during the Amateur Era) a total of ten times in the fifteen-year period between 1953 and 1967. This is more than triple the tally of the next best-performing country (the United States), as the following graph shows.

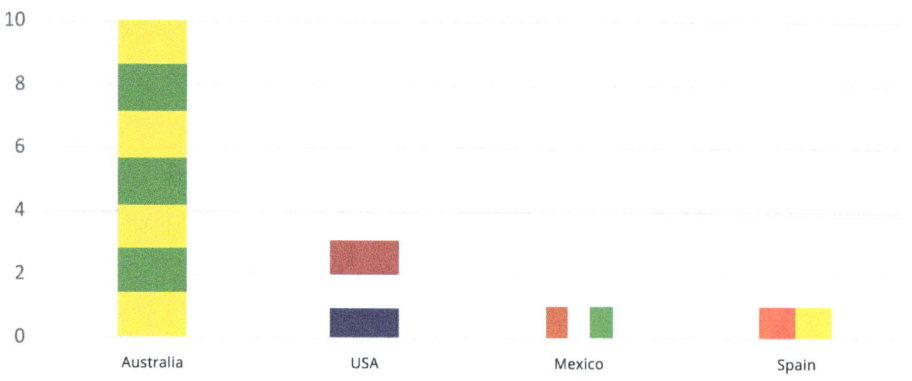

All of our Aussie men's singles winners at the US Championships from this era were:

- Neale Fraser (2)
- Roy Emerson (2)
- Ken Rosewall (1, and he won another in the Open Era – see Chapter 5)
- Rod Laver (1, and he won another in the Open Era – see Chapter 5)
- John Newcombe (1, and he won another in the Open Era – see Chapter 5)
- Mal Anderson
- Ashley Cooper
- Fred Stolle.

The tournament was still played on grass during this era. The US Championships were renamed as the US Open in 1968.[90]

Neale Fraser (2 titles)

Neale Fraser won back-to-back US Championships in 1959 and 1960. In 1959, he was 25 years old and the second seed behind American and local favourite Alex Olmedo. Results went as expected, and the pair met in the final. Olmedo had beaten Fraser in 4 sets in the final of the Australian Championships earlier that year, but Fraser turned the tables, winning the US title in 4.

Fraser entered the 1960 US Championships as the defending champion, top seed and the winner of Wimbledon 2 months earlier. The second seed was fellow Aussie Rod Laver, who had beaten him earlier in the year in a 5-set epic at the final of the Australian Championships. Both players won through to the final in the US, and Fraser played brilliantly to win in straight sets. Remarkably, he didn't drop a single set during the entire tournament, a rare feat in men's Grand Slam singles events both back then and today.[91]

Roy Emerson (2 titles)

Roy Emerson won the singles crown at the US Championships in 1961 and 1964.

In 1961, he was 24, the third seed and reigning Australian champion, having beaten top seed Rod Laver in the final. Laver was also the top seed at the US Championships after having won Wimbledon that year, and "Emmo" was seeded third. Emerson beat Laver in 4 sets in the final of the Australian Championships in 1961, and he went one better in the 1961 US Championships, beating him in straight sets in the final.

In 1962, Emmo returned to defend his title at the US Championships, but Laver was once again the top seed after having won the Australian, French and Wimbledon titles earlier in the year. Emerson was seeded second, and both players won their way through to what became an historic final. Laver beat Emmo in 4 sets to become only the second man in history (and the first Australian) to win a calendar year Grand Slam. There's more on that momentous achievement later in this chapter when we focus on Rod Laver again.

In 1964, Emerson won the men's singles at the US Championships for a second time. He was the top seed and beat fellow Aussie and fifth seed Fred Stolle in straight sets in the final. He won 3 of the 4 Grand Slam singles events that year, only missing out at the French Championships where he was the defending champion but beaten in the quarter-finals.[92]

Ken Rosewall

Ken Rosewall won the US Championships as an amateur in 1956 when he was just 21, denying a calendar year Grand Slam to Lew Hoad, his good friend and doubles partner. Hoad was the top seed having earlier won the Australian, French and Wimbledon titles earlier that year, beating Rosewall in 4 sets in the finals of both the Australian Championships and Wimbledon.

Rosewall was the second seed at the 1956 US Championships, and he turned the tables on Hoad with a 4-set victory in the final. It was a sweet victory after he'd finished runner-up at the US Championships the year before against American Tony Trabert.

Unfortunately, Rosewall didn't get a chance to defend his 1956 US title in 1957 due to turning pro. But as you'll see in Chapter 5, he returned as a pro in 1970 to win his second US crown at the renamed US Open. Had it not been for the pro ban that saw him miss all Grand Slam events for more than 11 years, who knows how many more Grand Slam titles he may have won.[93]

Rod Laver

It was a case of third-time lucky for Rod Laver at the 1962 US Championships. He had finished runner-up in straight sets in the 1960 and 1961 finals (to fellow Aussies Neale Fraser and Roy Emerson respectively).

But 1962 was to be the year when the then 24-year-old Rod Laver etched his name into tennis folklore. Winning the men's singles at the US Championships in 1962 made Laver the second man in history (and first Australian) to win a calendar year Grand Slam (the first was American Don Budge in 1938). He beat second seed Roy Emerson in 4 sets in the final.

Laver didn't get a chance to defend any of his 4 Grand Slam singles titles in 1963 after turning pro at the end of 1962 on a reported $100,000 contract (a HUGE amount of money at the time). He later explained his decision like this: *"I won Wimbledon in 1961 and 1962 and got a 15 pound voucher and a firm handshake."*[94]

He was subsequently banned from entering the next 21 Grand Slam events between the start of 1963 and April 1968 (when the Open Era began and professionals were allowed to compete). Like Ken Rosewall, who knows how many more Grand Slam titles he would have won but for his ban during the prime years of his career.

And as you'll see in Chapter 5, he won a second calendar year Grand Slam in the Open Era.

John Newcombe

"Newk" was the top seed in the men's draw at the 1967 US Championships after winning Wimbledon earlier that year. He beat seventh-seeded American Clark Graebner in the final in straight sets. It was the last US Championships that excluded the pros.

One year earlier, Newcombe finished runner-up to fellow Aussie Fred Stolle in the event, losing in 4 sets.

And as you'll see in Chapter 5, Newcombe won a second US singles crown in 1973 when he won the US Open (as it was renamed after the professional era started in 1968).[95]

Mal Anderson

Queenslander Mal Anderson won the men's singles at the US Championships as an unseeded 22-year-old in 1957.

He was the first unseeded player to ever achieve this feat when he beat fellow Aussie and top seed Ashley Cooper in straight sets in the final (though there were only 8 seeded players at the US Championships at the time). Cooper had won the singles at the Australian Championships and been a finalist at Wimbledon earlier that year.

Anderson's big scalps along the way to the final at the 1957 US Championships were American number 2 seed Dick Savitt in straight sets in the quarter-finals, and Swedish number 3 seed Sven Davidson in 5 sets in the semi-finals.

He just fell short of defending his US title in 1958 when he returned as the number one seed. Cooper was the second seed and beat him in the final in 5 sets. That event was to be his last Grand Slam event for nearly a decade. He turned pro shortly after, just like Cooper.[96]

Ashley Cooper

Ashley Cooper won the US Men's Singles Championship in 1958 just before he turned 22. It was a golden year for him where he won 3 of the 4 Grand Slam singles titles. The only one that eluded him was the French Championships where he bowed out in 5 sets in the semi-finals after winning the first 2.

His win in 5 sets over fellow Aussie, defending champion and top seed Mal Anderson for the 1958 US crown was sweet revenge after Anderson had beaten him in the US final a year earlier.

Unfortunately, Cooper never got the chance to defend his Australian, Wimbledon or US singles crowns in 1959 because he turned pro. He also never played another Grand Slam event. An arm injury forced him into premature retirement at the end of 1962 aged just 26, more than 5 years before pros were allowed to play in Grand Slam tournaments.[97]

Fred Stolle

Fred Stolle won the 1966 US men's singles title in 1966 when he was nearly 28 years old. Like Mal Anderson 9 years earlier, Stolle was unseeded when he won, despite having been a fifth-seeded finalist in 1964 when he finished runner-up in straight sets to fellow Aussie and doubles partner Roy Emerson.

He was obviously miffed at being unseeded in 1966, remarking that *"I guess they think I'm just an old hacker"* before the event started. Along the way to the final, he beat third-seeded American Richard Ralston in the fourth round in straight sets, and the second-seeded Emerson in straight sets in the semi-finals. That set him up for a meeting with another unseeded Aussie (then 22-year-old John Newcombe) in the final.

Newcombe won the first set, before Stolle won a tight second set 12-10 in the pre-tie-break era. It proved to be the turning point, as he went on to take the next 2 sets and the match 6-3, 6-4. *"Well, I guess the old hacker can still play a bit,"* he quipped afterwards.[98]

All Aussie US Championship Runners-Up (1953–1967)

Nine Aussie men finished runner-up a total of 10 times in the Wimbledon event in the 14-year amateur period between 1953 and 1967:

- Rod Laver (2)
- Ken Rosewall (1, and he finished runner-up once more in the Open Era – see Chapter 5)
- Rex Hartwig (1)
- Lew Hoad (1)
- Ashley Cooper (1)
- Mal Anderson (1)
- Roy Emerson (1)
- Fred Stolle (1)
- John Newcombe (1).

Rex Hartwig and Lew Hoad are the only 2 Aussie runners-up at the US Championships during our golden tennis era who didn't ever lift the men's singles trophy at the event, but like many of their contemporaries, they turned pro in the prime of their careers.

Rex Hartwig

New South Welshman Rex Hartwig finished runner-up at the 1954 US Championships when he was 25 and the fourth-seeded international player. He upset the top US seed Tony Trabert in the quarter-finals and second-seeded international and fellow Aussie Ken Rosewall in the semis.

That set him up for a showdown in the final against US second seed Vic Seixas. He won the first set, but ultimately went down in 4.

Earlier in 1954, Hartwig reached the only other Grand Slam final of his career, losing the men's singles at the Australian Championships in 4 sets to fellow Aussie and regular doubles partner Mervyn Rose. As you'll see in Chapter 8, the pair had plenty of Grand Slam doubles success around the world. Hartwig turned pro in late 1955 at the age of 26 and was never able to compete in another Grand Slam event before retiring.[99]

Lew Hoad

The stage was set for 21-year-old top seed Lew Hoad to become the second man in history (and first Aussie) to win a calendar year Grand Slam at the 1956 US Championships. He had already won the Australian, French and Wimbledon crowns earlier that year.

He won through to the US final to face his good friend, doubles partner and number 2 seed Ken Rosewall. Hoad had beaten Rosewall in 4 sets in both the Australian and Wimbledon finals in 1956. But Rosewall turned the tables in the US, beating Hoad in 4. As you've seen earlier in this chapter, it was fellow Aussie Rod Laver who became the second man in history (and first Aussie) to win a calendar year Grand Slam 6 years later in 1962.

Like many of his contemporaries, Hoad turned pro in the prime of his career in 1957 after defending his Wimbledon title. He received a then record sign-on fee of 56,000 British pounds.[100] He was immediately banned from playing in Grand Slam events, only returning very late in his career after the ban was lifted in 1968 when he was well past his best.[101]

The Aussie Pro Pioneers

As you've seen in this chapter, many of Australia's greats during this golden era between 1953 and April 1968 turned pro in the prime of their careers. In chronological order, they included Frank Sedgman, Ken Rosewall, Lew Hoad, Mal Anderson, Ashley Cooper and Rod Laver. They were banned from competing in Grand Slam events as a result. Many (if not all) would have likely had far more Grand Slam singles titles but for the ban.

These pro pioneers also blazed the trail for the earnings that all players have enjoyed ever since the Open Era began with the French Open in April 1968.

Many years later, Rod Laver recalled his pro tour experience: *"When I look back, when I turned pro I was shell-shocked. I played Ken Rosewall and Lew Hoad and all these guys and I realised that my game was so bad against the pros that I almost had to re-learn so much of the tennis. I could win in the amateurs and not really have to improve so much. When I turned pro I thought to myself I'm pretty good but I had a shock, I got beaten all the time. I played Lew Hoad 12 or 13 times when I first turned pro and couldn't beat him once."*[102]

Ken Rosewall also reflected on the struggles of life as an 'outcast' pro in the early days. Some of those struggles included:

- playing in any venues that would allow them (including covered ice rinks), as they were banned from using any facilities associated with national tennis associations.
- regularly travelling from city to city (often by car) to play in one-off exhibition matches that were in addition to their pro tournament schedule.

"There was a lot of opposition. We were not supported that much by tennis officials around the world, so it was a pretty hard slog."[103]

It's a far cry from the pro tennis tour today!

Chapter 4
Aussie Women at the Majors
(1960–January 1968)

The 1960s was the decade where Australian women really made their mark on Grand Slam events across the globe, as well as continuing on their winning ways at the Australian Championships. Unlike the men, there was no pro tennis tour for women at all pre-April 1968, All of the world's best players where still amateur until the Open Era started with the French Open in April 1968.

Two Australian women won Grand Slam singles events during this period – Margaret Smith (Court) and Lesley Turner (Bowrey). Smith (Court) won an incredible 13 titles, and Turner (Bowrey) 2. And as you'll see in Chapter 6, Court won another 11 more Grand Slam singles titles in the Open Era, giving her 24 in total, a record that still stands today for female players, and that was only equalled by Serbia's Novak Djokovic in 2023 among male players.[104]

The Australian Championships (1960–January 1968)

This was an era of near total dominance by Margaret Smith (Court). She was the only Australian woman to win the singles title at our local major during this time period, and as you'll see in Chapter 6, she won it another 4 times in the Open Era.

Margaret Smith (Court) – 7 titles

New South Wales' Margaret Smith (Court) won an incredible 7 straight women's singles titles at the Australian Championships between 1960 and 1966, not losing a single set in 4 of those tournaments. Tall and lean, she was known for her serve/volley style and high fitness level.

She was only 17 at the time of her first win in 1960. Despite her youth, she was still seeded seventh. Her breakthrough win came against the top-seeded Brazilian (and reigning Wimbledon and US champion) Maria Bueno in 3 sets in the quarter-finals. She then upset defending champion and fellow Aussie Mary Carter (Reitano) in 3 sets in the semi-finals, before beating another Aussie (and third seed) Jan Lehane (O'Neill) in straight sets in the final.

It was to be the first of 4 consecutive singles finals that Smith (Court) and Lehane (O'Neill) would play at the Australian Championships, and the result was the same every time. Smith (Court's) next 3 singles title wins in her home major came against fellow Aussie Lesley Turner (Bowrey) (1964), Brazilian Maria Bueno (1965) and Nancy Richey from the US in a walkover (1966).[105]

She missed the opportunity to win an eighth straight Australian Championship title in 1967 due to a brief retirement from the sport, and then finished runner-up to American Billie Jean Moffitt (King) in 1968. But as you'll see in Chapter 6, she won another 4 Australian singles crowns at the renamed Australian Open during the Open Era, giving her 11 in total. That's a record that still stands today.

And as you'll see in Chapters 9 and 10, Smith/Court's Grand Slam dominance during her era wasn't just confined to singles.[106]

Chapter 4 – Aussie Women at the Majors (1960–January 1968)

Two Aussie women finished as multiple runners-up to Margaret Smith (Court) during her golden reign at the Australian Championships in the 1960s when it was still an amateur event – Jan Lehane (O'Neill) and Lesley Turner (Bowrey). They were also the only Australian runners-up in the women's singles at our home Grand Slam during this time period.

Jan Lehane (O'Neill)

New South Wales' Jan Lehane (O'Neill) was a 4-time runner-up to Margaret Smith (Court) in the women's singles at the Australian Championships between 1960 and 1963. Unfortunately, that was as close as she got to a Grand Slam singles title during her career. However, she can lay claim to being the first leading female player to use a double-handed backhand, a technique that's very common today.[107]

Lesley Turner (Bowrey)

New South Wales' Lesley Turner (Bowrey) was a two-time runner-up in the women's singles at the Australian Championships. She was the second seed in 1964 and lost the final in straight sets to Margaret Smith (Court).

She was the second seed again in 1967 (during Margaret Smith/Court's brief retirement) when she finished runner-up to top-seeded American Nancy Richey.

Like Jan Lehane (O'Neill), being a runner-up was as close as Lesley Turner (Bowrey) got to winning the singles at her home Grand Slam. But as you'll see later in the chapter, she had more success at the French Open. And as you'll see in Chapters 9 and 10, she also had plenty of Grand Slam success in doubles, including with Margaret Smith (Court).[108]

Lesley Turner married Bill Bowrey in 1968, shortly after he had become the last man to win the men's singles at the Australian Championships in the Amateur Era.

The French Championships (1960–1967)

Two Aussie women won the singles at the French Championships in the 1960s when it was still an amateur event – Margaret Smith (Court) and Lesley Turner (Bowrey). Between them, they won 4 of the 8 French women's singles titles in this period. And as you'll see in Chapter 6, Court won the French Grand Slam event 3 more times in the Open Era.

Margaret Smith (Court) – 2 titles

Margaret Smith (Court) became Australia's first female international Grand Slam winner at an international event when she won the 1962 French Championships as a nineteen-year-old. The only Australian woman who had ever made it to an international Grand Slam final prior to Smith (Court) was Nancye Wynne (Bolton). She finished runner-up at the US Championships 24 years earlier in 1938.

Smith (Court) was already a 3-time winner at the Australian Championships by the time she arrived at Roland Garros in 1962 as the second seed. She had made the quarter-finals as the third seed the year before on her first visit. The top seed in 1962 was England's Ann Jones, but she was upset in the semi-finals by 13th-seeded fellow Aussie Lesley Turner (Bowrey), who was just 19 years old at the time like Smith (Court).

It was a hard-fought final between the 2 Australian teenagers, with Smith (Court) prevailing in 3 sets. She won the third set 7-5, after being down a match point.[109] As outlined in Chapter 3, fellow Aussie Rod Laver also beat Roy Emerson in the men's singles at the 1962 French Championships, making it a double triumph for Australia.

Smith (Court) won her second French Championship final 2 years later in 1964 as the top seed. She beat the second-seeded Brazilian Maria Bueno in 3 sets, after dropping the first. She returned to defend her title the following year, but as you'll see in the next boxed feature, she finished runner-up to Lesley Turner (Bowrey).

And as you'll see in Chapter 6, Court won another 3 French Opens in the Open Era.[110]

Lesley Turner (Bowrey) – 2 titles

Lesley Turner (Bowrey) had a strong baseline game that was well suited to the clay courts at Roland Garros. As you've seen in the previous boxed feature, she surprised everyone by making it to the 1962 French Championships final as a nineteen-year-old and came within a point of beating fellow Aussie teenager Margaret Smith (Court).

Turner (Bowrey) returned to Roland Garros the following year in 1963 as the second seed behind Smith (Court). However, Smith (Court) was knocked out in the quarter-finals. Turner (Bowrey) won her way through to the final without dropping a set. There she faced 24-year-old English fifth seed Ann Jones. Jones won the first set before Turner (Bowrey) stormed back to take the next 2 and the match. And as outlined in Chapter 3, fellow Aussie Roy Emerson won the men's singles title at the 1963 French Championships, making it an Australian double for the second year in a row after Margaret Smith (Court) and Rod Laver had done it the year before.

> Two years later, Turner (Bowrey) was the third seed at the 1965 French Championships. She upset the second-seeded Brazilian Maria Beuno in 3 sets in the semi-finals to set up a showdown in the final against top seed and defending champion Margaret Smith (Court). This time, Turner (Bowrey) beat Smith (Court) in straight sets to clinch her second French title. And as you'll see in Chapter 9, she then combined with Smith (Court) to win the women's doubles to cap off a remarkable tournament. Once again, it was also an Aussie double in the singles at the French Championships in 1965, with Fred Stolle winning the men's singles.
>
> Turner (Bowrey) finished runner-up for a second time at the French Championships in 1967, which was the last time it was an amateur event. She was the fourth seed, and lost the final in 3 sets to local French favourite 'Frankie' Dürr.[111]

Wimbledon (1960–1967)

Margaret Smith (Court) was the first Australian woman to reach a Wimbledon singles final. She did it 3 times in the Amateur Era, and as you'll see in Chapter 6, she played in 2 more Wimbledon singles finals in the Open Era.

> ### Margaret Smith (Court) – 2 titles
>
> Margaret Smith (Court) made 3 consecutive Wimbledon finals between 1963 and 1965, winning 2.
>
> In 1963, she was still just 20 years old and the top seed after having won her fourth consecutive Australian Championships on grass earlier that year. As expected, she won through to the final where she was due to face the giant-killing, 19-year-old American Billie Jean Moffitt (King).
>
> Moffitt (King) was unseeded and playing her first Grand Slam singles final, having beaten Aussie number 2 seed Lesley Turner (Bowrey) in 3 sets in the

fourth round, the seventh-seeded Brazilian Maria Bueno in straight sets in the quarter-finals, and England's number 3 seed Ann Jones in straight sets in the semi-finals. But Smith (Court) was too strong, winning her first Wimbledon singles crown in straight sets.

She went back to the All England Club to defend her title in 1964, again as the top seed after having won her fifth consecutive Australian singles crown and her second French singles title earlier that year. As expected, Smith (Court) won through to the final, as did the 24-year-old second-seed, Brazil's Maria Bueno (who had previously won consecutive women's singles at Wimbledon in 1959 and 1960).

Bueno won the first set, before Smith (Court) came back to win a hard-fought second set 9-7 (it was still the pre-tie-break era). It was anyone's match at 1-set all, but Beuno prevailed in the third set to win her third Wimbledon singles crown.

By the time the Wimbledon Grand Slam rolled around again in 1965, Smith (Court) had won her sixth consecutive singles title at the Australian Championships. She had beaten Maria Bueno in 3 sets in the Australian final, when Bueno retired with injury down 5-2 in the third set. However, Bueno was the top seed at Wimbledon as the defending champion, and Smith (Court) was seeded second.

Results went as expected, and the pair met in the final. This time, Smith (Court) won in straight sets to secure her second Wimbledon singles title. Fellow Aussie Roy Emerson won the men's singles in 1965 at Wimbledon as well, making it an Aussie double in the singles events at the tournament for the first time.

And as you'll see in Chapter 6, Smith (Court) won another Wimbledon singles title in the Open Era.[112]

Australia's Grand Slam Tennis Champions

The US Championships (1960–1967)

Margaret Smith (Court) was the only Australian woman to reach the singles final at the US Championships in the Amateur Era. She did it 3 times. She was only the second Aussie to ever reach the women's singles final there (after Nancye Wynne (Bolton's) runner-up effort in 1938).

And as you'll see in Chapter 6, Smith (Court) played in another 3 US women's singles finals in the Open Era, winning all of them.

Margaret Smith (Court) – 2 titles

Margaret Smith (Court) became the first Aussie woman to win the women's singles at the US Championships in 1962. The tournament was played on grass back then, and the then 20-year-old Smith (Court) had already won 3 Australian singles titles on the same surface when she arrived in the US as the top seed.

She won her way through to the final with a tough, 3-set semi-final win over her Brazilian rival Maria Bueno, the third seed. That set up a meeting with the fifth-seeded American Darlene Hard. Smith (Court) won the first set 9-7, before taking the second set 6-4 and her first US Grand Slam singles crown.

The 1962 US Championships was an historic tournament for Australian tennis for 2 reasons. Not only did Margaret Smith (Court) become the first Aussie woman to win it, but it was also the event where Rod Laver became the first Aussie man (and only the second person in history) to win a calendar year Grand Slam when he won the 1962 US men's singles crown.

Smith (Court) returned to defend her US title as the top seed in 1963 after she had won her fourth Australian and first Wimbledon titles earlier in the year. Once again, she won her way through to the final to play Brazilian number 4 seed Maria Bueno. However, this time Bueno proved to be too strong, winning in straight sets.

Smith (Court) would win her second US singles title in 1965 when she was 23 years old and again the top seed. Her opponent in the final was fifth-seeded American Billie Jean Moffitt (King). Smith (Court) won in 2 tough sets, 8-6, 7-5.[113]

Part 2
Singles in the Open Era
(April 1968 onwards)

Chapter 5
Aussie Men at the Majors
(April 1968–1986)

The Grand Slam Open Era began for both men and women with the renamed French Open in April 1968. Aussie professionals like Rod Laver and Ken Rosewall were finally welcomed back to the fold after years in the Grand Slam wilderness.

It had to happen. Many tennis associations around the world had been paying amateurs 'under the table' amounts anyway for years to try and keep top male players in their federations and away from the men's pro tour (as no women's pro tour existed prior to 1968).[114]

Eventually, common sense prevailed and the sport's governing global body (the International Lawn Tennis Federation) agreed to the birth of the Open Era. Both men and women would be able to compete for prizemoney in Grand Slam events and any other ILTF-sanctioned event. This decision paved the way for the sport as we know it today around the world. Another change that soon followed was the introduction of the tie-break in 1970 for all but the deciding sets in Grand Slam events.[115]

Our top Aussie men's players embraced the professional era with gusto. Between them, Rod Laver, John Newcombe and Ken Rosewall won 14 of the first 28 men's singles events in the Open Era between April 1968 and January 1975 – 5 of the 7 Australian Opens played during this period,[116] 4 of the 7 Wimbledon titles,[117] 3 of the 7 US Opens,[118] and 2 of the 7 French Opens.[119] This is more than double the tally of the next best-performing country (the United States), as the following graph shows.

Nationality of Men's Grand Slam Singles Winners (April 1968 — January 1975)

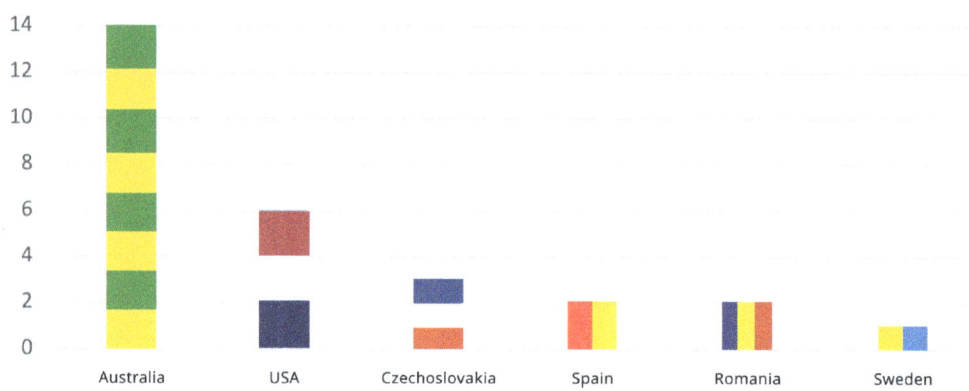

This tally is even more remarkable when you consider that Laver, Rosewall and Newcombe were all banned from competing at Wimbledon and the French Open in 1972. This was due to them playing on the World Championship Tennis (WCT) circuit. More on that later in this chapter.[120]

The mid-1970s certainly proved to be the end of our golden age in Grand Slam men's tennis. Other than an upset victory at the 1976 Australian Open by the unheralded Mark Edmondson (see the feature box later on this chapter), it would be more than a decade before an Australian man (Pat Cash) hoisted another Grand Slam singles trophy (see Chapter 7).

Let's look at our Aussie men's triumphs and near misses between April 1968 and the end of 1986.

The French Open (1968–1986)

Two Aussies won the first 2 men's singles titles at Roland Garros in the Open Era:

- Ken Rosewall (and he also won the men's singles at the French Championships as an amateur – see Chapter 3).
- Rod Laver (and like Rosewall, he also won the men's singles at the French Championships as an amateur – see Chapter 3).

Both finished runner-up to each other in their respective French Open Era finals. An Australian man has not won the French singles crown since, nor made the final.[121]

Ken Rosewall

Ken Rosewall won the 1968 French Open, the first Grand Slam event of the Open Era. He had spent more than a decade banned from competing in Grand Slam tournaments after turning pro at the end of 1956, missing 45 events.

His 1968 French Open singles victory at the age of 33 was his second at Roland Garros after having won the French Championships as an 18-year-old amateur in 1953 (see Chapter 3). He was the second seed in 1968, behind fellow Aussie and returning pro Rod Laver, who was 29 at the time. Fittingly, both won through to the final.

Their head-to-head singles record at the time in both amateur and professional events stood at 58-55 in favour of Laver, with the vast majority having been played as pros. But Rosewall made history as the first men's Grand Slam winner of the Open Era, beating Laver in 4 sets.[122] He pocketed 15,000 Francs, which was the French currency of the era.[123]

He returned to defend his title in 1969, but this time Laver turned the tables on him in the final as you'll see in the following feature box.

Rod Laver

Rod Laver won the 1969 French Open men's singles at the age of 30 after finishing runner-up to fellow Aussie and good friend Ken Rosewall at the 1968 event.

It was his second French title after he had won the French Championships as a 23-year-old amateur in 1962 on his way to a calendar year Grand Slam (see Chapter 3). He was banned from the next 21 Grand Slam events after he turned pro at the end of that year.

He entered the 1969 French Open as the top seed after having won the renamed Australian Open earlier that year. As expected, he won his way through to the final to face defending champion and the third-seeded Rosewall. He beat him in straight sets. 50 years later, both players reflected on their styles and tactics for the match.

Rosewall: *"I suppose we were opposites because he had a lot of power and variation, and my game was consistent."*

Laver: *"You think, how am I going to play this man because he beat me last year? The only thing I think I have is maybe I can hit the ball a bit harder, and put a little more spin on it.... Don't let him work me, let me work him over."*[124]

To this day, Laver is the last Aussie to have won a French Open title. No Aussie man has ever even reached the final since.

Wimbledon (1968–1986)

Like the French Open, an Aussie won the first 2 men's singles titles at Wimbledon in the Open Era. In fact, 2 Aussies won the first 4 men's Wimbledon singles titles in the Open Era:

- Rod Laver (2 wins to go with the 2 titles he won as an amateur – see Chapter 3).
- John Newcombe (2 wins to go with the 1 title he won as an amateur – see Chapter 3).

Three Aussies also finished as runner-up between 1968 and 1986 – Tony Roche and Newcombe (once each) and Ken Rosewall (twice).

Rod Laver

Rod Laver won the first Wimbledon men's singles title of the Open Era in 1968 at the age of 29, after having won the event as an amateur in both 1961 and 1962 (see Chapter 3).

He was the top seed for the 1968 tournament and the heavy favourite in the final against fellow Aussie and number 15 seed Tony Roche, who was 23 at the time. Laver won the match in straight sets and collected prizemoney of £2000.[125]

He was back to defend his title as the top seed in 1969 after having won both the Australian and French Opens earlier that year. He faced another Aussie in the final, the then 25-year-old and sixth-seeded John Newcombe. "Newk" pushed him to 4 sets, but Laver prevailed.

The win set him up for a shot at becoming the first person to win 2 calendar year Grand Slams (after winning his first in 1962, the year before he turned pro). He would have to travel to the US Open to make history as you'll see later in this chapter.[126]

John Newcombe

John Newcombe bounced back from his 1969 Wimbledon final loss against Rod Laver to win back-to-back Wimbledon titles in 1970 and 1971. The wins gave him 3 career Wimbledon singles titles, after he'd won the last amateur event in 1967 (see Chapter 3).

"Newk" was the second seed for the event in 1970 behind Laver, but became the favourite when Laver was bundled out in the fourth round in 4 sets by England's number 16 seed Roger Taylor.

Newk's opponent in the final was number 5 seed Ken Rosewall, who was 35 at the time and attempting to win the only Grand Slam singles title that had eluded him. He was the sentimental favourite, even though Newk was a very popular player in his own right. Newk was 9 years younger, and many years later, he recalled the atmosphere: *"When I got him down they were trying to will him to come back. If I would miss a shot they would applaud. When Ken hit a winner they applauded really loud."*[127]

Rosewall pushed him to 5 sets before he eventually claimed victory.

Newk came back to successfully defend his title in 1971. It was his third straight Wimbledon final. Even though he was the defending champion, Rod Laver was again the top seed. But for the second year in a row, Laver bowed out again in 4 sets in the fourth round, this time to unseeded Dutchman Tom Okker.

Newk's opponent in the 1971 Wimbledon final was fourth-seeded American Stan Smith. Just like his win a year earlier against Rosewall, he had to do it the hard way in 5 sets. He was even down 2 sets to 1 against Smith before winning the last 2 and the match. *"I rate my win over Ken higher since he was one of my boyhood heroes,"* Newk later recalled. *"It was a magic moment for me to play back-to-back Wimbledon finals against Laver and Rosewall."*

Sadly, Newcombe didn't get a chance to win 3 titles in a row in 1972. He was a contracted player for World Championship Tennis (WCT) in this era (as were Rod Laver, Ken Rosewall and Tony Roche), and the International Lawn Tennis Federation (ILTF) banned all WCT-contracted players from competing in all of its sanctioned events for a 6-month period in 1972.

The underlying issue was that the WCT wanted fees from tournament organisers to guarantee that their contracted players would compete. The ILTF wasn't prepared to do that. The ban resulted in WCT players missing both the 1972 Wimbledon and French Open tournaments.[128]

Decades later, Newcombe reiterated his frustration with the decision: *"All the WCT players realised they were not allowed to play, but being the two-time defending champion I put my entry form in and turned up at Wimbledon. They still would not allow me to play. That was devastating. Nobody had won Wimbledon 3 years in*

> *a row since Fred Perry from 1934-36, so I would have had a chance to make some history."*[129]

Tony Roche

Tony Roche was a giant-killing 23-year-old at the 1968 Wimbledon final. The left-handed number 15 seed upset the second-seeded Ken Rosewall (in straight sets) and US number 10 seed Butch Buchholz (in 4 sets) on his way to the final.

But his dream run ended in straight sets against Laver. It was the first and only Wimbledon singles final of Roche's career, though as you'll see in Chapter 8, he had plenty of Wimbledon success in doubles with John Newcombe.[130]

Ken Rosewall

Wimbledon is the only men's Grand Slam singles title that eluded Ken Rosewall during his decorated career (though he did miss a total of 12 Wimbledon tournaments due to the pro tour and WCT bans).

As outlined in Chapter 3, Rosewall finished runner-up in the Wimbledon men's singles twice as an amateur – 1954 and 1956. And as outlined earlier in this chapter, he lost in 5 sets a Wimbledon final at the age of 35 to John Newcombe in the Open Era in 1970.

Amazingly, he made his fourth Wimbledon final in 1974 at the age of 39, 20 years after his first Wimbledon final. He was the ninth seed and an underdog in 1974, but also the overwhelming sentimental favourite against third-seeded

American Jimmy Connors, who was 18 years younger and the reigning Australian Open champion.

Rosewall had beaten the top-seeded John Newcombe in the quarter-finals and the fourth-seeded American Stan Smith in 5 sets in the semi-finals, but there was no fairy tale ending in the final. Connors beat him in straight sets.[131]

The US Open (1968–1986)

The US Championships was rebranded as the US Open in 1968 when pros were first allowed to compete. Three Aussies won 3 of the first 6 men's singles titles at the US Open:

- Rod Laver (1 win to go with the 1 he won as an amateur – see Chapter 3).
- Ken Rosewall (1 win to go with the 1 he won as an amateur – see Chapter 3).
- John Newcombe (1 win to go with the 1 he won as an amateur – see Chapter 3).

Two Aussies also finished as runner-up between 1968 and 1986 – Tony Roche (twice) and Ken Rosewall. The US Open briefly switched from grass to clay for 3 years from 1975 before settling on a hard-court surface in 1978.[132]

Rod Laver

The stage was set at the US Open for Rod Laver to become the first person in tennis history to win 2 calendar year Grand Slams, having achieved the feat in 1962 as an amateur (see Chapter 3).

He duly delivered and is still to this day the only player to have achieved this feat. Laver is also the last male player to have won a calendar year Grand Slam, and the only player to have done it in the Open Era.

Not all of the best players in the world were competing in the Grand Slams in 1962 due to the professional ban in place at the time, but they all were in 1969. We'll never know if he'd have won any more calendar year Grand Slams during the 5 full years of his own pro ban between 1963 and 1967.

Three of his 4 finals' victories in his 1969 Grand Slam came against fellow Aussies: Ken Rosewall in the French Open, John Newcombe at Wimbledon, and Tony Roche at the US Open.

The eyes of the tennis world were on Laver as he attempted to make history in the US, and he almost stumbled in the fourth round. He was down 2 sets to 1 against local number 16 seed Dick Ralston, before storming back to win in 5.

Laver then beat fellow Aussie Roy Emerson in 4 sets in the quarters, and then followed up with a straight-sets win over the defending champion and local favourite Arthur Ashe in the semi-finals. That set up a meeting with Tony Roche, the third seed, who had beaten Laver 5 of the 8 times they had played that year, and who had also beaten second seed John Newcombe in the semi-finals.[133]

The final was scheduled for September 7, which was also the day Laver's wife was due to give birth to their first child. However, torrential rain delayed the final by a day, and Mary Laver's pregnancy also went into overtime.

The rain eased a little the following day, enabling the final to get under way. However, the court was still wet and slippery, despite a helicopter having hovered over it to try and dry it out. The US Open was still played on grass in 1969.

Both players found the slippery surface tough, and when Laver lost his footing when serving for the first set, he asked the match referee if he could wear spikes. As it was the last match of the tournament and there were no implications of any damage done to the court by the spikes, there was no objection.

However, Roche decided against donning spikes himself as he had a thigh injury from his semi-final win over Newcombe. He feared aggravating it by coming to sudden stops when wearing spikes.

The pair were locked at 1-set all when rain forced another delay. Laver emerged from the delay to blast his way through the next 2 sets to win the match and complete his second career Grand Slam.[134]

Laver reflected on his career and playing style on the 50th anniversary of his 1969 Grand Slam: *"I always found myself wanting to be the person that hits the winner, not just putting the ball back until somebody missed."*[135]

The 1969 US Open was to be Laver's final Grand Slam singles title. He elected not to even attempt to defend his titles at the Australian and French Opens in 1970, focusing on lucrative WCT events instead.[136]

Ken Rosewall

Ken Rosewall was attempting to win his second US Grand Slam singles title in the 1970 final at the age of 35. As outlined in Chapter 3, he won the event as an amateur way back in 1956.

He was the third seed at the 1970 US Open behind Rod Laver and John Newcombe. Earlier that year, he had finished runner-up to John Newcombe in 5 sets in the Wimbledon singles final. But Rosewall turned the tables on "Newk" in the US Open semi-finals, beating him in straight sets.

Laver had earlier been upset in 5 sets in the fourth round by American number 19 seed Dick Ralston, clearing the path for fourth seed Tony Roche to make the final. Roche won the first set, but Rosewall came back to win in 4 (including winning the third set in a tie-breaker). The 1970 US Open was the first Grand Slam event to feature tie-breakers. The tie-break format was slightly different to the one we know today. The winner was the first to 5 points, and there was no need to win by 2 points.[137]

Incredibly, Rosewall reached the US Open final 4 years later at the age of 39 in 1974. This was the last US Open tournament played on grass. He had finished runner-up at Wimbledon earlier that year as well.

Rosewall was the fifth seed at the US Open and won his way through to the final by beating Newk in 4 sets in the semi-finals. That set him up for a rematch in the final against the man who beat him at Wimbledon – 22-year-old local Jimmy Connors, who was the top seed who had also won the Australian Open earlier that year as well.[138]

Sadly, it was one-way traffic in the final. Rosewall only won 2 games in a straight sets' demolition by Connors. It was the last Grand Slam final that Ken Rosewall played in his legendary career.[139]

John Newcombe

John Newcombe won the 1973 US Open after having won the Australian Open earlier that year. It was his second US Grand Slam title after he'd won the event as an amateur back in 1967 (see Chapter 3).

Newcombe was the tenth seed at the 1973 US Open after only playing a light tournament schedule since the start of 1972.[140] He beat 21-year-old local favourite and ninth seed Jimmy Connors in the quarter-finals in straight sets, then fifth seed Ken Rosewall in straight sets in the semi-finals. Those wins set him up for a meeting with 27-year-old, sixth-seeded Czech Jan Kodeš in the final. He was 2 sets to 1 down before he came back to win in 5 sets.[141]

Tony Roche

As outlined earlier in the chapter, Tony Roche was on the other side of the net when Rod Laver won his 1969 calendar year Grand Slam by winning the US Open.

And as also outlined earlier in the chapter, he finished runner-up in the US Open a year later to Ken Rosewall. These 2 finals were the closest he came to lifting the US Open singles trophy.

The Australian Open (1969–1986)

The Australian Open was renamed in January 1969 when it included both professional players and prizemoney for the first time. However, scheduling and comparatively low prizemoney issues began to plague the tournament shortly afterwards for a decade. It resulted in fewer international players making the long trek to compete, despite it being a Grand Slam event.

Between 1972 and 1974, the Australian Open's January start date was moved to Boxing Day. This inconvenient start date was made worse in 1975 when it was moved to 21 December, before it moved back to Boxing Day in 1976. The tournament then had two 1977 editions – one in early January and the other in mid-to-late December. The poor timing over Christmas and New Year continued until 1982 (when it was moved to run between late November and mid-December until 1985). In 1986, the decision was made to not hold a November/December tournament and to move the permanent start date to January from 1987 onwards.

Four Aussies won the men's singles at our premier tennis tournament between the start of the Open Era and the end of 1986:

- Ken Rosewall (2 wins to go with the 2 titles he won as an amateur – see Chapter 3)
- John Newcombe (2)
- Rod Laver (1, to go with the 1 he won as an amateur – see Chapter 3).
- Mark Edmondson.

Aussies who finished runner-up at the Australian Open during this era were:

- Dick Crealy (1970)
- Mal Anderson (1972)
- Phil Dent (1974)
- John Newcombe (1976)
- John Marks (1978)
- Kim Warwick (1980).

For all but John Newcombe and Mal Anderson (who won the men's singles at the US Championships as an amateur in 1957), it was the closest they would ever come to a Grand Slam singles title.[142]

Let's take a closer look at the local Australian Open champions from this era, including some very familiar names from Chapter 4.

Ken Rosewall (2 titles)

Ken Rosewall achieved the rare feat of winning a men's Grand Slam singles title without dropping a single set when he won the Australian Open in 1971 at the age of 36.

He was the second seed at the tournament behind Rod Laver that year, but Laver was bundled out in the third round in 4 sets by Englishman Mark Cox, who was the number 15 seed.

Rosewall beat 27-year-old, third-seeded American Arthur Ashe in the 1971 final.

He went back-to-back at the 1972 Australian Open at the age of 37. Rosewall was the second seed behind a 27-year-old John Newcombe, but Newk was knocked out by the eighth-seeded Aussie Mal Anderson in 5 sets in the quarter-finals.

Anderson was 36 years old at the time and won his way through to the final by beating fourth-seeded Alex Metreveli from the Soviet Union. But Rosewall won the battle of the veterans in the final in straight sets. It was his last Grand Slam singles title, and his record of being the oldest man to win one in the Open Era at 37 years of age still stands to this day.

He also holds the record for winning Grand Slam singles titles 19 years apart. He won both the Australian and French Opens in 1953 as a fresh-faced 18-year-old (see Chapter 3), and then his final Australian Open in 1972. He won 4 Australian titles in total, 2 as an amateur and 2 as a pro.[143]

John Newcombe (2 titles)

John Newcombe won the first of his 2 Australian men's singles titles in 1973 when he was the second seed behind defending champion Ken Rosewall. The then 38-year-old Rosewall was knocked out in the second round by unseeded West German Karl Meiler in straight sets. "Newk" beat the New Zealand number 12 seed Onny Parun in 4 sets in the final.

He was the second seed again for the 1975 Australian Open behind American Jimmy Connors, who was the defending champion after having beaten Aussie Phil Dent in the final the year before. Connors was also the reigning Wimbledon and US Open champion at the time after having beaten veteran Ken Rosewall in both the year before.

As the 2 top seeds, Newk and Connors were expected to meet in the final. But Newk had a tough time getting there, being pushed to 5 sets 3 times. The first was against unseeded West German Rolf Gehring in the second round. Fellow Aussies Geoff Masters (the number 7 seed) and Tony Roche (the number 3 seed) then took him to 5 sets in the quarter and semi-finals respectively.

Connors by contrast had only dropped one set on the way to the final. He was fresher heading in and also more than 7 years younger than Newk (who was 30 at the time). But Newk found a way to win the last Grand Slam singles title of his career, beating Connors in 4 sets.

He came back to defend his title in 1976 but finished runner-up to fellow Aussie Mark Edmondson in an upset result.[144]

Rod Laver

Rod Laver won the first Australian Grand Slam event of the Open Era in 1969 as the first leg of his calendar year Grand Slam.

He was the top seed and beat 31-year-old, ninth-seeded Spaniard Andrés Gimeno in straight sets in the final. Gimeno set himself on the path to the final by upsetting second seed Ken Rosewall in straight sets in the third round.

The 1969 win was the third and final Australian title of

Laver's career after his amateur wins in 1960 and 1962 (see Chapter 3).[145]

Mark Edmondson

"Eddo" won the 1976 Australian Open as an unseeded 21-year-old from New South Wales who was ranked number 212 in the world at the time. In an interview with Pat Cash to recall his upset win 40 years later, Edmondson recalled how lucky he was to even get in the draw: *"I was the last or second last in. It was a 64-man draw then, not 128. With a 64 draw and not all the world's players coming to the Open like they do now, at the 11th hour someone pulled out and I was in."*[146]

Eddo's game was built around a big serve. His scalps on the way to the final included fellow Aussies Phil Dent (the number 5 seed and 1974 Australian Open finalist) in 4 sets in the second round, Dick Crealy (the number 13 seed and 1970 Australian Open finalist) in straight sets in the quarter-finals, and 41-year-old veteran Ken Rosewall in 4 sets in the semi-finals.

His semi-final win set him up for a showdown in the final with defending champion and top seed John Newcombe. Both had distinctive 'handlebar' moustaches that were in fashion at the time.

On a very windy summer's day, Edmondson's booming serve didn't let him down. He wasn't broken once during the match. He lost the first set in a tie-breaker before winning the next 3 sets and the title.

It was the only Grand Slam singles victory of Eddo's career, but he remains the last Australian to win the Australian Open men's singles to this day.[147]

Chapter 6
Aussie Women at the Majors
(April 1968–1986)

The Open Era began for both women and men with the renamed French Open in April 1968. For the first time, women would be able to compete for prizemoney in tournaments, including Grand Slam events. However, as you'll see later in this chapter, the gulf in prizemoney between men's and women's events was significant for a long time in the Open Era.

Margaret Smith (Court) led the Aussie women's charge into the professional era, and within a few years she was joined by Evonne Goolagong (Cawley). Between them, they won 18 Grand Slam singles titles between April 1968 and mid-1980, with each having a child along the way.

Court won 11 of the 12 Grand Slam singles finals she contested in the Open Era (4 Australian Opens, 3 French Opens, 3 US Opens and 1 Wimbledon crown), including 6 consecutive titles between 1969 and 1971. Her 11 Open Era Grand Slam singles titles gives her 24 in total when you factor in her amateur career. As highlighted in Chapter 4, this remains the all-time record for women to this day and was only equalled by Serbia's Novak Djokovic in 2023 for male players. She is also the only Australian woman to have won a calendar year Grand Slam, achieving the feat in 1970.[148] More on that later in this chapter.

Goolagong (Cawley) reached 18 Grand Slam singles finals, winning 7 (4 Australian Opens, 2 Wimbledon crowns, and 1 French Open). And as you'll see later in this chapter, she came agonisingly close to winning the US Open and achieving a career Grand Slam, finishing runner-up in that tournament 4 years in a row.[149]

However, 1980 proved to be the end of our golden age in women's tennis. It would be more than 3 decades before another Australian woman (Sam Stosur) hoisted another

Grand Slam singles trophy (see Chapter 7).

Let's look at our Aussie women's triumphs and near misses between April 1968 and the end of 1986.

The French Open (1968–1986)

Four Aussie women made at least one singles final at Roland Garros in this era – Margaret Smith (Court), Evonne Goolagong (Cawley), Helen Gourlay (Cawley) and Wendy Turnbull.

Margaret Smith (Court) – 2 titles

Margaret Smith (Court) won back-to-back French Opens in 1969 and 1970 after having previously won 2 French Championships as an amateur – see Chapter 4).

She didn't compete in the first French tournament of the Open Era in 1968 as she was temporarily retired at the time.[150] In 1969, she was back as the top seed at 26 years of age after having won the Australian Open earlier that year (see later feature box in this chapter).

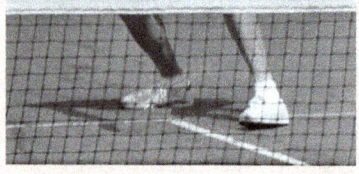

She didn't drop a set in 1969 on her way to the semi-finals where she met the fourth-seeded defending champion, 26-year-old American Nancy Richey. Court beat her in 3 tight sets. She then went on to defeat England's number 3 seed, 30-year-old Ann Jones, in 3 sets in the final. Rod Laver also won the men's singles at the French Open that year (see Chapter 5).

Court was back to defend her title in 1970 as the number one seed. Once again, she had won the Australian Open earlier that year. As expected, she won through to the final and beat West Germany's number 7 seed Helga Niessen in straight sets in the final. Niessen had earlier beaten American number 2 seed

Billie Jean Moffitt (King) in the quarter-finals.

Court won one more French Open singles title in her decorated career. It happened in 1973 after she had missed the 1972 tournament due to having her first child. Yet again she was the top seed at Roland Garros after winning the Australian Open earlier that year. The number 2 seed was an up-and-coming American Chris Evert, who was then just 18 years old and competing in her first Grand Slam singles final. Evert hadn't dropped a set getting to the final, and Court had only dropped one.

It was an epic final with the first 2 sets both going to tie-breakers. Evert won the first and 30-year-old Court won the second. She then went on to win the third set 6-4. It was the fifth and final French title of her career. She didn't defend her title in 1974 due to being pregnant with her second child.[151]

Evonne Goolagong (Cawley)

Born and raised in regional New South Wales where she began playing on ant-bed courts, Evonne Goolagong (Cawley) was only 19 years old when she entered the 1971 French Open as the third seed. Earlier that year she had finished runner-up to top seed Margaret Smith (Court) at the Australian Open.

But Court was bundled out in straight sets in the third round by unseeded local Gail Chanfreau, and England's number 2 seed Virginia Wade was upset in the first round.

Those 2 early exits paved the way for Goolagong (Cawley) and another Aussie to reach the final – unseeded 24-year-old Tasmanian giant killer, Helen Gourlay (Cawley). Gourlay (Cawley's) big scalp was 1968 French Open winner, American number 4 seed Nancy Richey. She beat her in straight sets in the semi-finals. That was the end of her dream run though. Goolagong beat her in straight sets in the final to win her first Grand Slam singles title.[152]

She was back to defend her Roland Garros title as the top seed in 1972. There was no Margaret Smith (Court) in the draw as she had her first child that year. Goolagong won her way through to the final to meet American number 3 seed Billie Jean Moffitt (King), who was 28 years old at the time and searching for the only Grand Slam singles title that had eluded her in her career to that point.

Neither player dropped a set on the way to the final, but King didn't drop a set winning her match against Goolagong either. She secured her career Grand Slam.[153]

Goolagong (Cawley) explained her fond memories of Roland Garros in an interview to mark the 50-year anniversary of her 1971 win: *"I loved the surface in Paris. It was slower and I thought 'Oh you can slide, you've got so much more time'... I felt very at home from the first day really,"* she said. *"I had plenty of time to get to the net, and just being able to get that variety of shots was very exciting for me."*[154]

Helen Gourlay (Cawley)

The French Open of 1971 was the first of 2 Grand Slam singles finals that Tasmania's Helen Gourlay (Cawley) reached in her career. The other was the December 1977 Australian Open (see feature box later in this chapter).[155]

As outlined in Evonne Goolagong (Cawley's) French Open feature box, Gourlay (Cawley) was an unseeded 24-year-old when she upset 1968 French Open winner, American number 4 seed Nancy Richey in straight sets in the 1972 French Open semi-finals. She was beaten by a 19-year-old Goolagong in straight sets in the final, though many years Goolagong recalled her as always being a tough opponent: *"She was a serve-and-volley player, she moved well, volleyed well, drop shots, she had the whole works."*[156]

As you'll see in Chapter 9, Gourlay (Cawley) had success in other Grand Slam events in doubles during her career.

Wendy Turnbull

Queenslander Wendy Turnbull was 26 years old when she finished runner-up in the 1979 French Open. It was the second of 3 Grand Slam finals in her career. The other 2 were in 1977 at the US Open and in 1980 at the Australian Open (see feature boxes later in this chapter).

Nicknamed 'rabbit' due to her court speed, Turnbull was the fourth seed at the 1979 French Open where she won her way through to the final against top-seeded American Chris Evert. Evert was 24 years old at the time and already a two-time French Open singles winner. She clinched her third title by beating Turnbull in straight sets.[157]

Wimbledon (1968–1986)

Three Aussie women made at least one singles final at Wimbledon in this era – Margaret Smith (Court), Evonne Goolagong (Cawley) and Judy Tegart (Dalton).

Evonne Goolagong (Cawley) – 2 titles

Evonne Goolagong (Cawley) made an incredible 5 Wimbledon finals between 1971 and 1980. She was fresh off her first Grand Slam singles victory at the French Open when she arrived at Wimbledon in 1971.

Still only 19 and the number 3 seed behind top seed Margaret Smith (Court) and American Billie Jean Moffitt (King), she won her way through to the final by beating King in straight sets in the semi-finals.

That victory put her into the final against Court, who had beaten her on grass in the Australian Open final earlier that year (see the feature box later in the chapter). But Goolagong turned the tables at Wimbledon, winning in straight sets.

On the 50th anniversary of her win, she recalled how she had dreamed of winning Wimbledon from the age of 8 after reading a magazine story about the famed centre court:

"Every time I hit the ball against the wall, I used to pretend I was there. And then I dreamt about it every night."

She also recalled how well she played in the final to achieve her childhood dream while still a teenager: *"There's been like 3 or 4 times in my life when I've been in complete control of my game – like in the zone, I guess. I think that was one of them."*[158]

John Newcombe also won the Wimbledon men's singles final in 1971, making it a double celebration for Australia. Goolagong returned in 1972 as the top seed, coming close to defending her title by reaching the final against a 28-year-old Billie Jean Moffitt (King), who was once again the second seed. King beat her in straight sets.

It was the first of 3 runner's up performances from Goolagong at Wimbledon in the women's singles. The second came in 1975 just after she married. She was the fourth seed, but again lost in straight sets against King, who was the third seed.

Cawley was runner-up for the third time in 1976. She was the second seed and went down in an epic 3-set battle against top seed Chris Evert, who was 21 years old at the time but already aiming for her second Wimbledon singles crown. She had won the 1974 title as a 19-year-old like Goolagong had in 1971.

The 1976 Wimbledon final between Evert and Cawley lasted for over 2 hours. Cawley was up 6-5 in the deciding third set before Evert stormed home to take the set 8-6, and the match.

Cawley's fifth and final Wimbledon final was when she was a 28-year-old mother of a three-year-old daughter in 1980. Seeded fourth, she won her way into the final by beating the second-seeded American teenage whiz kid Tracy Austin in 3 sets in the semi-finals. That win put her into the final against top seed Chris Evert. Cawley avenged her 1976 Wimbledon singles final defeat to Evert by beating her in straight sets.

She was the first mother to win the title since England's Dorothea Lambert Chambers in 1914, and to this day is still the last mother to do it.[159] She didn't defend her title in 1981 as she had just given birth to her second child.

Margaret Smith (Court)

Margaret Smith (Court) won a Wimbledon women's singles title in the Open Era to add to the 2 she won as an amateur – see Chapter 4.

Her Open Era win came in a golden year for her in 1970. She had already won the Australian Open that year (see the feature box later in this chapter) as well as the French Open (see the earlier feature box in this chapter) when she arrived at Wimbledon as the top seed ahead of American Billie Jean Moffitt (King). King had won 3 consecutive Wimbledon singles finals between 1966 and 1968, and she finished runner-up in 1969.

Both Court and King won their way through to the 1970 Wimbledon final and proceeded to play the longest final in the tournament's history in terms of games – 46, even though Court won in straight sets (14-12, 11-9).[160] Tie-breakers for non-deciding sets weren't introduced until the 1970 US Open a few months later.

Court and King's 46-game marathon is still the record for a Wimbledon women's singles final today. It won't be broken due to the introduction of tie-breakers for final sets in 2022.[161]

Court's 1970 Wimbledon win set her up for a tilt at a calendar year Grand Slam at the US Open just a few months later (see the feature box later in this chapter), and as outlined in Chapter 5, John Newcombe also won the Wimble-

> don men's singles final in 1970, making it an Australian double.
>
> 1970 proved to be the final Wimbledon crown of Margaret Smith (Court's) decorated career. She returned to defend her title as the top seed in 1971, but as outlined earlier in this chapter, she was beaten by the fellow Aussie and teenage third seed Evonne Goolagong (Cawley).[162]

Judy Tegart (Dalton)

Victorian Judy Tegart (Dalton) made the first Wimbledon final of the Open Era in 1968. It was the only Grand Slam singles final of her career. But as you'll see in Chapter 9, she had a lot of success in doubles, including a career Grand Slam with Margaret Smith (Court).

She had a serve-volley style and was the seventh seed in the Wimbledon women's singles draw in 1968 at the age of 28. Her path to the final included wins over second seed (and regular doubles partner) Margaret Smith (Court) in 3 sets in the quarter-finals, as well as third-seeded American Nancy Richey in straight sets in the semi-finals.

Her opponent in the final was top-seeded American Billie Jean Moffitt (King) who was aiming for her third straight Wimbledon title. King won the match in 2 tough sets, 9-7, 7-5.[163]

Judy Tegart (Dalton) can also be regarded as a pioneer of the women's pro tour. Along with fellow Aussie Kerry Melville (Reid), she joined with 7 American players led by Billie Jean Moffitt (King) to form a breakaway tour that later became the modern-day WTA, the governing body of contemporary women's tennis. The breakaway tour was formed in protest at the huge gulf that existed in men's and women's prizemoney for many tournaments in the early decades of the Open Era.[164]

And as you'll see in Chapter 9, Tegart (Dalton) also had plenty of Grand Slam doubles success in her career.

The US Open (1968–1986)

Four Aussie women made at least one US Open singles final in this era – Margaret Smith (Court), Evonne Goolagong (Cawley), Kerry Melville (Reid) and Wendy Turnbull.

Margaret Smith (Court) – 3 titles

Margaret Smith (Court) won 3 US women's singles titles in the Open Era to complement the 2 she won as an amateur – see Chapter 4.

She didn't lose a set during the entire tournament in 1969, beating sixth-seeded American Nancy Richey in the final. As outlined in Chapter 5, Rod Laver also won the US men's singles that year to give Australia the double.

1969 was a stellar year for Court where she won 3 of the 4 Grand Slam singles events (the Australian, French and US Opens), but she went one better in 1970. She became only the second woman in history to win a calendar year Grand Slam (and the first woman of the Open Era). American Maureen Connolly had done it in 1953 in the Amateur Era.

Court was obviously the first Australian woman to win a calendar year Grand Slam, and the second Australian after Rod Laver had done it in 1969. She is still the only Australian woman to have won a calendar year Grand Slam.

The 1970 US Open was the crowning moment of Margaret Smith (Court's) decorated singles career. She was 28 years old, and obviously the top seed after having won the Australian, French and Wimbledon titles earlier that year.

Everything went according to plan as she won her way through to the US Open final without dropping a set. There she faced the second-seeded American Rosie Casals in the final. Casals was only 21 and in the first Grand Slam singles final of her career.

She pushed Court to 3 sets, but ultimately the calendar year Grand Slam was Court's. And as outlined in Chapter 5, Ken Rosewall also won the men's singles in 1970 to give Australia a US open double for the second year in a row. Court didn't defend her US Open title in 1971 due to being pregnant with her first child.

Court won the fifth and final US title (and final Grand Slam singles title of her career) as a mother in 1973. It was another stellar year for her where she won 3 of the 4 Grand Slam singles events (and just like in 1969, it was the Australian, French and US Opens).

Despite Court having won all 3 Grand Slam events heading into the US Open, defending champion Billie Jean Moffitt (King) was the top seed and aiming for her third straight US title (and the fourth of her career). She was 29 years old at the time, and Court was 31.

However, King was bundled out in the third round in 3 sets by unseeded countrywoman Julie Heldman. King's exit cleared the way for fourth-seeded Aussie Evonne Goolagong (Cawley) to reach her first US Open final at the age of 22. Court won a hard-fought match in 3 sets. And as outlined in Chapter 5, John Newcombe also won the men's singles at the 1973 US open, giving Australia another double.

The 1973 US open was an historic event in terms of being the first Grand Slam that offered equal prizemoney for the men's and women's events. This decision was made in response to three-time winner and defending champion Billie Jean Moffitt (King) threatening to boycott the event. Both Margaret Smith (Court) and John Newcombe pocketed US$25,000 for their wins.[165] And as you'll see in Chapter 7, it took the other Grand Slam events decades to implement the same policy.

Court didn't defend her US Open title in 1974 due to the birth of her second child.[166] Years later she reflected on the challenges of playing in her era versus the modern day: *"How I would love to have taken family or friends along with me. But I couldn't. I had to go on my own or with the national team. People don't see all that. We didn't have psychologists or coaches with us."*[167]

Evonne Goolagong (Cawley)

The US Open was the only Grand Slam singles title that eluded Evonne Goolagong (Cawley) during her stellar career. But it wasn't for lack of trying. She finished runner-up a heart-breaking 4 years in a row between 1973 and 1976.

As outlined in the previous feature box, she was beaten by Margaret Smith (Court) in 3 tough sets in the 1973 final.

In 1974, she was the fifth seed and won her way through to the final by beating local favourite and top seed Chris Evert in 3 sets in the semi-finals. Evert was only 19 at the time but had won both the French Open and Wimbledon earlier that year. Goolagong had won the Australian Open (see later feature box in this chapter).

Goolagong's semi-final win over Evert put her into the final against another American, the second-seeded Billie Jean Moffitt (King). Moffitt (King) was 30 at the time and a three-time US Open champion. Goolagong won the first set before King came back to win the next 2 to secure her fourth US Open singles crown.

The 1974 US Open was the last time the tournament was played on grass. In 1975, the tournament switched to clay for a 3-year period. Goolagong had won the French Open on clay in 1971, so she had the game to do well on the surface. She had also married earlier in 1975.

She was the fourth seed and won her way into the 1975 US Open final after beating English second seed Virginia Wade in straight sets in the semi-finals. Chris Evert would be her next opponent. Like Cawley, she was also chasing her first US Open title. But just like she had in 1974, Cawley won the first set of the 1975 final before going down in 3.

She was seeded second behind Evert at the 1976 US Open. Both players won their way through to the final without losing a set, and Evert managed to keep that clean record intact when she won the final in straight sets as well. It was to be the last US Open final of her career.[168]

Kerry Melville (Reid)

Kerry Melville (Reid) was the ninth seed at the 1972 US Open. Raised in New South Wales, she was 25 at the time and her previous best performance at a Grand Slam had been her runner-up finish to Margaret Smith (Court) at the Australian Open 2 years earlier (see later feature box in this chapter).

Known for her solid baseline game, Melville beat the seventh-seeded Frenchwoman 'Frankie' Dürr and third-seeded teenage local Chris Evert on her way to the final to face Billie Jean Moffitt (King). Moffitt (King) beat her in straight sets to win her third US Open title.[169]

As mentioned earlier in this chapter, Melville can be regarded as a pioneer for women achieving more equal prizemoney on the pro tour. Along with fellow Aussie Judy Tegart (Dalton), she joined with 7 American players led by Billie Jean Moffitt (King) to form a breakaway tour that later became the modern-day WTA. The rebel tour was formed in protest at the huge gulf that existed in men's and women's prizemoney for many tournaments in the early decades of the Open Era.[170]

Wendy Turnbull

Wendy Turnbull reached the first Grand Slam singles titles of her career as a 24-year-old in 1977. It was the last year that the tournament was played on clay.

Turnbull was the number 12 seed and beat 3 higher seeds on her way to the final – sixth-seeded American Rosie Casals in 3 sets in the fourth round, English third seed Virginia Wade in straight sets in the quarter-finals, and Czech-born American second seed Martina Navratilova in 3 sets in the semi-finals.

Those wins set her up for a showdown with American top seed Chris Evert in the final. Evert was just 22 years old but was aiming for her third straight US open title and she beat a gallant Turnbull in straight sets.[171]

And as you 'll see in Chapter 7, Turnbull would be the last Australian woman to feature in a US Open singles final for another 34 years.

Although Turnbull never won a Grand Slam singles title during her career despite reaching the finals at the French, US and Australian Opens, you'll see in Chapter 9 that she had plenty of Grand Slam doubles success.

The Australian Open (1969–1986)

As mentioned in Chapter 6, scheduling and comparatively low prizemoney issues plagued the Australian Open during these early years of the Open Era. Fewer international players made the long trek to compete, despite it being a Grand Slam event.

Between 1972 and 1974, the Australian Open's January start date was moved to Boxing Day. This inconvenient start date was made worse in 1975 when it was moved to 21 December, before it moved back to Boxing Day in 1976. The tournament then had two 1977 editions – one in early January and the other in mid-to-late December. The poor timing over Christmas and New Year continued until 1982 (when it was moved to run between late November and mid-December until 1985). In 1986, the decision was made to not hold a November/December tournament and to move the permanent start date to January from 1987 onwards.[172]

Four Aussies won the women's singles at our premier tennis tournament between the start of the Open Era and the end of 1986:

- Margaret Smith (Court) (4 wins to go with the 7 titles she won as an amateur – see Chapter 4)
- Evonne Goolagong (Cawley) (4)

- Kerry Melville (Reid)
- Chris O'Neil.

Aussies who finished runner-up at the Australian Open during this era were:

- Evonne Goolagong (Cawley) (3 years in a row: 1971 –73)
- Margaret Smith (Court) (1968)
- Kerry Melville (Reid) (1970)
- Dianne Fromholtz (Balestrat) (January 1977)
- Helen Gourlay (Cawley) (December 1977)
- Wendy Turnbull (1980).

For Wendy Turnbull, it was her third and final Grand Slam singles runner-up performance after having finished runner-up in the US Open in 1977 and the French Open in 1979 (see feature boxes earlier in this chapter).

For Helen Gourlay (Cawley), it was her second and final Grand Slam runner-up performance after having finished runner-up to Evonne Goolagong (Cawley) at the 1971 French Open (see feature box earlier in this chapter).

For Dianne Fromholtz (Balestrat), it was the best-ever Grand Slam singles performance of her career.[173]

Let's take a closer look at our local Australian Open champions from this era.

Margaret Smith (Court) – 4 titles

Margaret Smith (Court) won 3 straight Australian Open singles finals between 1969 and 1971. She then missed the 1972 tournament due to being pregnant with her first child, before returning to win the last Australian Open of her career in 1973.

Court's combined 11 singles wins as an amateur and pro in Australia's premier tennis tournament is an all-time record for both men and women.

Her first Australian Open final win in the Open Era in 1969 was a straight sets victory over American top seed and defending champion Billie Jean

Moffitt (King). Court was the second seed that year.

She was back to defend her title in 1970 as the top seed and didn't drop a set for the entire tournament, beating fellow Aussie and second seed Kerry Melville (Reid) in the final. It was the first leg of her calendar year Grand Slam.

Court made it 3 Australian Open wins in a row in 1971 when she was once again the top seed. She beat second seed Evonne Goolagong (Cawley) in 3 sets in the final after dropping the first set.

Following her childbirth break from tennis in 1972, Court became the first mother to win a Grand Slam singles event at the Australian Open in 1973.[174] And as outlined earlier in this chapter, she also won the French and US Open titles that same year.

Court didn't defend her Australian Open title in 1974 due to being pregnant with her second child.[175]

Evonne Goolagong (Cawley) – 4 titles

Fittingly, Evonne Goolagong (Cawley) won 3 consecutive Australian Opens between 1974 and 1976 after having lost 3 consecutive Australian Open finals between 1971 and 1973.

She was the number 2 seed behind American Chris Evert in 1974 but broke through at last for her first Australian Open win in 3 sets in the final.

She returned in 1975 as the third seed and successfully defended her title by beating number 8 seed Martina Navratilova in straight sets in the final. Navratilova was 18 years old and still a Czech citizen at the time, but she had shown her immense potential by upsetting top seed Margaret Smith (Court) in the quarter-finals.

In 1976, Evonne Goolagong (Cawley) won her third straight Australian Open singles title as the top seed. She didn't drop a set the entire way and beat Czech fifth seed Renáta Tomanová in straight sets in the final.

Cawley didn't get the opportunity to win 4 consecutive Australian Open singles titles due to being pregnant when the first 1977 tournament was held in January. However, a change in scheduling for the event saw another Australian Open tournament held in December that year when she was back playing.

Once again Cawley was the top seed, and she didn't drop a set winning the fourth and final Australian Open of her career. She beat number 5 seed Helen Gourlay (Cawley) in the final in straight sets.[176]

Kerry Melville (Reid)

Kerry Melville (Reid) won the January 1977 Australian Open after having finished runner-up in the event 7 years earlier in the first Grand Slam singles final of her career.

She was 30 years old and the second seed in 1977 behind fellow Aussie Dianne Fromholtz (Balestrat). Both won their way through to the final as expected, but Reid beat the left-handed Fromholtz (Balestrat) in straight sets.[177]

Chris O'Neil

Unseeded Chris O'Neil from New South Wales had an amazing run to reach and win the only Grand Slam singles title of her career at the Australian Open in 1978. She was just 22 at the time and didn't drop a single set in the entire tournament.

Her first test was expected to be against American third seed Beth Norton in the second round, but O'Neil opened her path in the draw by winning in straight sets. Fellow unseeded Aussie Dianne Evers then did O'Neil a favour by knocking out English top seed and 1976 French Open winner Sue Barker in the quarter-finals.

O'Neil then dispatched Evers in straight sets in the semi-finals to set up a meeting with American number 8 seed Betsy Nagelsen in the final. Nagelsen was 32 years old and it would be the only Grand Slam singles final of her career. O'Neil beat her in straight sets.[178]

As you'll see in Chapter 7, it would be more than 4 decades before another Australian woman won the Australian Open.

Chapter 7
Aussie Men and Women at the Majors
(1987–Present Day)

Chapters 5 and 6 highlighted that Aussie success on the Grand Slam stage started to wane from the mid-1970s onwards. The decline followed a golden run for both our men and women over a long period. This chapter looks at the Grand Slam singles triumphs and near misses of both our men and women from 1987 to the present day. The 4 Grand Slam events have been played in the following calendar year order in the Open Era since 1987.

- the Australian Open
- the French Open
- Wimbledon
- the US Open.

Let's take a look at each tournament in that order.

The Australian Open (1987–Present Day)

The Australian Open was moved to start and finish in January from 1987 onwards. No tournament was played in 1986 to accommodate the change. The scheduling change followed years of awkward late-year scheduling that often saw the tournament played over the Christmas/New Year period.

Prizemoney improvements soon followed to help the Australian Open to attract as many of the best players as possible. The event also moved from grass to a hard-court surface in 1988 when it was moved to its current-day venue, Melbourne Park.[179] The

Australian Open became the second of the 4 Grand Slam tournaments to offer equal prizemoney for men and women in 2001.[180]

Only one able-bodied Australian has won a singles event at the Australian Open since unseeded Chris O'Neil won the women's title in 1978 (see Chapter 6). Ash Barty broke a 44-year drought when she lifted the trophy in 2022.[181]

Prior to Barty's appearance in the 2022 final, no Australian woman had made it to the last match of the Australian Open women's singles since Wendy Turnbull in 1980 (see Chapter 6).[182]

Ash Barty

There was huge expectation on Queenslander Ash Barty when she entered the 2022 Australian Open as the number one seed. She was 25 years old, the world number one and reigning Wimbledon champion at the time (see feature box later in this chapter).

Everything went to plan as she stormed through the draw without dropping a set. She was the red-hot favourite against 28-year-old American Danielle Collins in the final. Collins was the number 27 seed but won her way through to the final by beating Poland's seventh seed Iga Świątek in straight sets in the semi-finals.[183]

Barty absorbed all the hometown pressure to win the final in straight sets. Less than 2 months later, she shocked the tennis world by announcing her retirement despite being at the peak of her game: *"I know how much work it takes to bring the best out of yourself. And I've said it to my team multiple times; I don't have that in me anymore. I don't have the physical drive, the emotional want, and kind of everything it takes to challenge yourself at the very top of the level anymore. And I think I just know that I'm absolutely spent; I just know physically I have nothing more to give. That for me is success – I've given absolutely everything I can to this beautiful sport of tennis. And I'm really happy with that."*[184]

She retired having won 3 of the 4 Grand Slam singles majors in her shortened career. Her French Open and Wimbledon wins are featured later in this chapter.

Chapter 7 – Aussie Men and Women at the Majors (1987–Present Day)

After dominating the tournament for the first 7 decades of its existence, no Australian man has won the men's singles at the Australian Open since the unseeded Mark Edmondson did it in 1976 (see Chapter 5). Only 2 Aussie men have made the men's singles final since 1980, and both finished runner-up – Pat Cash (twice) and Lleyton Hewitt.

Pat Cash

Victorian Pat Cash finished as the men's singles runner-up at back-to-back Australian Opens in 1987 and 1988. The 1987 tournament was the last played on grass at Melbourne's Kooyong Stadium. Cash was 22 years old and the number 11 seed, and he had led Australia to a Davis Cup final win over Sweden a few weeks earlier in late 1986.

His first big scalp was French number 3 seed Yannick Noah in 4 sets in the quarter-finals. Unfortunately, he aggravated a shoulder injury during the match which hampered the pace of his serving for the rest of the tournament.[185]

Cash faced top-seeded Czech Ivan Lendl in the semi-finals. Lendl was 26 years old and the reigning US and French Open champion at the time, but Cash beat him in 4 sets with his crisp volleying being a feature of his game.

The win over Lendl put him into the final against 21-year-old Swede Stefan Edberg, the number 4 seed who had won the Australian Open singles title as a teenager in 1985. Cash had beaten Edberg in straight sets in the Davis Cup final a few weeks before the 1987 final. But that statement makes the win sound easier than it was. He won 13-11, 13-11, 6-4![186]

The Australian Open final was another epic 5-setter between the 2, with Cash coming back from 2 sets down to square the match before losing the fifth set and the match.

Cash returned to the Australian Open in 1988 as the reigning Wimbledon champion (see feature box later in this chapter) and the number 4 seed. It was the first time the tournament was played on a hard-court surface at Melbourne

Park.

Once again, Cash came up against top seed Ivan Lendl in the semi-finals and this time he won an epic 5-setter. And once again, the semi-final win put him into the final against a Swede, but this time it was 23-year-old Mats Wilander, the number 3 seed and a two-time Australian Open singles winner as a teenager.

Wilander had beaten his fellow countryman, defending Australian Open champion and number 2 seed Stefan Edberg in 5 sets in the semi-finals. Like the year before, the 1988 final was another 5-set marathon, but Wilander won the fifth set 8-6 to take the match and his third Australian Open men's singles title in just under four-and-a-half hours. Cash would never make another Australian Open final.[187]

Lleyton Hewitt

South Australian Lleyton Hewitt was 23 years old and the third seed at the 2005 Australian Open. He was desperate to win his home major after having already won both the US Open and Wimbledon earlier in his career (see feature boxes late in this chapter).

His first big challenge at the 2005 Australian Open was a tough 5-setter in the fourth round against unseeded Spanish teenager Rafael Nadal that lasted nearly 4 hours.

His next opponent was Argentinian number 9 seed David Nalbandian and it was another 5-set epic with Hewitt winning the final set 10-8.

The top 4 seeds all reached the semi-finals. Hewitt faced 22-year-old American number 2 seed Andy Roddick in his match and beat him in 4 sets.

Third-seeded Russian 25-year-old Marat Safin upset top seed Roger Federer in a 5-set marathon in the other semi-final, saving a match point along the way. Federer was 23 years old at the time.

Safin had previously finished runner-up at the Australian Open men's singles twice, but he wasn't to be denied a third time. After dropping the first set, he beat Hewitt in 4. It was the closest Hewitt would ever come to winning the singles at his home major.[188]

The French Open (1987–Present Day)

Only 2 Australian women have made the French Open singles final since Wendy Turnbull finished runner-up in 1979 (see Chapter 6) – Ash Barty and Sam Stosur. Equal prizemoney for men and women was introduced at the French Open in 2006.[189]

And after a promising start to the Open Era where Ken Rosewall and Rod Laver won the first 2 French Open singles titles (see Chapter 5), the tournament has proved to be a graveyard for Australian men ever since. No Aussie man has made the final since 1969.[190]

Ash Barty

Her French Open win in 2019 was the first Grand Slam singles title of Ash Barty's career. She was 23 years old at the time and arrived at Roland Garros as the number 8 seed.

It was a tournament of upsets, with most of the top seeds falling in the early rounds. Top seed Naomi Osaka was knocked out in straight sets in the third round, opening up Barty's draw.

The only seed Barty had to face on her way to the final was American number 14 seed Madison Keys in the quarter-finals. Barty beat her in straight sets. She followed that with a 3-set win over unseeded American Amanda Anisimova in the semi-finals, despite dropping the first set.

That win put her into the final against unseeded Czech teenager Markéta Vondroušová in the final. The left-handed Vondroušová had beaten 4 seeds on her way to the final, including Latvian number 12 seed Anastasija Sevastova in the fourth round. She hadn't dropped a set over the entire 2 weeks.

But Vondroušová's fairy-tale run ended in the final with Barty winning in straight sets. She became the first Australian woman to win a French Open singles title since Margaret Smith (Court) in 1973 (see Chapter 6).

Her breakthrough Grand Slam singles win came just 3 years after she took a 21-month break from the sport after having spent a lifetime on the court and travelling. During her break, she took up cricket and played a season for the Brisbane Heat, as well as living a more balanced life than the pro tennis circuit allows.[191]

Sam Stosur

Queenslander Sam Stosur became the first Australian to reach the French Open singles final in 31 years when she reached the 2010 decider. She was 26 years old and the number 7 seed at the event.

Stosur came from a set down to beat Belgium's 4-time French Open champion Justine Henin in the fourth round. She then upset 28-year-old American top seed Serena Williams in an epic quarter-final, winning the third and deciding set 8-6.

A straight sets semi-final victory over Serbian number 4 seed Jelena Janković followed to set up a meeting with Italian number 17 seed Francesca Schiavone in the final. Schiavone was 29 at the time and like Stosur, it was her first Grand Slam singles final. No Italian player had ever won a Grand Slam singles title, but Schiavone made history by winning in straight sets.

Stosur later reflected on what turned out to be the best French Open performance of her career: *"It's an event I can look back on and be very proud about how I played, who I beat, where I got to. A Grand Slam final, it's not something to be ashamed of."*

And as you'll see later in this chapter, Stosur did claim a Grand Slam singles title a year later.

Wimbledon (1987–Present Day)

Three Aussies have won Wimbledon singles finals since 1987 – Pat Cash, Lleyton Hewitt and Ash Barty. Three other Aussies have finished runner-up at Wimbledon singles events over the same period – Pat Rafter (twice), Mark Philippoussis and Nick Kyrgios.[192]

Wimbledon was the last of the Grand Slam events to introduce equal prizemoney for men and women in 2007, and it was the only Grand Slam tournament that wasn't played in 2020 due to the COVID-19 pandemic.[193]

Pat Cash

Pat Cash had already finished runner-up at the Australian Open on grass earlier in the year when he arrived at Wimbledon as a 22-year-old in 1987 (see earlier feature box in this chapter). Like the Australian Open, he was the number 11 seed.

Wearing his trademark black and white chequered headband, Cash worked his way through the early rounds without any fuss. He only dropped one set. Fellow Aussie Peter Doohan did everyone in the draw a favour when he upset Germany's teenage defending champion and top seed Boris Becker in 4 sets in the second round.

Cash's first big test was expected to be against Swedish number 3 seed Mats Wilander in the quarter-finals, but he played brilliantly to beat him in straight sets.

His semi-final opponent was seventh-seeded American Jimmy Connors, who was 34 at the time and a two-time Wimbledon singles champion. Once again, Cash played superbly to win in straight sets. That win set him up for a showdown with Czech number 2 seed Ivan Lendl in the final. Cash was in the best form of his career and beat Lendl in straight sets.

Cash famously climbed over the commentary box roof and into the Wimbledon stands to hug family, friends and his team immediately after sealing his win with a cross-court forehand volley. It was a significant break from Wimbledon traditions at the time: *"I was regretting it midway up, but I thought I was going to make myself the biggest fool of all time. I was thinking about turning around, going down and back onto the court. But I knew I couldn't do that, so it took me a while to test out the strength of the commentary box roof."*[194]

Lleyton Hewitt

Lleyton Hewitt was the reigning US champion (see later feature box in this chapter) when he arrived at Wimbledon in 2002 as the top seed for the men's singles.

He didn't drop a set in the first 4 rounds before coming up against Dutchman Sjeng Schalken in the quarter-finals. Schalken was the number 18 seed but pushed Hewitt to 5 sets before going down 7-5 in the fifth.

Hewitt then beat local number 4 seed Tim Henman in straight sets in the semi-finals to set up a meeting with Argentina's David Nalbandian in the final. Nalbandian was 20 years old and the number 28 seed. He didn't cause any major upsets on his way to the final. He benefited from a lot of the top seeds being knocked out early.

As expected, Hewitt was too strong for Nalbandian in the final, winning in straight sets. He later reflected on what it meant to him: *"Winning the title is an amazing feeling, it is the greatest tennis club in the world. You go there as a junior and you feel that tradition and get the goose bumps. But to go back there knowing you have been able to hold up that great gold trophy is an amazing feeling, and to walk through and see your name on the boards as a member is incredible. Something I never forget."*[195]

No Aussie has won the Wimbledon men's singles title since Hewitt.

Ash Barty

Like most Aussie tennis players, Ash Barty had always dreamed of winning a Wimbledon singles title. She won the Wimbledon girls' singles title in 2011 when she was a 15-year-old junior.

The 2021 Wimbledon tournament was the first for 2 years after the scheduled 2020 event had been cancelled due to the COVID-19 pandemic.

The 2021 Wimbledon tournament also marked the 50th anniversary of Evonne Goolagong (Cawley's) first Wimbledon singles title in 1971. Goolagong (Cawley) had long been an idol of Barty's, so she came up with a tribute idea. She wanted to wear a 'scallop' dress in her matches at the tournament that was similar to the one Goolagong had worn at Wimbledon 50 years earlier, and she called Goolagong (Cawley) beforehand to get her blessing for the idea. Goolagong (Cawley) was touched and excited. Barty later recalled: *"... her favourite dress, probably her most iconic dress, is something that inspired me and inspired our generation of Indigenous youth. I hope that my version of it, my outfit, can do the same for the next generation of Indigenous youth coming forwards."*[196]

Barty arrived as the top seed for the 2021 Wimbledon women's singles and survived a first-round scare against Spain's Carla Suárez Navarro when she was pushed to 3 sets.

But she didn't drop another set on her way to the final. There she faced 29-year-old Czech number 8 seed Karolína Plíšková who had upset second seed Aryna Sabalenka from Belarus in the semi-finals. Barty won the match in 3 sets, and her Wimbledon-winning dress is now housed at the National Museum of Australia.[197] Her win broke a 41-year drought for Australia in the Wimbledon women's singles. Evonne (Goolagong) Cawley's famous second Wimbledon singles title as a mother in 1980 (see Chapter 6) was the last Aussie win at the event before Barty.

Pat Rafter

Queenslander Pat Rafter was already a two-time US Open winner (see later feature box in this chapter) when he arrived at Wimbledon in 2000 as the 27-year-old number 12 seed. A shoulder injury that ultimately required surgery had restricted his appearances over the previous 12 months.

His big test came in the semi-final against second-seeded American Andre Agassi, who was 30 years old at the time and in the prime of his career. Rafter's serve-volley style against Agassi's blistering service returns and solid all-round baseline game ensured a great match-up. He won a see-sawing 5-set match to avenge his straight-set semi-final loss to Agassi at Wimbledon the year before, later reflecting: *"Today was a match that I couldn't have played any better under the circumstances, on a big court against one of the best players ever."*[198]

Rafter's Wimbledon semi-final win in 2000 put him up against American top seed Pete Sampras in the final. Sampras was 28 years old and chasing his seventh Wimbledon title. He was also attempting to break the record of 12 Grand Slam singles titles that he jointly held with Aussie Roy Emerson at the time.

Rafter started well by winning the first set in a tie-break, but Sampras steadied to take the second in a tie-break himself before running away with the match to make history as the greatest Grand Slam singles winner of all time to that point.[199]

Rafter returned as the number 3 seed for the 2001 Wimbledon men's singles. Sampras was once again the top seed, but he was beaten by Switzerland's Roger Federer in 5 sets in the fourth round. Federer was only 20 years old at the time and the number 15 seed. Even though Federer was beaten in the quarter-finals by England's Tim Henman, his win over Sampras was a sign of things to come for the tennis world.

For the third year in a row, Rafter won his way through to the 2001 Wimbledon semi-finals to face Andre Agassi. And just like he had in 2000, Rafter won the 2001 semi-final in 5 sets, winning the fifth 8-6.

His opponent in the final was big-serving Croatian wildcard Goran Ivanišević, who was 30 years old, unseeded, and ranked 125 in the world after having battled a shoulder injury for some time. But Ivanišević had cut a swathe of destruction through the draw, beating Spanish number 21 seed Carlos Moyá in 4 sets in the second round, Russian fourth seed Marat Safin in 4 sets in the quarter-finals, and England's sixth seed and great hope Tim Henman in 5 sets in the semi-finals.

It turned out to be a fitting Wimbledon men's final after so many great matches had been played throughout the tournament. Ivanišević beat Rafter in 5 sets, taking the decider 9-7. He made history by becoming the lowest world-ranked player to win Wimbledon and the first wildcard entrant to ever win a Grand Slam event. It would be the only Grand Slam singles title of his career.[200]

Mark Philippoussis

Big-serving Victorian Mark Philippoussis was 26 years old and unseeded when he made the 2003 Wimbledon final. After promising early signs (including a US Open finals appearance in 1998 that is featured later in this chapter), his career had been hampered by 3 knee surgeries, although earlier that year he had helped Australia to a Davis Cup final victory over Spain.[201]

Nicknamed 'the Scud', Philippoussis' breakthrough win at the 2003 Wimbledon tournament came in the fourth round against American number 2 seed Andre Agassi. He came back from 2 sets to 1 down to win in 5.

His quarter-final was another 5-setter against unseeded German Alexander Popp. This time Philippoussis lost the first 2 sets before storming back to win the match 8-6 in the fifth set.

That win put him into the semi-final against French number 13 seed Sébastien Grosjean. Philippoussis beat him in straight sets to set up a showdown with 21-year-old Swiss fourth seed Roger Federer. Like Philippoussis, Federer was aiming to win his first Grand Slam singles title in 2003. He did by beating Philippoussis in straight sets.

Philippoussis would never make another Grand Slam singles final.[202]

Nick Kyrgios

Canberra's Nick Kyrgios was 27 years old and unseeded at the 2022 Wimbledon men's singles event. He really opened up his draw by beating Greek number 4 speed Stefanos Tsitsipas in 4 sets in the third round.

No more seeds stood in the way of him reaching a potential semi-final with Spanish legend and number 2 seed Rafael Nadal, provided both kept winning.

Chapter 7 – Aussie Men and Women at the Majors (1987–Present Day)

They did, but the then 35-year-old Nadal tore an abdominal muscle in a hard-fought, 5-set semi-final win over American number 11 seed Taylor Fritz.

The injury forced Nadal to withdraw from his semi-final, gifting Kyrgios a walkover into his first Grand Slam singles final against Serbian top seed, defending champion and 6-time Wimbledon singles winner Novak Djokovic. Djokovic was 35 years old at the time and engaged in his running battle with Nadal for the record number of men's Grand Slam singles wins. Djokovic's pursuit of that record was hampered by him being banned from playing the Australian Open earlier that year due to his steadfast refusal to be vaccinated against COVID-19. It also cost him a spot in the US Open draw later that year.

Kyrgios won the first set of his 2022 Wimbledon final against Djokovic, but he was beaten in 4 sets. It was Djokovic's 21st Grand Slam singles title, surpassing Roger Federer' career tally of 20, and putting him one behind Nadal at the time. [203] He would go on to surpass Nadal at the 2023 French Open when he won his 23rd career title. [204]

The US Open (1987–Present Day)

Three Aussies have won US Open singles finals since 1987 – Pat Rafter (twice), Lleyton Hewitt and Sam Stosur. Two Aussies have finished runner-up at US Open singles events over the same period – Mark Philippoussis and Lleyton Hewitt. [205]

As highlighted in Chapter 6, the US Open was the first of the Grand Slam events to offer equal prizemoney for men and women in 1973, largely due to the lobbying of defending champion Billie Jean Moffitt (King) who was prepared to boycott the tournament if the change wasn't made. [206]

Pat Rafter (2 titles)

Pat Rafter broke a 24-year drought for Australia when he won the US Open men's singles title in 1997. He was the first Aussie man to do it since John Newcombe in 1973 (see Chapter 5).

Rafter was 24 years old at the time and the number 13 seed for the event. His first big win came in 4 sets in the fourth round against Andre Agassi, who was battling injury and personal problems at the time before his career resurgence shortly afterwards. Agassi was asked after the match if Rafter could go all the way and win the title. *"No,"* was his blunt response.[207]

Many of the higher seeds at the 1997 US open were bundled out early (including top seed Pete Sampras in the fourth round). The only seed that stood in the way of Rafter making it to the final was American number 2 seed Michael Chang who he was drawn to play in the semi-finals. Rafter played a brilliant serve-volley match to beat noted baseliner Chang in straight sets.

That put him into his first Grand Slam final as the favourite against the unseeded, Canadian-born Englishman Greg Rusedski. Rusedski was a noted big server, but Rafter held his nerve and won in 4 sets. He did a 'Pat Cash', climbing to enter the guest box where his family and friends were seated. *"Cashy did it,"* he said shortly afterwards at the presentation. *"I thought it was pretty cool."*[208]

Later on, John Newcombe was on hand to celebrate with him well into the early hours at a Manhattan bar, along with Tony Roche.

Rafter was back to defend his title in 1998 as the number 3 seed behind Pete Sampras and Chile's Marcelo Rios. He suffered a scare almost straight away, having to come back from 2 sets down to beat unseeded Moroccan Hicham Arazi in 5 sets. Had he lost, he would have become the first defending champion to be knocked out in the first round.[209]

Everything went to plan on Rafter's side of the draw and he won his way through to play Sampras in the semi-final. It turned out to be an epic 5-setter, with Rafter coming back to win the final 2 sets and the match.

Rafter had one final hurdle to overcome to win back-to-back titles – fellow Aussie Mark Philippoussis. The 'Scud' was 21 years old the time and unseeded, but he had beaten 2 seeds on the way to the final – English number 13 seed Tim Henman in 4 sets in the fourth round and Spanish tenth seed Carlos Moyá in 4 sets in the semi-finals.

Rafter and Philippoussis split the opening sets of the final before Rafter powered away to win in 4 sets.

There was certainly no love lost between Rafter and Sampras after the tournament ended. Sampras said that the difference between him and Rafter was *"10 Grand Slams"* and that the sight of Rafter holding his US Open trophies *"pisses me off"*. Rafter responded by calling Sampras a *"cry baby"*.[210]

Lleyton Hewitt

Lleyton Hewitt won the first of the 2 Grand Slam singles titles of his career at the 2001 US Open. He was just 20 years old at the time and the number 4 seed. No Aussie man has won the US Open since.

Hewitt's toughest match to get to the final was a 5-set marathon against teenage American number 18 seed Andy Roddick. His opponent in the final was American number 10 seed Pete Sampras, who hadn't lost a single game on serve since the second round of the tournament.

Although Sampras was 30 years old and his career was starting to wind down, he had beaten number 2 seed Andre Agassi in 4 sets in the quarter-finals and third-seeded Russian Marat Safin in straight sets in the semi-finals. He would also go on to win the 2002 US Open as his final Grand Slam singles title.

But he was no match for Hewitt in 2001. After winning the first set in a tie-break, Hewitt raced away with the match 6-1, 6-1.[211] Just 2 days later, New York and the rest of the world was rocked by the 9/11 terrorist attacks on the World Trade Center.[212]

Three years later in 2004, Hewitt reached the US Open singles final once again. He was the fourth seed and didn't drop a set on his way to the semi-finals. Second-seeded American Andy Roddick was expected to be his semi-final opponent, but he was knocked out in 5 sets in the quarter-finals by Swedish number 28 seed Joachim Johansson.

But Hewitt continued his good form, beating Johansson in straight sets in the semi-final to set up a showdown with Swiss top seed Roger Federer. Federer was 23 years old at the time, just like Hewitt. He had only won 3 of his 20 career Grand Slam singles titles at the time, including both the Australian Open and Wimbledon earlier that year.

Hewitt had an 8-5 winning record against Federer heading into the match, though in an ominous sign of things to come, Federer had won their previous 3 meetings. Federer had survived a 5-set scare in the quarter-finals against local favourite and number 6 seed Andre Agassi. But even though Hewitt hadn't dropped a set on the way to the final, Federer proved far too strong. He won in straight sets, including 6-0 in both the first and third sets. The second went to a tie-breaker.[213]

Sam Stosur

Sam Stosur broke a 38-year drought for Aussie women at the US Open singles when she won the 2011 tournament. She was the first Aussie winner since Margaret Smith (Court) in 1973. She was also the first Aussie Grand Slam winner for any women's singles event since Evonne Goolagong (Cawley) won her second Wimbledon title in 1980 (see Chapter 6).

Stosur was 27 years old and the number 9 seed at the 2011 US Open. In the third round, she played the longest women's singles match in US Open history when won a tough 3-setter against Russian number 24 seed Nadia Petrova. The match lasted for 3 hours and 16 minutes.[214]

She followed that marathon with another tight, 3-set, record-breaking victory over Russian number 25 seed Maria Kirilenko in the fourth round. It featured the longest tie-breaker in US Open history (32 points), with Kirilenko winning it to take the match to a deciding set.[215] Stosur steadied to win the match.

Her breakthrough win came in the quarter-finals against yet another Russian – second seed Vera Zvonareva. But this time, Stosur won in straight sets to book a semi-final meeting against unseeded German Angelique Kerber. It was another 3-setter, but Stosur came up trumps yet again. She was on a roll, but her opponent in the final would be local favourite Serena Williams.

Williams was 29 years old at the time and a three-time US Open winner, but she was seeded 28 due to having played limited tournaments during the year because of injury. However, most pundits still expected her to win.

But Stosur started strongly and won the first set. The match then featured a controversial moment where Stosur was awarded a point that broke Williams' serve in the opening game of the second set. Williams shouted 'Come on' as Stosur attempted to return a forehand that looked like it was going to be a winner. The chair umpire ruled that Williams' shouting had hindered Stosur's unsuccessful return. She awarded the point and the game to Stosur, who went on to win the second set and the US Open title.

Williams was left fuming by the controversial decision, verbally abusing the umpire and refusing to shake her hand at the end of the match. However, in the post-match press conference, she didn't blame her defeat on the incident: *"I hit a winner, but I guess it didn't count. It wouldn't have mattered in the end. Sam played well."*[216]

Stosur's post-match interview revealed that she understood the significance of the win both for herself and Australian women's tennis: *"To actually do it, it's unbelievable. Being Australian with that great history and now to break that drought is obviously very special."*

It was the only Grand Slam singles win of Stosur's career.

Mark Philippoussis

As mentioned earlier in the chapter, Mark Philippoussis finished runner-up to Pat Rafter in the men's singles at the 1998 US Open. He was gracious in defeat, acknowledging how well Rafter played on the day: *"You've got to hand it to Pat. Five unforced errors in 4 sets, that's pretty impressive,"* he said in the post-match interview.[217]

However, he was annoyed that Australia's Davis Cup coach Tony Roche sat in Rafter's support box during the final, even though Roche and Rafter had a strong friendship. He boycotted the Davis Cup team for the next year but returned to lead Australia to a Davis Cup final victory on clay against France in 1999 when Rafter was injured.[218]

Aussie Wheelchair and Quad Tennis Pioneers at the Majors (2002–Present Day)

Wheelchair and quad wheelchair tennis emerged at the Grand Slams in the early 2000s. The 2 categories reflect the different functional impairments of participants. Wheelchair tennis is for players with the permanent impairment of one or both legs, but who have normal arm function. Quad tennis is for players who have a permanent impairment of one or both legs, plus an impairment of their playing arm that restricts their ability to handle a racquet and move their wheelchair.[219]

There are Grand Slam events for both wheelchair and quad categories for men, and wheelchair only for women. All matches for both genders are best of 3 sets. The Australian Open was the first Grand Slam tournament to introduce wheelchair events in 2002, followed by the US Open in 2006, the French Open in 2007 and finally Wimbledon in 2016.[220]

The US Open was the first Grand Slam event to introduce quad tournaments for men in 2007, followed by the Australian Open in 2008, and both the French Open and Wimbledon in 2019.[221]

David Hall – Wheelchair Tennis

New South Welshman David Hall was a pioneer of Australian wheelchair tennis who won 3 consecutive Australian Open singles titles between 2003 and 2005.[222]

All 3 victories were over Dutchman Robin Ammerlaan who had beaten him in the first official Australian Open men's wheelchair singles final in 2002.

Hall was 33 at the time of his first Australian Open win and had been a dominant force in wheelchair tennis around the world since 1995. Even though he only has 3 official Grand Slam titles for his Australian Open wins, he won the event another 6 times prior to it being recognised as a Grand Slam title. He also won the US Open 8 times prior to its official recognition as Grand Slam title, as well as Australia's first ever wheelchair tennis gold medal at the 2000 Paralympic Games in Sydney.[223]

He began playing tennis at 19 after losing his legs 3 years earlier when hit by a car: *"I played tennis as a kid but after the accident I went through all the phases,"* he later said when reflecting on his career. *"You go through the 'why me' phase. Then the anger phase. At some point you accept it. I don't think everyone accepts it,*

> *but once you move through those different phases you see those doors open again. When I discovered tennis, it opened up a whole new world."*[224]

Dylan Alcott – Wheelchair Quad Tennis

Victorian Dylan Alcott won his first quad Grand Slam singles title at the 2015 Australian Open when he was 24. It was the first of 7 consecutive Australian Open titles for him before his streak was finally broken in 2022 when Dutchman Sam Schröder beat him in the final. A year earlier, Alcott had beaten Schröder to win his seventh Australian Open title.[225]

Four of Alcott's 7 Australian Open final wins came against American David Wagner, who was a three-time previous winner of the event himself. The other 2 were against England's Andy Lapthorne.

In 2019, Alcott won the first French Open quad singles event ever held. He beat American David Wagner in 3 sets in the final.[226] It was the first of 3 consecutive French Open titles at Roland Garros for him. In 2020, he beat England's Andy Lapthorne in the final in straight sets.[227] In 2021, he beat Dutchman Sam Schröder in straight sets to win the title.[228] It was the second leg of a calendar year Grand Slam that Alcott achieved that year.

Alcott also won the first ever Wimbledon quad singles event in 2019. He beat local favourite Andy Lapthorne in straight sets in the final: *"Dream come true to be here. Wearing the whites, strawberries and cream, everyone drinking Pimm's. It was so cool,"* he said after the match.[229]

Two years later, he defended his title after Wimbledon was abandoned in 2020 due to the COVID-19 pandemic.[230] He beat Dutchman Sam Schröder in straight sets in the final.[231]

Alcott won his first US Open singles title in 2015 when he beat local favourite

David Wagner in 3 tough sets in the final.[232] He won 2 more US Opens in his career. In 2018, he beat Wagner in the final again, but this time Wagner was the defending champion and Alcott won in straight sets.[233]

He finished runner-up at the US Open in 2019 when attempting to both defend his title and achieve a calendar year Grand Slam. He had won the Australian, French and Wimbledon titles earlier in the year, but lost the US Open final in straight sets to England's Andy Lapthorne.[234]

But in 2021, Alcott did achieve a calendar year Grand Slam by beating Dutch teenager Niels Vink in straight sets in the US Open final after once again having won the Australian, French and Wimbledon titles earlier that year. Reflecting on his achievement after his win, Alcott said: *"I used to hate myself so much, I hated my disability. I didn't even want to be here anymore. Then I found tennis and it changed and saved my life."*[235]

Alcott became a paraplegic after having surgery in the first few weeks of his life to remove a tumour that was wrapped around his spinal cord.[236]

All up, Alcott won 15 Grand Slam singles titles in his decorated career before he retired at the end of the Australian Open in 2022.[237] He was named the 2022 Australian of the Year during the Australian Open tournament that year.[238]

Incredibly, tennis wasn't the first sport where Alcott achieved the ultimate success. He won a gold medal as a 17-year-old as a member of Australia's paralympic basketball team ('The Rollers') at the 2008 Beijing Paralympic Games and a silver at the 2012 London Paralympic Games before focusing solely on tennis. He then won the gold medal in the quad singles tennis event at the 2016 Paralympic Games and the 2020 Tokyo Paralympic Games (held in 2021 due to the COVID-19 pandemic).[239]

Danni Di Toro – Wheelchair Tennis

Victorian Danni Di Toro was a pioneer in wheelchair tennis, finishing runner-up at the Australian Open 4 times and runner-up at the US Open once.

She was runner-up at the Australian Open in the first 3 women's wheelchair singles events ever played between 2002 and 2004, as well as in 2011. Each time she lost to Dutch legend Esther Vergeer, who won an incredible 21 Grand Slam singles titles in her career. But Di Toro pushed her to 3 sets in both the 2003 and 2004 finals. Di Toro also finished runner-up to Vergeer in the US Open final in 2010.

However, like Aussie male wheelchair tennis pioneer David Hall, Di Toro won several Australian and US Open singles titles before they were officially designated as Grand Slam wheelchair events. She won 11 Australian Opens and 2 US Opens prior to their official Grand Slam classification. She also won 2 French Open titles during this time.[240]

Di Toro became a paraplegic at the age of 13 when a retaining wall collapsed on her at a school swimming carnival and landed on her back.[241] She had been playing tennis since she was 9, and within 2 months of her accident, she was playing wheelchair tennis: *"I knew I was relatively technically sound, so being in a wheelchair I just thought that should be easy. I was a total 13-year-old punk who just thought I can do it all,"* she laughed when reflecting on her transition many years later.[242]

Danni Di Toro has also represented Australia in table tennis at multiple Paralympic Games.[243]

Heath Davidson – Wheelchair Quad Tennis

Victorian Heath Davidson finished runner-up in the 2023 Wimbledon quad singles final, going down to Dutchman Niels Vink. And as you'll see in Chapter 11, he also finished runner-up in the quad doubles event at Wimbledon that year.

However, as you'll also see in Chapter 11, Davidson had plenty of Grand Slam doubles success in earlier years with his good friend and fellow Victorian Dylan Alcott. Davidson's paraplegia was caused by a virus affecting his spinal cord soon after birth.[244]

Top All-Time Aussie Grand Slam Singles Winners (Men and Women)*

Player	Total Number of Grand Slam Singles Title Wins	Total Number of Amateur Era Grand Slam Singles Title Wins	Total Number of Open Era Grand Slam Singles Title Wins
Margaret Smith (Court)	24	13	11
Dylan Alcott	15		15
Roy Emerson	12	12	
Rod Laver**	11	6	5
Ken Rosewall **	8	4	4
John Newcombe ***	7	2	5
Evonne Goolagong (Cawley)	7		7
Jack Crawford	6	6	
Nancye Wynne (Bolton)****	6	6	
Daphne Akhurst (Cozens)	5	5	
Frank Sedgman **	5	5	

Australia's Grand Slam Tennis Champions

Player	Total Number of Grand Slam Singles Title Wins	Total Number of Amateur Era Grand Slam Singles Title Wins	Total Number of Open Era Grand Slam Singles Title Wins
Lew Hoad **	4	4	
Ashley Cooper **	4	4	
Norman Brookes	3	3	
Gerald Patterson	3	3	
James Anderson	3	3	
Joan Hartigan (Bathurst)	3	3	
Adrian Quist****	3	3	
Neale Fraser	3	3	
David Hall	3		3
Ash Barty	3		3
Rodney Heath	2	2	
Pat O'Hara Wood	2	2	
Margaret Mutch (Molesworth)	2	2	
Coral McInnes (Buttsworth)	2	2	
John Bromwich****	2	2	
Thelma Coyne (Long)*****	2	2	
Mervyn Rose	2	2	
Mary Carter (Reitano)	2	2	
Lesley Turner (Bowrey)	2	2	
Fred Stolle	2	2	
Pat Rafter	2		2
Lleyton Hewitt	2		2

* Minimum 2 Grand Slam Singles title wins. Players listed in order of the number of Grand Slam events won. Where that number is equal, they are listed in chronological order.

** **Rod Laver** was banned from competing in 21 Grand Slam tournaments between the start of 1963 when he turned pro and April 1968 when the Open Era commenced. He was also banned from competing in 2 Open Era Grand Slam tournaments in 1972 due to being a part of World Championship Tennis (WCT).

** **Ken Rosewall** was banned from competing in 45 Grand Slam tournaments between the start of 1957 when he turned pro and April 1968 when the Open Era commenced. He was also banned from competing in 2 Open Era Grand Slam tournaments in 1972 due to being a part of World Championship Tennis (WCT).

** **Frank Sedgman** was banned from competing in 52 Grand Slam tournaments between the start of 1953 when he turned pro and the end of 1965 when he retired. However, he briefly returned to play in Grand Slam events in the early years of the Open Era when he was in his early forties.

** **Lew Hoad** was banned from competing in 41 Grand Slam tournaments between mid-1957 when he turned pro and the end of 1967 when he retired. However, he briefly returned to play in Grand Slam events in the early years of the Open Era when he was in his mid-thirties.

** **Ashley Cooper** was banned from competing in 16 Grand Slam tournaments between the start of 1959 when he turned pro and the end of 1962 when he retired.

*** **John Newcombe** was banned from competing in 2 Open Era Grand Slam tournaments in 1972 due to being a part of World Championship Tennis (WCT).

**** **Nancye Wynne (Bolton), John Bromwich, Adrian Quist** and **Thelma Coyne (Long)** missed the opportunity to add to their respective Grand Slam tallies due to 5 Australian, 6 Wimbledon and 1 French Championship/s being cancelled during World War II.

Australia's Grand Slam Tennis Champions

Aussie Winners of at least 2 of the 4 Grand Slam Singles Titles*

Player	Australian Open	French Open	Wimbledon	US Open
Rod Laver	✓	✓	✓	✓
Margaret Smith (Court)	✓	✓	✓	✓
Dylan Alcott	✓	✓	✓	✓
Roy Emerson	✓	✓	✓	✓
Jack Crawford	✓	✓	✓	
Frank Sedgman	✓		✓	✓
Ken Rosewall	✓	✓		✓
Lew Hoad	✓	✓	✓	
Ashley Cooper	✓		✓	✓
John Newcombe	✓		✓	✓
Evonne Goolagong (Cawley)	✓	✓	✓	
Ash Barty	✓	✓	✓	
Norman Brookes	✓		✓	
Gerald Patterson	✓		✓	
Mervyn Rose	✓	✓		
Neale Fraser			✓	✓
Fred Stolle		✓		✓
Lleyton Hewitt			✓	✓

* Players listed in order of the number of different Grand Slam events won (i.e. 4, 3 or 2). Where that number is equal, they are listed in chronological order.

Chapter 7 – Aussie Men and Women at the Majors (1987–Present Day)

Top Aussie Australian Open Singles Winners (Men and Women)* 245

Player	Total Number of Australian Open Singles Title Wins	Total Number of Amateur Era Australian Open Singles Title Wins	Total Number of Open Era Australian Open Singles Title Wins
Margaret Smith (Court)	11	7	4
Dylan Alcott	7		7
Nancye Wynne (Bolton)**	6	6	
Roy Emerson	6	6	
Daphne Akhurst (Cozens)	5	5	
Jack Crawford	4	4	
Ken Rosewall	4	2	2
Evonne Goolagong (Cawley)	4	4	
James Anderson	3	3	
Joan Hartigan (Bathurst)	3	3	
Adrian Quist**	3	3	
Rod Laver	3	2	1
David Hall	3		3
Rodney Heath	2	2	
Pat O'Hara Wood	2	2	
Margaret Mutch (Molesworth)	2	2	
Coral McInnes (Buttsworth)	2	2	
John Bromwich**	2	2	
Frank Sedgman	2	2	
Thelma Coyne (Long)	2	2	

Player	Total Number of Australian Open Singles Title Wins	Total Number of Amateur Era Australian Open Singles Title Wins	Total Number of Open Era Australian Open Singles Title Wins
Mary Carter (Reitano)	2	2	
Ashley Cooper	2	2	
John Newcombe	2		2

* Minimum 2 Australian Open singles title wins. Players listed in order of the number of Australian Singles titles won. Where that number is equal, they are listed in chronological order.

** **Adrian Quist** won the Australian Championships (as the Australian Open was then known) on either side of World War II. The tournament was cancelled due to World War II between 1941 and 1945.

** **John Bromwich** won the Australian Championships (as the Australian Open was then known) on either side of World War II. The tournament was cancelled due to World War II between 1941 and 1945.

** **Nancye Wynne (Bolton)** won the Australian Championships (as the Australian Open was then known) on either side of World War II. The tournament was cancelled due to World War II between 1941 and 1945.

Top Aussie French Open Singles Winners (Men and Women)* 246

Player	Total Number of French Open Singles Title Wins	Total Number of Amateur Era French Open Singles Title Wins	Total Number of Open Era French Open Singles Title Wins
Margaret Smith (Court)	5	2	3
Dylan Alcott	3		3
Ken Rosewall	2	1	1
Rod Laver	2	1	1
Roy Emerson	2	2	

Player	Total Number of French Open Singles Title Wins	Total Number of Amateur Era French Open Singles Title Wins	Total Number of Open Era French Open Singles Title Wins
Lesley Turner (Bowrey)	2	2	
Jack Crawford	1	1	
Lew Hoad	1	1	
Mervyn Rose	1	1	
Fred Stolle	1	1	
Tony Roche	1	1	
Evonne Goolagong (Cawley)	1		1
Ash Barty	1		1

* Players listed in order of the number of French Singles titles won. Where that number is equal, they are listed in chronological order.

Top Aussie Wimbledon Singles Winners (Men and Women)* [247]

Player	Total Number of Wimbledon Singles Title Wins	Total Number of Amateur Era Wimbledon Singles Title Wins	Total Number of Open Era Wimbledon Singles Title Wins
Rod Laver	4	2	2
Margaret Smith (Court)	3	2	1
John Newcombe	3	1	2
Norman Brookes	2	2	
Gerald Patterson	2	2	
Lew Hoad	2	2	
Roy Emerson	2	2	
Evonne Goolagong (Cawley)	2		2

Player	Total Number of Wimbledon Singles Title Wins	Total Number of Amateur Era Wimbledon Singles Title Wins	Total Number of Open Era Wimbledon Singles Title Wins
Dylan Alcott	2		2
Jack Crawford	1	1	
Frank Sedgman	1	1	
Ashley Cooper	1	1	
Neale Fraser	1	1	
Pat Cash	1		1
Lleyton Hewitt	1		1
Ash Barty	1		1

* Players listed in order of the number of Wimbledon Singles titles won. Where that number is equal, they are listed in chronological order.

Top Aussie US Open Singles Winners (Men and Women)* [248]

Player	Total Number of US Open Singles Title Wins	Total Number of Amateur Era US Open Singles Title Wins	Total Number of Open Era US Open Singles Title Wins
Margaret Smith (Court)	5	2	3
Dylan Alcott	3		3
Frank Sedgman	2	2	
Ken Rosewall	2	1	1
Neale Fraser	2	2	
Roy Emerson	2	2	
Rod Laver	2	1	1
John Newcombe	2	1	1
Pat Rafter	2		2
Mal Anderson	1	1	

Chapter 7 – Aussie Men and Women at the Majors (1987–Present Day)

Player	Total Number of US Open Singles Title Wins	Total Number of Amateur Era US Open Singles Title Wins	Total Number of Open Era US Open Singles Title Wins
Ashley Cooper	1	1	
Fred Stolle	1	1	
Lleyton Hewitt	1		1
Sam Stosur	1		1

* Players listed in order of the number of US Singles titles won. Where that number is equal, they are listed in chronological order.

Part 3
Doubles in the Amateur Era
(pre-April 1968)

Chapter 8
Aussies in Grand Slam Men's Doubles
(Amateur Era)

Men's doubles events have been a feature of both the US Championships (as the US Open was called in the pre-Open Era) and the Australasian and Australian Championships (the forerunners to today's Australian Open) ever since those tournaments were founded in 1881[249] and 1905 respectively.[250]

Wimbledon added the men's doubles event in 1884, 7 years after the men's singles event was first played there.[251] Men's doubles was added to the French Championships (as the French Open was originally called) in 1925 when the tournament was first designated as a major by the International Lawn Tennis Federation.[252]

As you'll see later in this chapter, 2 Aussies were the first players in history to win a calendar year Grand Slam in doubles. Let's first take a look at our most successful Grand Slam men's doubles players of the Amateur Era, starting with our local event.

Multiple Aussie Men's Doubles Champions
Australasian/Australian Championships: 1905–1968

As you would expect in the early days of international travel during the Amateur Era, Aussies initially had the most success at our local major. The pairings and individuals in the feature boxes that follow are listed in order of the highest number of local Grand Slam doubles titles won (by the most successful of a regular pair in some cases), and where that number is equal, chronologically.

Adrian Quist (10 titles) and John Bromwich (8 titles)

South Australian Adrian Quist and New South Welshman John Bromwich had an incredible record as a doubles combination at the Australian Championships, winning 8 consecutive titles together either side of World War II. Their winning streak was interrupted at 3 (1938-1940) due to the tournament being suspended for 5 years during the War, but they returned afterwards to add another 5 victories (1946-1950).

Prior to teaming up with Bromwich in 1938, Quist also won 2 doubles titles at the Australian Championships with fellow Aussie Don Turnbull in 1936 and 1937, giving him 10 consecutive titles.[253] He also won the singles titles at the Australian Championships in 3 of those years – 1936, 1940 and 1948 (see Chapter 1).

John Bromwich won the singles titles in 2 of his successful doubles years at the Australian Championships – also see Chapter 1.[254]

Gerald Patterson (5 titles) and John Hawkes (3 titles)

Victorians Gerald Patterson (pictured) and John Hawkes won 3 doubles titles as partners at the Australasian/Australian Championships – 1922, 1926 and 1927. Patterson won the singles crown at the 1927 event as well (beating Hawkes, who had won the singles title himself in 1926, see Chapter 1).

Patterson also won 2 more doubles titles either side of World War 1 with different partners – in 1914 with Ashley Campbell and 1925 with Pat O'Hara Wood.[255]

Pat O'Hara Wood (4 titles) and Ron Thomas (2 titles)

Victorian Pat O'Hara Wood (pictured) and South Australian Ron Thomas won consecutive Australasian doubles championships in the first 2 events held after World War I in 1919 and 1920 (and in 1920, O'Hara Wood beat Thomas for the singles crown as well).

O'Hara Wood also won a further 2 Australasian doubles titles in 1923 (with Queenslander Bert St. John, who he beat in the singles final that year) and 1925 (with Gerald Patterson).[256]

Jack Crawford (4 titles) and Harry Hopman (2 titles)

New South Welshmen Jack Crawford and Harry Hopman won 2 consecutive Australian doubles titles as partners in 1929 and 1930.[257]

Crawford also won 2 more titles with different partners from New South Wales (1932 with Edgar Moon and 1935 with Vivian McGrath),[258] along with his 4 wins in the singles event in the Australian Championships (1931-33 and 1935, beating Hopman in 2 of those finals – see Chapter 1).

Lew Hoad (3 titles) and Ken Rosewall (2 titles)

Great mates and New South Welshmen Lew Hoad and Ken Rosewall won 2 Australian Championships as doubles partners – in 1953 (when Rosewall also won the Aussie singles title, see Chapter 3) and 1956. In 1956, the pair also played each other in the singles final, with Hoad winning, see Chapter 3).

Hoad won a third Aussie doubles title in 1957 with Victorian Neale Fraser after Rosewall had turned pro and was banned from competing. Hoad turned pro himself later in 1957.[259]

And as you'll see in Chapter 11, Rosewall also won a third Grand Slam doubles title at his home major in the Open Era after the pros were allowed back to compete.[260]

Neale Fraser (3 titles)

Victorian Neale Fraser won 3 Aussie doubles titles, and all 3 were with different Aussie partners – in 1957 with Lew Hoad before he turned pro later that year, in 1958 with the Melbourne-born, Queensland-raised Ashley Cooper before he turned pro in 1959, and in 1962 with Roy Emerson.

His 1959 doubles win with Emerson gave him a career Grand Slam in doubles, as he had already won the French, Wimbledon and US doubles titles earlier in his career (as you'll see later in this chapter). This was a feat that Emerson would also achieve 3 years later when he and Fraser won the 1962 Australian doubles title.[261]

Rod Laver and Bob Mark (3 titles)

Queenslander Rod Laver and New South Welshman Bob Mark won 3 doubles titles in a row at the Australian Championships – 1959, 1960 and 1961. They formed a potent left-hand/right-hand combination. In 1960, Laver got the double in the event by winning the singles as well (see Chapter 3).

And as you'll see in Chapter 11, Laver also won a fourth Aussie Grand Slam doubles title in the Open Era.[262]

Fred Stolle (3 titles) and Bob Hewitt (2 titles)

New South Welshmen Fred Stolle (pictured) and Bob Hewitt paired up to win consecutive Australian Championships in doubles in 1963 and 1964. Both finals were 5-set marathons.

Stolle also won a third Aussie doubles title in 1966 with Roy Emerson. The final was another 5-set epic. They beat John Newcombe and Tony Roche.[263]

Rodney Heath (2 titles)

Victorian Rodney Heath won 2 doubles titles in the very early years of the Australasian Championships, and unusually, both were with international partners.

His first win came in the second event ever held in 1906, when he partnered New Zealander Anthony Wilding when the event was held 'across the ditch' in Christchurch. His second doubles victory came in 1911 when he joined forces with Englishman Randolph Lycett in Melbourne.[264]

Ernie Parker (2 titles)

Western Australian Ernie Parker won 2 doubles titles at the Australasian Championships in 1909 and 1913. The tournament was held in Perth in both years. In 1909, he partnered J.P. Keane to victory and in 1913 he was with New South Welshman Alf Hedeman (when he also won the men's singles event).

Parker was also a talented cricketer who represented WA. Sadly, he was killed in World War 1 while serving in France in 1918 at the age of 34.[265]

Ashley Campbell (2 titles) and Horace Rice (2 titles)

Ashley Campbell won 2 doubles titles at the Australasian Championships. The first was in 1910 with fellow New South Welshman Horace Rice (pictured) and the second was with Victorian Gerald Patterson in 1914.

Horace Rice won his second doubles title in 1915 with another New South Welshman, Clarence Todd.[266]

Frank Sedgman and Ken McGregor (2 titles)

Victorian Frank Sedgman and South Australian Ken McGregor were the first male players in history to win a calendar year Grand Slam in doubles in 1951.[267] That was also the year they ended Adrian Quist and John Bromwich's 8-year winning streak at the Australian Championships (and Quist's 10-year streak, see the boxed feature earlier in this chapter). They won the 1951 Australian doubles final in 5 sets over the long-time defending champions.

Sedgman and McGregor also won the doubles at the Australian Championships in 1952 (and McGregor also won the singles title that year by beating Sedgman in the final, see Chapter 1).[268] The pair turned pro in 1953 and never played another Grand Slam doubles event together.

To this day, Sedgman and McGregor are the only male players from any country to have won a calendar year Grand Slam in doubles.

Roy Emerson (2 titles)

Queenslander Roy Emerson won 2 doubles titles at his home Grand Slam, and both with a different partner. The first was with left-hander Neale Fraser in 1962, and the second with Fred Stolle in 1966 (when he also won the singles event, see Chapter 3).

His 1962 doubles win at the Australian Championships with Fraser gave him a career Grand Slam in doubles, as he had already won the French, Wimbledon and US doubles titles earlier in his career (as you'll see later in this chapter). As mentioned earlier in this chapter, this was a feat that Fraser had achieved himself 3 years earlier when he and Emerson won the 1962 Australian doubles title.

And as you'll see in Chapter 11, "Emmo" also won a third Aussie Grand Slam doubles title in the Open Era.[269]

John Newcombe and Tony Roche (2 titles)

Yet another successful left-hand/right-hand pairing, New South Welshmen "Newk" and Tony Roche won the doubles at the Australian Championships in 1965 and 1967. And as you'll see in Chapter 11, both Newcombe and Roche won 3 more Aussie doubles titles in the Open Era, including 2 with each other.[270]

All Aussie Men's Doubles Champions
Australasian/Australian Championships: 1905–1968

The following table lists all of the Aussie men's doubles winners of our local major during the Amateur Era). Where only a single player is listed, the player had an international partner.

No Australians competed at the 1912 event as it was held in New Zealand. Excluding the years when the event wasn't held during World War I and World War II, there were only 5 years during the Amateur Era when at least 1 Australian (and usually 2 Aussie partners) didn't win the doubles at Australia's premier tennis tournament. This was due to limited international participants in the early years when long-distance travel was more difficult, and the dominance of Australian players in world tennis during the latter part of the Amateur Era.[271]

Year	Winner/s
1905	Tom Tachell
1906	Rodney Heath
1907	William Gregg
1908	Alfred Dunlop
1909	Ernie Parker/J.P. Keane
1910	Horace Rice/Ashley Campbell
1911	Rodney Heath
1913	Ernie Parker/Alf Hedeman
1914	Gerald Patterson/Ashley Campbell
1914	Horace Rice/Clarence Todd
1919	Pat O'Hara Wood/Ron Thomas
1920	Pat O'Hara Wood/Ron Thomas
1921	Stanley Eaton/Rice Gimmell
1922	Gerald Patterson/John Hawkes
1923	Pat O'Hara Wood/Bert St. John
1924	Norman Brookes/James Anderson
1925	Gerald Patterson/ Pat O'Hara Wood
1926	Gerald Patterson/John Hawkes
1927	Gerald Patterson/John Hawkes
1929	Jack Crawford/Harry Hopman
1930	Jack Crawford/Harry Hopman
1931	Charles Donohoe/Ray Dunlop
1932	Jack Crawford/Edgar Moon
1935	Jack Crawford/Vivian McGrath
1936	Adrian Quist/Don Turnbull
1937	Adrian Quist/Don Turnbull
1938	Adrian Quist/John Bromwich
1939	Adrian Quist/John Bromwich
1940	Adrian Quist/John Bromwich
1946	Adrian Quist/John Bromwich
1947	Adrian Quist/John Bromwich
1948	Adrian Quist/John Bromwich
1949	Adrian Quist/John Bromwich
1950	Adrian Quist/John Bromwich
1951	Frank Sedgman/Ken McGregor

Chapter 8 – Aussies in Grand Slam Men's Doubles (Amateur Era)

Year	Winner/s
1952	Frank Sedgman/Ken McGregor
1953	Lew Hoad/Ken Rosewall
1954	Mervyn Rose/Rex Hartwig
1956	Lew Hoad/Ken Rosewall
1957	Lew Hoad/Neale Fraser
1958	Neale Fraser/Ashley Cooper
1959	Rod Laver/Bob Mark
1960	Rod Laver/Bob Mark
1961	Rod Laver/Bob Mark
1962	Neale Fraser/Roy Emerson
1963	Fred Stolle/Bob Hewitt
1964	Fred Stolle/Bob Hewitt
1965	John Newcombe/Tony Roche
1966	Fred Stolle/Roy Emerson
1967	John Newcombe/Tony Roche
1968	Allan Stone/Dick Crealy

Aussie Men's Doubles Runners-Up
Australasian/Australian Championships: 1905–1968

The following table lists all of the Aussie doubles runners-up in our premier tennis event of the Amateur Era. Again, where only one player is listed, the Aussie player had an international partner.[272]

Year	Runners-Up
1905	Edgar Barnard/Basil Spence
1907	Horace Rice/George Wright
1908	Granville Sharp
1909	Tom Crooks
1910	Rodney Heath/John Odea
1911	Norman Brookes/John Addison
1913	Ray Taylor
1914	Rodney Heath/Arthur O'Hara Wood
1915	Bert St. John
1919	James Anderson/Arthur Lowe
1920	Horace Rice/Ray Taylor
1921	N. Brearley/Edward Stokes
1922	James Anderson/Norman Peach
1923	Dudley Bullough/Horace Rice
1924	Gerald Patterson/Pat O'Hara Wood
1925	James Anderson/Fred Kalms
1926	James Anderson/Pat O'Hara Wood
1927	Pat O'Hara Wood/Ian McInnes
1928	James Willard/Edgar Moon
1929	Jack Cummings/Edgar Moon
1930	John Hawkes/Tim Fitchett
1931	Jack Crawford/Harry Hopman
1932	Harry Hopman/Gerald Patterson
1933	Jack Crawford/Edgar Moon
1934	Adrian Quist/Don Turnbull
1936	Jack Crawford/Vivian McGrath
1937	John Bromwich/Jack Harper

Year	Runners-Up
1939	Colin Long/Don Turnbull
1940	Jack Crawford/Vivian McGrath
1946	Max Newcombe/Leonard Schwartz
1947	Frank Sedgman/George Worthington
1948	Frank Sedgman/Colin Long
1949	Geoff Brown/Bill Sidwell
1951	Adrian Quist/John Bromwich
1952	Don Candy/Mervyn Rose
1953	Don Candy/Mervyn Rose
1954	Neale Fraser/Clive Wilderspin
1955	Lew Hoad/Ken Rosewall
1956	Don Candy/Mervyn Rose
1957	Mal Anderson/Ashley Cooper
1958	Roy Emerson/Bob Mark
1959	Don Candy/Bob Howe
1960	Roy Emerson/Neale Fraser
1961	Roy Emerson/Marty Mulligan
1962	Bob Hewitt/Fred Stolle
1963	John Newcombe/Ken Fletcher
1964	Roy Emerson/Ken Fletcher
1965	Roy Emerson/Fred Stolle
1966	John Newcombe/Tony Roche
1967	Bill Bowrey/Owen Davidson
1968	Terry Addison/Ray Keldie

Aussie Men's Doubles Champions
French Championships: Amateur Era pre-1968

Australia's first doubles success at the French Championships came in 1935 (2 years after our first singles success in the event with Jack Crawford in 1933, see Chapter 1). The 1935 French doubles final was an all-Australian affair. Jack Crawford and Adrian Quist beat Vivian McGrath and Don Turnbull in straight sets to give Crawford the distinction of being the first Aussie to win both the singles and the doubles title at Roland Garros.

Crawford and Quist's 1935 win followed 3 unsuccessful French doubles finals' appearances by Aussies (Harry Hopman and Jim Willard in 1930, Adrian Quist and Vivian McGrath in 1933 and Jack Crawford and Vivian McGrath in 1934).[273] The tournament wasn't played between 1940 and 1945 due to World War II.

Let's take a look at our most successful French Championships doubles players in the Amateur Era. Once again, the pairings and individuals in the feature boxes in this section are listed in order of the highest number of French doubles titles won during this period (including by the most successful of a regular pair in some cases), and where that number is equal, chronologically.

Roy Emerson (6 titles)

Roy Emerson won an incredible 6 doubles titles in a row at the French Championships between 1960 and 1965. He partnered fellow Aussies in 5 of those victories – Neale Fraser twice (1960 and 1962), Rod Laver (1961), Queenslander Ken Fletcher (1964) and Fred Stolle (1965).

"Emmo's" other French doubles victory was in 1963 (the same year he also won the French singles title, see Chapter 3) when he paired with Spaniard Manuel Santana.

Two of Emerson's doubles finals victories at the French Championships were in all-Aussie finals. In 1961, he and Laver beat Bob Howe and Bob Mark, while in 1964 he and Fletcher beat a young John Newcombe and Tony Roche.

Emerson was also a French doubles runner-up twice in the Amateur Era (in 1959 with Neale Fraser and 1967 with Ken Fletcher), as and another 2 times in the Open Era (see Chapter 11).[274]

Neale Fraser (3 titles)

Neale Fraser won his first French doubles titles in 1958 with Ashley Cooper (the same year the pair also won the Australian doubles title).

After Cooper turned pro in 1959, he paired up with Roy Emerson. They finished runners-up at the French Championships at their first tilt together in 1959, before winning the event in 1960 and 1962 (the same year they also won the Australian doubles title together).[275]

Frank Sedgman and Ken McGregor (2 titles)

Frank Sedgman and Ken McGregor won back-to-back French doubles titles in 1951 and 1952 before turning pro in 1953 (and then being barred from competing in all amateur events, including all 4 Grand Slams). Their 1951 win was the second leg of their calendar year Grand Slam, and in 1952 they also won the Australian doubles event earlier in the year.

Sedgman had earlier finished runner-up at the doubles at the French Championships in 1948 when he partnered Harry Hopman.[276]

Ashley Cooper (2 titles)

Ashley Cooper won back-to-back French doubles titles with different Aussie partners in 1957 and 1958 before turning pro in 1959. His partner in 1957 was Queenslander Mal Anderson and in 1958 it was Neale Fraser (who he also partnered to win the 1958 Aussie doubles title).

Cooper had earlier finished runner-up in the doubles at the 1956 French Championships when he partnered Lew Hoad.[277]

Jack Crawford and Adrian Quist

As mentioned in the introduction to this section, Jack Crawford and Adrian Quist won Australia's first ever French doubles title in 1935.[278] They won the final in straight sets against fellow Aussies – New South Welshman Vivian McGrath and Western Australian Don Turnbull.

Both Crawford and Quist had finished runner-up in the event with Vivian McGrath in earlier years – Quist in 1933 and Crawford in 1934.[279]

Ken Rosewall and Lew Hoad

Ken Rosewall and Lew Hoad won the French doubles titles as teenagers in 1953, beating fellow Aussies Mervyn Rose and Clive Wilderspin. Rosewall was just 18 (and won the French singles title the same year, see Chapter 3), and Hoad was

19. The pair had already won the Australian doubles title earlier that year.

They returned to defend their French doubles title in 1954 but finished runners-up. Hoad also finished runner-up in the doubles at Roland Garros in 1956 when he partnered with Ashley Cooper.[280]

And as you'll see in Chapter 11, Rosewall won a second French doubles title in the Open Era.[281]

Don Candy

South Australian Don Candy won the 1956 doubles title at the French Championships when he partnered American Bob Perry to beat Lew Hoad and Ashley Cooper in straight sets. He finished runner-up the following year with fellow Aussie Mervyn Rose.[282]

Mal Anderson

Mal Anderson won the 1957 French doubles title with Ashley Cooper, beating fellow Aussies Don Candy (the defending champion) and Mervyn Rose in the final.

Cooper had lost the French doubles final to Candy and American Bob Perry a year earlier when he was partnering Lew Hoad.[283]

Rod Laver

Rod Laver won the doubles at the French Championships in 1961 with Roy Emerson, beating fellow Aussies Bob Howe and Bob Mark. Ironically, Laver had partnered Mark to beat Emerson and Marty Mulligan in the doubles at the Australian Championships earlier that year.

And as you'll see in Chapter 11, he also finished as a doubles runner-up twice at the French Open in the Open Era.[284]

Ken Fletcher

Queenslander Ken Fletcher won his French doubles title as Roy Emerson's 1964 partner. The following year, he finished runner-up to Emerson and Fred Stolle at Roland Garros in the doubles.

Fletcher also teamed up with Emerson for a runner-up finish in 1967 to fellow Aussies John Newcombe and Tony Roche in the last French Championships of the Amateur Era.[285]

Fred Stolle

Fred Stolle added the French doubles title to his singles win at the 1965 event (see Chapter 3). His doubles partner was Roy Emerson in what turned out to be the last of "Emmo's" 6 French doubles titles.

And as you'll see in Chapter 11, Stolle won a second French doubles title in the Open Era when he partnered Ken Rosewall in 1968.[286]

John Newcombe and Tony Roche

John Newcombe and Tony Roche won the last French doubles title of the Amateur Era in 1967, ending Roy Emerson's run of 6 straight doubles crowns at Roland Garros. The win avenged their defeat in the French doubles final 3 years earlier against "Emmo" and his partner in both of those finals, Ken Fletcher.

And as you'll see in Chapter 11, Newcombe and Roche also won another French title together in the Open Era, and "Newk" won a third French doubles title.[287]

Aussie Men's Doubles Runners-Up
French Championships: Amateur Era pre–1968

The following table lists all of the Aussie doubles runners-up in the French Championships of the Amateur Era. Special mention should be made of multiple runners-up Vivian McGrath (3), Harry Hopman (2), Mervyn Rose (2) and Bob Howe (2). Those runner-up performances were as close as they each came to winning the French men's doubles title.

Where only one player is listed, the Aussie player had an international partner.[288]

Year	Runners-Up
1930	Harry Hopman/Jim Willard
1933	Vivian McGrath/Adrian Quist
1934	Jack Crawford/Vivian McGrath
1935	Vivian McGrath/ Don Turnbull

Chapter 8 – Aussies in Grand Slam Men's Doubles (Amateur Era)

Year	Runners-Up
1947	Bill Sidwell
1948	Harry Hopman/Frank Sedgman
1953	Mervyn Rose/Clive Wilderspin
1954	Lew Hoad/Ken Rosewall
1956	Ashley Cooper/Lew Hoad
1957	Don Candy/Mervyn Rose
1958	Bob Howe
1959	Roy Emerson/Neale Fraser
1961	Bob Howe/Bob Mark
1964	John Newcombe/Tony Roche
1965	Ken Fletcher
1967	Roy Emerson/Ken Fletcher

Aussie Men's Doubles Champions
Wimbledon: Amateur Era pre–1968

Australia's first doubles success at Wimbledon came in 1907, the same year we had our first singles success there with Norman Brookes (see Chapter 1). Brookes won both the singles and the doubles at Wimbledon that year to cement his place as an Australian tennis pioneer.

Let's take a look at our most successful Wimbledon doubles players in the Amateur Era. Once again, the pairings and individuals in the feature boxes in this section are listed in order of the highest number of Wimbledon doubles titles won during this period (including by the most successful of a regular pair in some cases), and where that number is equal, chronologically. There were 10 years in the Amateur Era when the tournament wasn't played (1915-1918 due to World War I and 1940-1945 due to World War II).[289]

Frank Sedgman (3 titles) and Ken McGregor (2 titles)

Frank Sedgman and Ken McGregor won back-to-back Wimbledon doubles titles together in 1951 and 1952. As outlined earlier in the chapter, 1951 was the year that they became the first (and still the only) men's doubles players to win a calendar year Grand Slam.

Their doubles win at Wimbledon in 1952 set them up for a chance to win back-to-back calendar year Grand Slams, but they fell at the last hurdle when they lost the doubles final at the US Championships. Sedgman achieved the Wimbledon trifecta in 1952, winning the singles and mixed doubles titles as well (see Chapters 1 and 10 respectively).

And prior to teaming up with McGregor in 1951, Sedgman won a Wimbledon doubles title with Aussie doubles legend John Bromwich in 1950, giving him a hat-trick of doubles wins at the famous venue.[290]

Lew Hoad (3 titles) and Ken Rosewall (2 titles)

Lew Hoad and Ken Rosewall joined forces to win 2 Wimbledon doubles titles. The first was in 1953 in an all-Aussie final when they beat Rex Hartwig and Mervyn Rose.

They won a second Wimbledon doubles title in 1956 (and Hoad also won the Wimbledon singles title in 1956, see Chapter 3). The pair won 3 of the 4 calendar year Grand Slam doubles titles in both 1953 and 1956.

Hoad also won another Wimbledon doubles title in 1955 with Rex Hartwig. They beat Rosewall and Neale Fraser in the final. Hoad later went on to lose a Wimbledon doubles final with Fraser as well in 1957 after Rosewall had turned pro.[291]

And as you'll see in Chapter 9, Rosewall also finished as a Wimbledon doubles runner-up twice in the Open Era.[292]

Norman Brookes (2 titles)

Aussie tennis pioneer Norman Brookes won 2 Wimbledon doubles titles, and both were with New Zealander Anthony Wilding. The pair formed a formidable left-hand/right hand combination.

As mentioned earlier in the chapter, Brookes was the first Aussie to win the Wimbledon doubles title in 1907 (the same year he also became the first Aussie to win the Wimbledon singles title, see Chapter 1).

He and Wilding won their second Wimbledon doubles title in 1914 (when Brookes yet again won the Wimbledon singles title, ironically beating Wilding in the final – see also Chapter 1).[293]

1914 was the last Wimbledon tournament for 4 years because the event was suspended during World War I. Sadly, Wilding was killed in France during the War.[294]

Adrian Quist (2 titles)

Adrian Quist won his first Wimbledon doubles title in 1935 with Jack Crawford, just months after the pair had become the first Aussies to win the doubles at the French Championships.

Quist won his second Wimbledon doubles title 15 years later in 1950 with long-time partner John Bromwich. They beat fellow Aussies Geoff Brown and Bill Sidwell.[295]

John Bromwich (2 titles)

John Bromwich won 2 Wimbledon doubles titles – the first was with Frank Sedgman in 1948, and the second with long-time partner Adrian Quist in 1950.

He reached all 3 Wimbledon finals in 1948, losing the singles (see Chapter 1), but winning both the men's doubles and the mixed doubles (see Chapter 10).[296]

Rex Hartwig (2 titles)

Rex Hartwig made 3 consecutive Wimbledon doubles finals, winning back-to-back titles with 2 different Aussie partners – the first was in 1954 with Mervyn Rose and the second was with Lew Hoad a year later.

The 1955 final was an all-Aussie affair, with Hartwig and Hoad downing Neale Fraser and Ken Rosewall on one of the rare occasions that Hoad and Rosewall weren't doubles partners in a Grand Slam event.

Hartwig's first doubles finals appearance with Mervyn Rose in 1953 was unsuccessful, ironically being beaten by future partner Lew Hoad and his partner Ken Rosewall.[297]

Roy Emerson and Neale Fraser (2 titles)

Roy Emerson and Neale Fraser won the 1959 and 1961 Wimbledon doubles titles together, and as you'll see in Chapter 9, "Emmo" also won a third Wimbledon doubles title in the Open Era.[298]

Both of their Wimbledon doubles titles in the Amateur Era were in all-Aussie finals. They beat Rod Laver and Bob Mark in 1959, and Bob Hewitt and Fred Stolle in 1961.

The 1959 win gave Fraser a career Grand Slam in men's doubles. He tasted defeat in a Wimbledon doubles final 4 times with 4 other Aussie partners (3 in the Amateur Era and one in the Open Era), while Emerson was a Wimbledon doubles runner-up twice with fellow Aussie Ken Fletcher.[299]

Fred Stolle and Bob Hewitt* (2 titles)

Fred Stolle (pictured) and Bob Hewitt won Wimbledon doubles titles together in 1962 and 1964. The 1964 final was another all-Aussie affair, with Stolle and Hewitt beating Roy Emerson and Ken Fletcher.[300]

*Bob Hewitt later became a South African citizen and won 3 further Wimbledon titles (1 more in the Amateur Era and another 2 in the Pro Era).[301]

John Newcombe (2 titles) and Tony Roche (1 title)

John Newcombe won back-to-back Wimbledon doubles titles as an amateur, and as you'll see in Chapter 9, another 4 in the Open Era (all with his great mate Tony Roche). "Newk's" first Wimbledon doubles title was in 1965 with Roche. They beat Ken Fletcher and Bob Hewitt in yet another all-Australian final.

His second title in 1966 was with Ken Fletcher when Roche chose to focus his efforts solely on the singles event instead. Newk and Fletcher were too strong for fellow Aussies Bill Bowrey and Owen Davidson.[302]

Pat O'Hara Wood and Ron Thomas

Pat O'Hara Wood and Ron Thomas won the Wimbledon doubles in 1919, the first time the event was held after a 4-year break due to World War I. Later, they won the 1919 Australasian doubles title together (it was played after Wimbledon that year).

O'Hara Wood didn't return to Wimbledon again until 1922 with fellow Aussie Gerald Patterson as his doubles partner. They finished runners-up.[303]

James Anderson

New South Welshman James Anderson won the 1922 Wimbledon doubles title with Englishman Randolph Lycett.

They beat Aussie defending champions Pat O'Hara Wood and Gerald Patterson in the final, coming from 2 sets down to win in 5 sets. The fifth set was an 11-9 marathon.[304]

Jack Crawford

Jack Crawford won the only Wimbledon doubles title of his career in 1935 with Adrian Quist, just months after the pair had won the French doubles title, and 2 years after he had won the Wimbledon singles crown (see Chapter 1).[305]

Mervyn Rose

Mervyn Rose won the 1954 Wimbledon doubles title with Rex Hartwig, a year after the left-hand/right-hand combination had finished runner-up to fellow Aussies Lew Hoad and Ken Rosewall.

Rose and Hartwig also won the doubles title at the Australian Championships in 1954.[306]

Chapter 8 – Aussies in Grand Slam Men's Doubles (Amateur Era)

Ken Fletcher

Ken Fletcher won the 1966 Wimbledon doubles title with John Newcombe, the same year he also won the Wimbledon mixed doubles title (see Chapter 10).

Fletcher was also a 3-time Wimbledon men's doubles runner-up (in 1964 and 1967 with Roy Emerson, and in 1965 with Bob Hewitt).[307]

Aussie Men's Doubles Runners-Up
Wimbledon: Amateur Era pre–1968

The following table lists all of the Aussie doubles runners-up in the Wimbledon Championships of the Amateur Era. Special mention should be made of two-time runners-up Gerald Patterson, Geoff Brown and Bill Sidwell. Those runner-up performances were as close as they each came to winning the Wimbledon men's doubles title.

Where only one player is listed, the Aussie player had an international partner.[308]

Year	Runners-Up
1909	Stanley Doust
1919	Rodney Heath
1922	Pat O'Hara Wood/Gerald Patterson
1928	John Hawkes/Gerald Patterson
1946	Geoff Brown/Dinny Pails
1947	Bill Sidwell
1950	Geoff Brown/Bill Sidwell
1953	Rex Hartwig/Mervyn Rose
1955	Neale Fraser/Ken Rosewall
1957	Neale Fraser/Lew Hoad
1958	Ashley Cooper/Neale Fraser
1959	Rod Laver/Bob Mark
1961	Bob Hewitt/Fred Stolle
1964	Roy Emerson/Ken Fletcher
1965	Ken Fletcher/Bob Hewitt
1966	Bill Bowrey/Owen Davidson
1967	Roy Emerson/Ken Fletcher

Aussie Men's Doubles Champions
US Championships: Amateur Era pre–1968

Australia's first doubles success at the US Championships came in 1919 with pioneers Norman Brookes and Gerald Patterson, and it was also the event where Frank Sedgman and Ken McGregor became the first (and still the only) male tennis players from any country to win a calendar year Grand Slam in doubles.

Several other Aussie players achieved a career Grand Slam in doubles by winning the US Championships as their fourth and final leg, including Adrian Quist, Lew Hoad, Ken Rosewall, Fred Stolle, John Newcombe and Tony Roche.[309]

Unlike the other Grand Slam events, the US Championships was played every year during both World War I and World War II. Let's take a look at our most successful doubles players at the tournament in the Amateur Era. Once again, the pairings and individuals in the feature boxes in this section are listed in order of the highest number of US doubles titles won during this period (including by the most successful of a regular pair in some cases), and where that number is equal, chronologically.

Roy Emerson (4 titles)

Roy Emerson won 4 doubles titles at the US Championships – back-to-back victories with Neale Fraser in 1959 and 1960, and back-to-back wins with Fred Stolle in 1965 and 1966.

And as outlined earlier in this chapter, "Emmo" and Fraser also won Wimbledon together in 1959 and the French doubles in 1960. Victory in the US Championships in both years gave them 2 of the 4 calendar year Grand Slam doubles titles. Their 1960 US doubles win was an all-Australian final. They beat Rod Laver and Bob Mark.

As also mentioned earlier in the chapter, Emmo and Stolle won the doubles at the French Championships in 1965 and the Australian Championships in 1966, giving them 2 of the 4 calendar year Grand Slam doubles titles.[310]

John Bromwich (3 titles)

John Bromwich won 3 US doubles titles with 3 different Aussie partners. The first was in 1939 in the early days of his long-time partnership with Adrian Quist (and as mentioned earlier in the chapter, they also won the second of their 8 consecutive Australian doubles titles earlier that year). They had finished runners-up at the US Championships the year before.

Bromwich won his second US doubles title a decade later in 1949 with fellow Aussie Bill Sidwell. They beat fellow Aussies Frank Sedgman and John Worthington.

A year later, Bromwich teamed up with Sedgman to win his third US doubles title.[311]

Neale Fraser (3 titles)

Neale Fraser won the first of his 3 US doubles titles in 1957 with Ashley Cooper, followed by his back-to-back victories with Roy Emerson in 1959 and 1960. Fraser had the unique distinction of winning back-to-back US singles titles in 1959 and 1960 (see Chapter 3) to go with his doubles victories.

And as outlined in "Emmo's" US feature box, Fraser and Emerson won 2 of the 4 Grand Slam doubles titles in

both of those years – the US and Wimbledon in 1959 and the US and French in 1960.[312]

Frank Sedgman (2 titles) and Ken McGregor (1 title)

Frank Sedgman and Ken McGregor famously completed their calendar year Grand Slam at the US Championships in 1951. They beat fellow Aussies Don Candy and Mervyn Rose, and Sedgman also won the US singles title that year (see Chapter 1). As mentioned earlier, they are still the only men's doubles players to have ever achieved this feat.

In 1952, they narrowly missed out on a back-to-back Grand Slam when they went down to Mervyn Rose and American Vic Seixas in 5 sets in the US doubles final.

Prior to teaming up with McGregor, Sedgman won the 1950 US doubles title with John Bromwich. He also finished runner-up in the US doubles in 1949 with Aussie partner John Worthington.[313]

Mervyn Rose (2 titles)

Mervyn Rose won back-to-back US doubles titles in 1952 and 1953.

As outlined in the previous feature box, his first US doubles title denied his fellow Aussies Frank Sedgman and Ken McGregor back-to-back calendar year Grand Slams. His partner was American Vic Seixas.

The year before, he had been on the court when Sedgman and McGregor completed their Grand Slam. He and his Aussie partner Don Candy lost the final in 4 sets.

Rose successfully defended his 1952 US doubles title in 1953 when he partnered Rex Hartwig.[314]

Fred Stolle (2 titles)

Fred Stolle won back-to-back US doubles titles in 1965 and 1966 with Roy Emerson. Both were memorable years for Stolle at the US Championships. The 1965 win gave him a career Grand Slam in men's doubles, while he also won the US singles title in 1966.

Stolle and Emerson also won the doubles at the French Championships in 1965 and the Australian Championships in 1966, giving them 2 of the 4 Grand Slam doubles titles in both of those years.

And as you'll see in Chapter 11, Stolle also won a third US doubles title in the Open Era.[315]

Gerald Patterson and Norman Brookes

Aussie tennis pioneers Gerald Patterson and Norman Brookes combined as a right-hand/left-hand duo to win the 1919 US doubles title.

Patterson also finished as a runner-up in the men's doubles at the US Championships 4 more times (twice with Pat O'Hara Wood in 1922 and 1924, and twice with John Hawkes in 1925 and 1928).[316]

Adrian Quist

Adrian Quist won the 1939 US doubles final with his long-time doubles partner in Australia, John Bromwich (and they had won their second Australian doubles titles earlier that year as well).

They beat fellow Aussies Jack Crawford and Harry Hopman in the US final, after finishing as runners-up the year before.

The 1939 US title gave Quist a career Grand Slam in doubles, after he'd won the Australian, French and Wimbledon titles earlier in his career.[317]

Chapter 8 – Aussies in Grand Slam Men's Doubles (Amateur Era)

Bill Sidwell

Bill Sidwell won the 1949 US doubles with fellow New South Welshman John Bromwich, after finishing runner-up 2 years earlier when he partnered American Bill Talbert.

Sidwell and Bromwich beat Frank Sedgman and John Worthington in an all-Aussie US doubles final in 1949. Sidwell's tennis career had earlier been interrupted by World War I where he served as a pilot. He lived to the ripe old age of 101.[318]

Rex Hartwig

Rex Hartwig partnered with Mervyn Rose to win the doubles at the 1953 US Championships.

It was the first Grand Slam title of his career in men's doubles. As outlined earlier in the chapter, he went on to win 3 others – 2 at Wimbledon and 1 in Australia.[319]

Ken Rosewall and Lew Hoad

Ken Rosewall and Lew Hoad won the 1956 US doubles title, after finishing runners-up 2 years earlier. Rosewall also won the US singles in 1956 (ironically, beating Hoad in the final and denying him a calendar year singles Grand Slam – see Chapter 3).

Their doubles win at the US Championships gave them a career Grand Slam in men's doubles, after having won the Australian, French and Wimbledon titles earlier in their careers. And as you'll see in Chapter 11, Ken Rosewall also won another US doubles title in the Open Era, and he finished runner-up once as well.[320]

Ashley Cooper

Ashley Cooper won the doubles at the 1957 US Championships with Neale Fraser as his partner.

It was the second of 4 Grand Slam doubles titles that he won in his career before turning pro and being barred from competing in Grand Slam events for the rest of his career.[321]

John Newcombe and Tony Roche

John Newcombe and Tony Roche won the last US doubles title of the Amateur Era, beating Bill Bowrey and Owen Davidson in an all-Aussie final. The win gave them a career Grand Slam in men's doubles, after they had won the Australian, French and Wimbledon titles earlier in their careers.

The 1967 US tournament was a great success for Newcombe, as he won the singles as well – see Chapter 3. And as you'll see in Chapter 11, "Newk" also won 2 more US doubles titles in the Open Era, as well as finishing runner-up once.[322]

Aussie Men's Doubles Runners-Up
US Championships: Amateur Era pre–1968

The following table lists all of the Aussie doubles runners-up in the US Championships of the Amateur Era. Special mention should be made of two-time runners-up Pat O'Hara Wood and John Hawkes. Those runner-up performances were as close as they each came to winning the US men's doubles title.

Where only one player is listed, the Aussie player had an international partner.[323]

Year	Runners-Up
1922	Pat O'Hara Wood/Gerald Patterson
1924	Pat O'Hara Wood/Gerald Patterson
1925	Gerald Patterson/John Hawkes
1928	Gerald Patterson/John Hawkes
1938	John Bromwich/Adrian Quist

Australia's Grand Slam Tennis Champions

Year	Runners-Up
1939	Jack Crawford/Harry Hopman
1947	Bill Sidwell
1949	Frank Sedgman/John Worthington
1951	Don Candy/Mervyn Rose
1952	Ken McGregor/Frank Sedgman
1954	Lew Hoad/Ken Rosewall
1960	Rod Laver/Bob Mark
1967	Bill Bowrey/Owen Davidson

Chapter 9
Aussies in Grand Slam Women's Doubles
(Amateur Era)

Women's doubles events were a feature of the Australasian and Australian Championships (the forerunners to today's Australian Open) ever since women first competed at the tournament in 1922.[324]

Women's doubles was added to the French Championships (as the French Open was originally called) in 1914, 17 years after the first women's singles event at Roland Garros, but the tournament didn't officially become a Grand Slam event until 1925.[325]

Wimbledon added the women's doubles event in 1913, 29 years after the first Wimbledon women's singles tournament.[326] It became an annual feature of the US Championships in 1889, 2 years after the first US women's singles event.[327]

Let's first take a look at our most successful Grand Slam women's doubles players of the Amateur Era, starting with our local event.

Multiple Aussie Women's Doubles Champions
Australasian/Australian Championships: 1922–1968

As you would expect in the early days of international travel during the Amateur Era, Aussies initially had the most success at our local major. The pairings and individuals in the feature boxes that follow are listed in order of the highest number of local Grand Slam doubles titles won (by the most successful of a regular pair in some cases), and where that number is equal, chronologically.

Thelma Coyne (Long) – 12 titles and Nancye Wynne (Bolton) – 10 titles

Sydney's Thelma Coyne (Long) and Melbourne's Nancye Wynne (Bolton) had an incredible run of success as a doubles pairing at the Australian Championships in the Amateur Era, combining to win 10 titles.

Wynne (Bolton) also won the Australian women's singles crown in 5 of those years (including 2 wins over Coyne (Long) – see Chapter 2), as well as both the women's singles and mixed doubles in 3 of those years – see Chapters 2 and 10.

Their first 5 Aussie doubles titles came in consecutive years between 1936 and 1940, just prior to the tournament being suspended for 5 years due to World War II. Tragically, as highlighted in Chapter 2, Wynne (Bolton) lost her husband during the War, while Coyne (Long) served in the Australian Women's Army Service.

Coyne (Long) and Wynne (Bolton) lost the first women's doubles final at the Australian Championships after World War II, before winning the next 3 titles from 1947 to 1949. They then lost the 1950 final before winning back-to-back crowns in 1951 and 1952.

Coyne (Long) also won the singles event at the Australian Championships in 1952, as well as the mixed doubles to give her a triple celebration that year – see Chapters 2 and 10.[328]

But for the World War II break, who knows how many more Australian doubles titles they would have won together. Coyne (Long) went on to win a further 2 titles with Mary Bevis (Hawton) in 1956 and 1958.³²⁹

Mary Bevis (Hawton) – 5 titles

Sydney's Mary Bevis (Hawton) won 5 Aussie women's doubles titles with 3 different local partners and finished runner-up another 7 times.

Her first success in the tournament came when she and Victorian Joyce Fitch (Rymer) interrupted Thelma Coyne (Long) and Nancye Wynne (Bolton)'s 5-year winning streak in the 1946 Australian Championship final, the first one held after World War II.

It would be another 8 years and 5 finals defeats before Bevis (Hawton) held the trophy aloft again, but she then won 4 of the 5 doubles events at the Australian Championships between 1954 and 1958 – back-to-back titles with fellow Sydneysider Beryl Penrose (Collier) in 1954 and 1955, and a further 2 titles with Thelma Coyne (Long) in 1956 and 1958 (after Coyne Long's long-time partner Nancye Wynne (Bolton) had retired).

Bevis (Hawton) finished runner-up in the Aussie women's doubles twice more before retiring.³³⁰

Esna Boyd (Robertson) – 4 titles

Victorian pioneer Esna Boyd (Robertson) won the first 2 women's doubles titles ever played at the then Australasian Championships in 1922 and 1923.

Her partner in the first victory was Marjorie Mountain and a year later it was Sylvia Lance (Harper). She was the women's singles runner-up at the tournament in both of those years – see Chapter 2.

Boyd won a further 2 Aussie doubles titles in 1926

(with Meryl Waxman (O'Hara Wood)) and 1928 (partnering Daphne Akhurst (Cozens)), as well as finishing runner-up twice (in 1925 and again in 1927, when she won her only Aussie women's singles title – also see Chapter 2).[331]

Daphne Akhurst (Cozens) – 4 titles

Sydney's Daphne Akhurst (Cozens) won back-to-back women's doubles titles at the Australasian Championships in 1924 and 1925 with Sylvia Lance (Harper), as well as 2 more back-to-back titles in 1928 (with Esna Boyd (Robertson), who she beat in the singles final that year, see Chapter 2) and 1929 (with Louie Bickerton (Cozens). She finished runner-up in 1926 with Marjorie Cox (Crawford).[332]

Akhurst also won the Australian women's singles event in 1924 to give her a double celebration in that year. She went one better in 1925, 1928 and 1929 – winning the women's singles, women's doubles and the mixed doubles at her home Grand Slam – see Chapters 2 and 10.

Margaret Smith (Court) – 4 titles

Margaret Smith (Court) appeared in 7 Aussie women's doubles finals in the Amateur Era, winning 4.

She won 3 consecutive titles between 1961 and 1963, the first with Mary Carter (Reitano) and the next 2 with Robyn Ebbern (Vincenzi). Her fourth and final doubles crown as an amateur came in 1965 with Lesley Turner (Bowrey). Smith (Court) won the Aussie women's singles each year that she won the doubles event in the Amateur Era.

And as you'll see in Chapter 12, she won another 4 Aussie women's doubles titles in the Open Era, as well as finishing runner-up once.[333]

Chapter 9 – Aussies in Grand Slam Women's Doubles (Amateur Era)

Louie Bickerton (Cozens) – 3 titles

Victorian pioneer Louie Bickerton (Cozens) won 3 women's doubles titles at the Australian Championships. The first was with Meryl Waxman (O'Hara Wood) in 1927, and the other 2 were with Daphne Akhurst (Cozens) in 1929 and 1931.

She later finished runner-up at the tournament in 1935 with partner Nell Hall (Hopman).[334]

Margaret Mutch (Molesworth) and Emily Hood (Westacott) – 3 titles

Pioneering Brisbane pair Margaret Mutch (Molesworth) and Emily Hood (Westacott) won the 1930, 1933 and 1934 Aussie women's double titles.[335]

Mutch (Molesworth) had finished as an Aussie doubles runner-up earlier in her career in 1923, while Hood (Westacott) finished runner-up twice after Mutch (Molesworth) retired.[336]

Lesley Turner (Bowrey) – 3 titles and Judy Tegart (Dalton) – 2 titles

Lesley Turner (Bowrey) won 3 Aussie doubles titles – back-to-back victories in 1964 (with Judy Tegart (Dalton)) and 1965 (with Margaret Smith (Court)), and another in 1967 (with Judy Tegart (Dalton)).

She also finished runner-up 3 times in the Amateur Era with 3 different partners (Jan Lehane (O'Neill), Margaret Smith (Court) and Judy Tegart (Dalton)), as well as once more in the Open Era – see Chapter 12.[337]

Sylvia Lance (Harper) – 2 titles

Pioneer Sylvia Lance (Harper) won back-to-back Aussie doubles titles in 1924 and 1925 with Daphne Akhurst (Cozens).

1924 was an especially memorable year for her as she won the Aussie women's singles event as well (see Chapter 2).

She finished as the Aussie doubles runner-up 3 more times later in her career with 3 different partners (in 1927 with Esna Boyd (Robertson), 1929 with Meryl Waxman (O'Hara Wood) and 1930 with Marjorie Cox (Crawford)).[338]

Meryl Waxman (O'Hara Wood) – 2 titles

Meryl Waxman (O'Hara Wood), wife of fellow Aussie tennis pioneer Pat O'Hara Wood, was yet another Aussie who won back-to-back Aussie doubles titles – in 1926 (with Esna Boyd (Robertson)) and 1927 (with Louie Bickerton (Cozens)).

She also finished runner-up in 1923 (with Kathleen Le Messurier) and 1929 (with Sylvia Lance (Harper)).[339]

Beryl Penrose (Collier) – 2 titles

Sydney's Beryl Penrose (Collier) was another who won back-to-back Aussie women's doubles titles, and both were with Mary Bevis (Hawton) in 1954 and 1955. She also finished runner-up twice (in 1953 with Bevis (Hawton) and 1956 with Mary Carter (Reitano).

1955 was a dream tournament for Penrose. She won the women's singles, women's doubles and mixed doubles (with Neale Fraser) at her home Grand Slam.[340]

Robyn Ebbern (Vincenzi) – 2 titles

Brisbane's Robyn Ebbern (Vincenzi) made 4 Aussie women's doubles titles in a row, winning the first 2 with Margaret Smith (Court) in 1962 and 1963 before the pair finished runner-up in 1964.

The following year, she partnered American Billie Jean Moffitt (King) and finished runner-up to Smith (Court) and Lesley Turner (Bowrey).[341]

Judy Tegart (Dalton) – 2 titles

Victorian Judy Tegart (Dalton) won 2 Aussie women's doubles titles in the Amateur Era, and both were with Lesley Turner (Bowrey) – 1964 and 1967.

And as you'll see in Chapter 12, Tegart (Dalton) won 2 more Aussie women's doubles titles in the Open Era.[342]

All Aussie Women's Doubles Champions
Australasian/Australian Championships: 1905–1968

The following table lists all of the Aussie women's doubles winners during the Amateur Era. Excluding the 5 years when the event wasn't held during World War II, there were only 7 years during the Amateur Era when a non-Australian doubles team won at Australia's premier tennis tournament. This domination is largely due to limited international participants in the early years when long-distance travel was more difficult.[343]

Australia's Grand Slam Tennis Champions

Year	Winner/s
1922	Esna Boyd (Robertson)/Marjorie Mountain
1923	Esna Boyd (Robertson)/Sylvia Lance (Harper)
1924	Daphne Akhurst (Cozens)/Sylvia Lance (Harper)
1925	Daphne Akhurst (Cozens)/Sylvia Lance (Harper)
1926	Esna Boyd (Robertson)/Meryl Waxman (O'Hara Wood)
1927	Meryl Waxman (O'Hara Wood)/Louie Bickerton (Cozens)
1928	Esna Boyd (Robertson)/Daphne Akhurst (Cozens)
1929	Daphne Akhurst (Cozens)/Louie Bickerton (Cozens)
1930	Margaret Mutch (Molesworth)/ Emily Hood (Westacott)
1931	Daphne Akhurst (Cozens)/Louie Bickerton (Cozens)
1932	Coral McInnes (Buttsworth)/Marjorie Cox (Crawford)
1933	Margaret Mutch (Molesworth)/Emily Hood (Westacott)
1934	Margaret Mutch (Molesworth)/Emily Hood (Westacott)
1936	Thelma Coyne (Long)/Nancye Wynne (Bolton)
1937	Thelma Coyne (Long)/Nancye Wynne (Bolton)
1938	Thelma Coyne (Long)/Nancye Wynne (Bolton)
1939	Thelma Coyne (Long)/Nancye Wynne (Bolton)
1940	Thelma Coyne (Long)/Nancye Wynne (Bolton)
1946	Joyce Fitch (Rymer)/Mary Bevis (Hawton)
1947	Thelma Coyne (Long)/Nancye Wynne (Bolton)
1948	Thelma Coyne (Long)/Nancye Wynne (Bolton)
1949	Thelma Coyne (Long)/Nancye Wynne (Bolton)
1951	Thelma Coyne (Long)/Nancye Wynne (Bolton)
1952	Thelma Coyne (Long)/Nancye Wynne (Bolton)
1954	Mary Bevis (Hawton)/Beryl Penrose (Collier)
1955	Mary Bevis (Hawton)/Beryl Penrose (Collier)
1956	Mary Bevis (Hawton)/Thelma Coyne (Long)
1958	Mary Bevis (Hawton)/Thelma Coyne (Long)
1961	Mary Carter (Reitano)/Margaret Smith (Court)

Chapter 9 – Aussies in Grand Slam Women's Doubles (Amateur Era)

Year	Winner/s
1962	Margaret Smith (Court)/Robyn Ebbern (Vincenzi)
1963	Margaret Smith (Court)/Robyn Ebbern (Vincenzi)
1964	Judy Tegart (Dalton)/Lesley Turner (Bowrey)
1965	Margaret Smith (Court)/Lesley Turner (Bowrey)
1967	Judy Tegart (Dalton)/Lesley Turner (Bowrey)
1968	Karen Krantzcke/Kerry Melville (Reid)

Aussie Women's Doubles Runners-Up
Australasian/Australian Championships: 1922–1968

The following table lists all of the Aussie doubles runners-up in our premier tennis event of the Amateur Era. Where only one player is listed, the Aussie player had an international partner.[344]

Year	Runners-Up
1922	Floris St. George (Conway)/Gwen Chiplin (Utz)
1923	Margaret Mutch (Molesworth)/Beryl Spowers (Turner)
1924	Kathleen Le Messurier/Meryl Waxman (O'Hara Wood)
1925	Esna Boyd (Robertson)/Kathleen Le Messurier
1926	Daphne Akhurst (Cozens)/Marjorie Cox (Crawford)
1927	Esna Boyd (Robertson)/Sylvia Lance (Harper)
1928	Kathleen Le Messurier
1929	Sylvia Lance (Harper)/Meryl Waxman (O'Hara Wood)
1930	Marjorie Cox (Crawford)/Sylvia Lance (Harper)
1931	Nell Lloyd/Gwen Chiplin (Utz)
1932	Kathleen Le Messurier
1933	Joan Hartigan (Bathurst)
1934	Joan Hartigan (Bathurst)/Ula Valkenburg
1935	Louie Bickerton (Cozens)/Nell Hall (Hopman)
1936	May Blick/Katherine Woodward
1937	Nell Hall (Hopman)/Emily Hood (Westacott)

Australia's Grand Slam Tennis Champions

Year	Runners-Up
1939	Emily Hood (Westacott)/May Hardcastle
1940	Joan Hartigan (Bathurst)/Emily Niemeyer
1946	Thelma Coyne (Long)/Nancye Wynne (Bolton)
1947	Joyce Fitch (Rymer)/Mary Bevis (Hawton)
1948	Mary Bevis (Hawton)/Pat Jones
1949	Marie Toomey
1950	Thelma Coyne (Long)/Nancye Wynne (Bolton)
1951	Joyce Fitch (Rymer)/Mary Bevis (Hawton)
1952	Allison Burton (Baker)/Mary Bevis (Hawton)
1953	Mary Bevis (Hawton)/Beryl Penrose (Collier)
1955	Nell Hall (Hopman)/Gwen O'Halloran (Thiele)
1956	Mary Carter (Reitano)/Beryl Penrose (Collier)
1957	Mary Bevis (Hawton)/Fay Muller (Colthorpe)
1958	Lorraine Coghlan (Robinson)
1959	Mary Carter (Reitano)/Lorraine Coghlan (Robinson)
1960	Lorraine Coghlan (Robinson)/Margaret Smith (Court)
1961	Mary Bevis (Hawton)/Jan Lehane (O'Neill)
1962	Mary Carter (Reitano)
1963	Jan Lehane (O'Neill)/Lesley Turner (Bowrey)
1964	Margaret Smith (Court)/Robyn Ebbern (Vincenzi)
1965	Robyn Ebbern (Vincenzi)
1966	Margaret Smith (Court)/Lesley Turner (Bowrey)
1967	Lorraine Coghlan (Robinson)
1968	Judy Tegart (Dalton)/Lesley Turner (Bowrey)

Aussie Women's Doubles Champions
French Championships: Amateur Era pre–1968

Australia's first women's doubles success at the French Championships came in 1954 when pioneer Nell Hall (Hopman) partnered with American Maureen Connolly to win the title. Her doubles triumph came 8 years before our first women's singles victory at the French event with Margaret Smith (Court) – see Chapter 4.[345]

Let's take a look at our most successful French Championships doubles players in the Amateur Era. Once again, the pairings and individuals in the feature boxes in this section are listed in order of the highest number of French doubles titles won during this period (including by the most successful of a regular pair in some cases), and where that number is equal, chronologically.

Margaret Smith (Court) – 3 titles and Lesley Turner (Bowrey) – 2 titles

Margaret Smith (Court) and Lesley Turner (Bowrey) won back-to-back French doubles championships in 1964 and 1965.

Smith (Court) also won the French singles (see Chapter 4) and mixed doubles titles (see Chapter 10) to cap off a dream Roland Garros tournament in 1964, while Turner (Bowrey) also won the French singles title in 1965 to give her a double celebration (also see Chapter 4).

Smith (Court) then won a third consecutive doubles title at Roland Garros in

1966 with Judy Tegart (Dalton). And as you'll see in Chapter 12, Smith (Court) also won another French doubles title in the Open Era.

Earlier in her career, Smith (Court) finished as a runner-up in back-to-back French doubles championships in 1962 (with American Justina Bricka) and 1963 (with fellow Aussie Robyn Ebbern (Vincenzi)).[346]

Nell Hall (Hopman)

As mentioned at the start of this section, pioneer Nell Hall (Hopman) was the first Australian to win a Grand Slam women's double event outside of Australia. She did it in 1954 with American Maureen Connolly at the age of 45.

Hall (Hopman) was employed by the United States Tennis Association at the time to act as companion and chaperone to the-then 20-year-old Connolly, who was also being coached by Hall (Hopman)'s husband and fellow Aussie tennis pioneer Harry.

And as you'll see in Chapter 10, Nell and Harry had plenty of success as a mixed doubles pairing.[347]

Judy Tegart (Dalton)

Judy Tegart (Dalton) won the 1966 French doubles title with Margaret Smith (Court), beating fellow Aussies Jill Blackman (Emmerson) and Fay Toyne (Moore) in 3 sets in the final. It was her second Grand Slam win in women's doubles, after she and Lesley Turner (Bowrey) had won the 1964 Australian doubles title.

> It was the only French doubles title of Tegart (Dalton)'s career, but as you'll see in Chapter 12, it enabled her to become one of the select group of Aussies to achieve a career Grand Slam in women's doubles when she won both the Wimbledon and US doubles titles in the Open Era.[348]

Aussie Women's Doubles Runners-Up
French Championships: Amateur Era pre–1968

The following table lists all of the Aussie doubles runners-up in the French Championships of the Amateur Era. Where only one player is listed, the Aussie player had an international partner.[349]

Year	Runners-Up
1958	Thelma Coyne (Long)
1962	Margaret Smith (Court)
1963	Margaret Smith (Court)/ Robyn Ebbern (Vincenzi)
1966	Jill Blackman (Emmerson)/Fay Toyne (Moore)

Aussie Women's Doubles Champions
Wimbledon: Amateur Era pre–1968

Australia's only women's doubles success at Wimbledon in the Amateur Era came with Margaret Smith (Court) and Lesley Turner (Bowrey) in 1964,[350] the year after Smith (Court) became the first Aussie woman to win a Wimbledon singles title – see Chapter 4.

But there were plenty of near misses by Aussie women at the Wimbledon doubles in the pre-Open Era. Let's take a look at our most successful amateur doubles players at the All England Club.

Margaret Smith (Court) and Lesley Turner (Bowrey)

Margaret Smith (Court) and Lesley Turner (Bowrey) won the 1964 Wimbledon women's doubles title to make them the first Australian women to achieve a career Grand Slam in doubles.[351] They had won the Australian, French and US doubles titles earlier in their careers (though their US doubles titles were with different partners, see feature boxes later in this chapter).

Smith (Court) had previously finished runner-up in the Wimbledon doubles event in 1961 (with fellow Aussie Jan Lehane (O'Neill)) and in 1963 (with Robyn Ebbern (Vincenzi)). She later finished runner-up a third time in 1966 with Judy Tegart (Dalton).

And as you'll see in Chapter 12, Smith (Court) also won a second Wimbledon doubles title in the Open Era, as well as finishing runner-up for a fourth time.[352]

Aussie Women's Doubles Runners-Up
Wimbledon: Amateur Era pre–1968

Although only 2 Aussies lifted the Wimbledon women's doubles trophy in the Amateur Era, we had another 9 runners-up, including Margaret Smith (Court). The following table lists them all.[353]

Year	Runners-Up
1956	Fay Muller (Colthorpe)/Daphne Seeney
1957	Mary Bevis (Hawton)/Thelma Coyne (Long)
1961	Margaret Smith (Court)/Jan Lehane (O'Neill)
1963	Margaret Smith (Court)/Robyn Ebbern (Vincenzi)
1966	Margaret Smith (Court)/Judy Tegart (Dalton)

Aussie Women's Doubles Champions
US Championships: Amateur Era pre–1968

Australia's first doubles success at the US Championships came in 1961 when Lesley Turner (Bowrey) partnered with American Darlene Hard to win the title.[354] Her doubles triumph came a year before our first women's singles victory at the US event with Margaret Smith (Court) – see Chapter 4.

Let's take a look at our most successful doubles players at the tournament in the Amateur Era.

Lesley Turner (Bowrey)

Lesley Turner (Bowrey) chose her partner wisely for the 1961 US women's doubles event.

She had just turned 19 at the time and paired up with American Darlene Hard who had won the previous 3 US doubles titles. Hard was also the defending US singles champion.[355]

Margaret Smith (Court) and Robyn Ebbern (Vincenzi)

Margaret Smith (Court) (pictured) and Robyn Ebbern (Vincenzi) won the 1963 US doubles title, beating Americans Darlene Hard and Brazilian Maria Beuno in 3 tough sets in the final.

Their win broke Hard's 5-year winning streak in the event (which included her win with Lesley Turner (Bowrey) in 1961.

And as you'll see in Chapter 12, Smith (Court) also won 4 more US doubles titles in the Open Era, as well as finishing runner-up twice.[356]

Aussie Women's Doubles Runners-Up
US Championships: Amateur Era pre–1968

Only 2 Aussie women reached a US doubles final in the Amateur Era and finished runners-up – Margaret Smith (Court) and Lesley Turner (Bowrey) when they paired up at the US event in 1964.

Smith (Court) was attempting to go back-to-back after winning her first US doubles title with Robyn Ebbern (Vincenzi) in 1963. Turner (Bowrey) was searching for her second US doubles crown after her breakthrough 1961 win. They were beaten in 3 sets by Americans Billie Jean Moffitt (King) and Karen Susman in the final.[357]

Chapter 10
Aussies in Grand Slam Mixed Doubles
(Amateur Era)

Mixed doubles events were a feature of the Australasian and Australian Championships (the forerunners to today's Australian Open) ever since women first competed at the tournament in 1922.[358]

Mixed doubles was added to the French Championships (as the French Open was originally called) in 1902, 5 years after women first competed in singles at Roland Garros, but the tournament didn't officially become a Grand Slam event until 1925.[359]

Wimbledon added the mixed doubles event in 1913, 29 years after the first Wimbledon women's singles tournament.[360] It became an annual feature of the US Championships in 1887, the same year as the first US women's singles event.[361]

Let's first take a look at our most successful Grand Slam mixed doubles players of the Amateur Era, starting with our local event.

Multiple Aussie Mixed Champions
Australasian/Australian Championships: 1922–1968

As you would expect in the early days of international travel during the Amateur Era, Aussies initially had the most success at our local major. The pairings and individuals in the feature boxes that follow are listed in order of the highest number of local Grand Slam mixed doubles titles won (by the most successful of a regular pair in some cases), and where that number is equal, chronologically.

Daphne Akhurst (Cozens) – 4 titles

Pioneer Daphne Akhurst (Cozens) won 4 Aussie mixed doubles titles – back-to-back victories with fellow New South Wales player Jim Willard in 1924 and 1925, followed by back-to-back wins in 1928 (with Frenchman Jean Borotra, the first non-Australian to win the Australasian mixed doubles title) and 1929 with Edgar Moon, another New South Welshman.

1925, 1928 and 1929 were magic years for Akhurst at the Australasian/Australian Championships – she not only won the mixed doubles in each of those years, but also the women's singles (see Chapter 2) and the women's doubles as well (see Chapter 9).[362]

Nell Hall (Hopman) and Harry Hopman (4 titles)

Nell Hall (Hopman) and her husband Harry Hopman had a great partnership both on and off the court. Both from New South Wales, they won 4 Aussie mixed doubles titles together (1930, 1936, 1937 and 1939) and were runners-up once. They were married in 1934 and spent the next 34 years together before Nell passed away in 1968.[363]

Nancye Wynne (Bolton) and Colin Long (4 titles)

Victorian pair Nancye Wynne (Bolton) and Colin Long also won 4 Aussie mixed doubles titles (1940, 1946, 1947 and 1948) and finished runners-up once. They dethroned defending champions Nell Hall (Hopman) and Harry Hopman in 1940 for their first title, and but for the 5-year tournament break for World War II, it's highly likely they would have won many more titles together.

Wynne (Bolton) won all 3 Aussie women's titles on offer in 1940, 1947 and 1948 – the singles (see Chapter 2), the women's doubles (see Chapter 9) and the mixed doubles.[364]

Thelma Coyne (Long) – 4 titles and George Worthington (3 titles)

New South Wales partners Thelma Coyne (Long) and George Worthington won 3 mixed doubles titles at the Australian Championships – 1951, 1952 and 1955.

In 1952, Coyne (Long) also won the Aussie women's singles (see Chapter 2) and women's doubles events (see Chapter 9).

She won a fourth Aussie mixed doubles title with another New South Welshman, Rex Hartwig, in 1954.

Esna Boyd (Robertson) and John Hawkes (3 titles)

Victorian tennis pioneers Esna Boyd (Robertson) and John Hawkes won the first mixed doubles event ever held at the Australasian Championships in 1922. They followed it up with back-to-back titles in 1926 and 1927 before finishing as runners-up in 1928.

Hawkes won all 3 men's titles at the Australasian Championships in 1926 – the singles, men's doubles (see Chapter 8) and mixed doubles.[365]

Marjorie Cox (Crawford) and Jack Crawford (3 titles)

Marjorie Cox (Crawford) and her husband Jack Crawford played in 5 consecutive mixed doubles finals at the Australian Championships between 1929 and 1933. They finished runners-up in the first 2 years, but bounced back to win the 1931, 1932 and 1933 events.

They married in 1930.

In 1932, Jack Crawford won the Australian men's singles (see Chapter 1) and men's doubles events (see Chapter 8), in addition to the mixed doubles title.[366]

Margaret Smith (Court) – 3 titles and Ken Fletcher (2 titles)

New South Wales' Margaret Smith (Court) and Queenslander Ken Fletcher won back-to-back Australian mixed doubles titles together in 1963 and 1964. As you'll see later in this chapter, the 1963 win was the first leg of a calendar year Grand Slam for the pair. They were the first players in world tennis to achieve this feat.

Smith (Court) also won all 3 Australian women's titles in 1963 – the singles (see Chapter 2), the women's doubles (see Chapter 9), along with the mixed doubles.

She also shared an Aussie mixed doubles title in 1965 when she and partner John Newcombe reached the final, but the match wasn't played due to bad weather. Smith (Court), Newcombe and their fellow Aussie opponents Robyn Ebbern (Vincenzi) and Owen Davidson were declared joint winners. Once again Smith (Court) had earlier won both the women's singles and women's doubles at the 1965 event.[367]

Jim Willard (2 titles)

New South Welshman Jim Willard made 4 consecutive mixed doubles finals at the Australasian championships. As mentioned earlier in the chapter, he partnered Daphne Akhurst (Cozens) in 2 of her 4 Australian mixed doubles victories.

The wins came back-to-back in 1924 and 1925, and he followed them up with consecutive Aussie mixed doubles runner-up performances (once with Akhurst in 1926, and the other with Youtha Anthony in 1927).[368]

Edgar Moon (2 titles)

New South Welshman Edgar Moon won 2 Aussie mixed doubles titles. As mentioned earlier in the chapter, he partnered Daphne Akhurst (Cozens) to victory in 1929 for his first title. They beat Marjorie Cox (Crawford) and Jack Crawford in the final.

His second victory came 5 years later when he and fellow New South Wales player Joan Hartigan (Bathurst) joined forces to win the title.[369]

Frank Sedgman (2 titles)

Frank Sedgman won back-to-back Aussie mixed doubles titles with American Doris Hart in 1950. Hart was the first non-Australian woman to win the Australian mixed doubles title.

And as you'll see later in this chapter, Sedgman and Hart combined to win a career Grand Slam prior to Sedgman turning pro in 1953 and subsequently being banned from all Grand Slam events.[370]

Rex Hartwig (2 titles)

Rex Hartwig won back-to-back Aussie mixed doubles titles in 1953 and 1954.

The first was with American Julia Sampson (Hayward), and the second with fellow New South Wales player Thelma Coyne (Long), as mentioned earlier in the chapter.[371]

Jan Lehane (O'Neill) – 2 titles

New South Wales' Jan Lehane (O'Neill) won back-to-back Aussie mixed doubles titles in 1960 and 1961, the first with South African Trevor Fancutt, and the second with Bob Hewitt. [372]

Lesley Turner (Bowrey) – 2 titles

Lesley Turner (Bowrey) won the mixed doubles twice at the Australian Championships, partnering fellow New South Wales player Fred Stolle to victory in 1962, and Victorian Owen Davidson in 1967.[373]

Owen Davidson (2 titles)

New South Welshman Owen Davidson shared the Aussie mixed doubles title with Brisbane partner Robyn Ebbern (Vincenzi) and their finals' opponents Margaret Smith (Court) and John Newcombe in 1965. The final was abandoned due to bad weather.

Davidson teamed with Lesley Turner (Bowrey) in 1967 to win the mixed doubles event outright. And as you'll see later in the chapter, he achieved a calendar year Grand Slam in mixed doubles by also winning the French, Wimbledon and US mixed doubles titles during his career.[374]

All Aussie Mixed Doubles Champions
Australasian/Australian Championships: 1922–1968

The following table lists all of the Aussie mixed doubles winners during the Amateur Era. Where only one player is listed, the Aussie had an international partner. Excluding the 5 years when the event wasn't held during World War II, there were only 8 years during the Amateur Era when an Australian pairing didn't win at Australia's premier tennis tournament, and in those years, one of the partners was an Aussie anyway. This domination is largely due to limited international participants in the early years when long-distance travel was more difficult.[375]

Year	Winner/s
1922	Esna Boyd (Robertson)/John Hawkes
1923	Sylvia Lance (Harper)/Horace Rice
1924	Daphne Akhurst (Cozens)/Jim Willard
1925	Daphne Akhurst (Cozens)/Jim Willard
1926	Esna Boyd (Robertson)/John Hawkes

Chapter 10 – Aussies in Grand Slam Mixed Doubles (Amateur Era)

Year	Winner/s
1927	Esna Boyd (Robertson)/John Hawkes
1928	Daphne Akhurst (Cozens)
1929	Daphne Akhurst (Cozens)/Edgar Moon
1930	Nell Hall (Hopman)/Harry Hopman
1931	Marjorie Cox (Crawford)/Jack Crawford
1932	Marjorie Cox (Crawford)/Jack Crawford
1933	Marjorie Cox (Crawford)/Jack Crawford
1934	Joan Hartigan (Bathurst)/Edgar Moon
1935	Louie Bickerton (Cozens)
1936	Nell Hall (Hopman)/Harry Hopman
1937	Nell Hall (Hopman)/Harry Hopman
1938	Margaret Wilson/John Bromwich
1939	Nell Hall (Hopman)/Harry Hopman
1940	Nancye Wynne (Bolton)/Colin Long
1946	Nancye Wynne (Bolton)/Colin Long
1947	Nancye Wynne (Bolton)/Colin Long
1948	Nancye Wynne (Bolton)/Colin Long
1949	Frank Sedgman
1950	Frank Sedgman
1951	Thelma Coyne (Long)/George Worthington
1952	Thelma Coyne (Long)/George Worthington
1953	Rex Hartwig
1954	Thelma Coyne (Long)/Rex Hartwig
1955	Thelma Coyne (Long)/George Worthington
1956	Beryl Penrose (Collier)/Neale Fraser
1957	Fay Muller (Colthorpe)/Mal Anderson
1958	Mary Bevis (Hawton)/Bob Howe
1959	Bob Mark
1960	Jan Lehane (O'Neill)
1961	Jan Lehane (O'Neill)/Bob Hewitt

Year	Winner/s
1962	Lesley Turner (Bowrey)/Fred Stolle
1963	Margaret Smith (Court)/Ken Fletcher
1964	Margaret Smith (Court)/Ken Fletcher
1965	Margaret Smith (Court)/John Newcombe and Robyn Ebbern (Vincenzi)/Owen Davidson (shared)
1966	Judy Tegart (Dalton)/Tony Roche
1967	Lesley Turner (Bowrey)/Owen Davidson
1968	Dick Crealy

Aussie Mixed Doubles Runners-Up
Australasian/Australian Championships: 1922–1968

The following table lists all of the Aussie doubles runners-up in our premier tennis event of the Amateur Era. Where only one player is listed, the Aussie player had an international partner.[376]

Year	Runners-Up
1922	Gwen (Chiplin) Utz/Harold Utz
1923	Margaret Mutch (Molesworth)/Bert St. John
1924	Esna Boyd (Robertson)/Garton Hone
1925	Sylvia Lance (Harper)/Richard Schlesinger
1926	Daphne Akhurst (Cozens)/Jim Willard
1927	Youtha Anthony/Jim Willard
1928	Esna Boyd (Robertson)/John Hawkes
1929	Marjorie Cox (Crawford)/Jack Crawford
1930	Marjorie Cox (Crawford)/Jack Crawford
1931	Emily Hood (Westacott)/Aubrey Willard
1932	Meryl Waxman (O'Hara Wood)
1934	Emily Hood (Westacott)/Ray Dunlop
1935	Birdie Bond

Chapter 10 – Aussies in Grand Slam Mixed Doubles (Amateur Era)

Year	Runners-Up
1936	May Blick/Abe Kay
1937	Dorothy Stevenson (Waddell)/Don Turnbull
1938	Nancye Wynne (Bolton)/Colin Long
1939	Margaret Wilson/John Bromwich
1940	Nell Hall (Hopman)/Harry Hopman
1946	Joyce Fitch (Rymer)/John Bromwich
1947	Joyce Fitch (Rymer)/John Bromwich
1948	Thelma Coyne (Long)/Bill Sidwell
1949	Joyce Fitch (Rymer)/John Bromwich
1950	Joyce Fitch (Rymer)
1951	Clare Proctor (Copeman)/Jack May
1952	Gwen O'Halloran (Thiele)/Tom Warhurst
1954	Beryl Penrose (Collier)/John Bromwich
1955	Jenny Staley (Hoad)/Lew Hoad
1956	Mary Bevis (Hawton)/Roy Emerson
1957	Jill Langley
1958	Peter Newman
1959	Rod Laver
1960	Marty Mulligan
1961	Mary Carter (Reitano)/John Pearce
1963	Lesley Turner (Bowrey)/Fred Stolle
1964	Jan Lehane (O'Neill)
1966	Robyn Ebbern (Vincenzi)/Bill Bowrey
1967	Judy Tegart (Dalton)/Tony Roche
1968	Margaret Smith (Court)/Allan Stone

Aussie Mixed Doubles Champions
French Championships: Amateur Era pre-1968

Australia's first mixed doubles success at the French Championships came in 1933 when pioneer Jack Crawford partnered with England's Margaret Scriven to win the title. Crawford also became the first international player to win the French men's singles title that same year (see Chapter 1).

We had to wait another 23 years before an Australian woman won the French mixed doubles title. Thelma Coyne (Long) joined forces with Chilean Luis Ayala to claim victory. Margaret Smith (Court) and Ken Fletcher became the first Aussie pair to win the mixed doubles at Roland Garros 10 years later in 1963.

Let's take a look at our most successful French Championships mixed doubles players in the Amateur Era. Once again, the pairings and individuals in the feature boxes in this section are listed in order of the highest number of French mixed doubles titles won during this period (including by the most successful of a regular pair in some cases), and where that number is equal, chronologically.[377]

Margaret Smith (Court) and Ken Fletcher (3 titles)

Margaret Smith (Court) and Ken Fletcher won 3 consecutive French mixed doubles titles between 1963 and 1965. Their first French title in 1963 was the second leg of their calendar year Grand Slam that year. They beat fellow Aussies Lesley

Turner (Bowrey) and Fred Stolle in the final, as they did again in 1964.

And as you'll see in Chapter 13, Smith (Court) also won a French mixed doubles title in the Open Era.[378]

Frank Sedgman (2 titles)

Frank Sedgman won back-to-back French mixed doubles titles in 1951 and 1952 with American Doris Hart before turning pro in 1953. They beat the Aussie pair of Thelma Coyne (Long) and Mervyn Rose in the 1951 final.

Three years earlier, Sedgman and Hart finished runners-up in the 1948 French mixed doubles event.[379]

Bob Howe (2 titles)

New South Welshman Bob Howe won 2 French mixed doubles titles, both with international partners. He and Brazilian Maria Beuno won the 1960 Roland Garros final, beating Roy Emerson and England's Ann Jones. His second title came in 1962 with South African partner Renée Schuurman, beating Aussies Lesley Turner (Bowrey) and Fred Stolle in the final.

Howe had earlier lost 2 mixed doubles finals at Roland Garros (in 1956 with American Darlene Hard and 1958 with fellow Aussie Lorraine Coghlan (Robinson)). [380]

Jack Crawford

As mentioned at the start of this section, Jack Crawford was the first Aussie to win the French mixed doubles title. The year was 1933, and his partner was England's Margaret Scriven. Crawford also became the first Aussie man to win the French singles title in 1933 (see Chapter 1), and Scriven also won the French women's singles in the same year.[381]

Lew Hoad

Lew Hoad won the 1954 French mixed doubles final with American Maureen Connolly. He was only 19 at the time, as was Connolly. They defeated Aussie Rex Hartwig and French player Jacqueline Patorni in straight sets.[382]

Thelma Coyne (Long)

As mentioned at the start of this section, Thelma Coyne (Long) was the first Aussie woman to win the French mixed doubles title. It happened in 1956 when she partnered Chile's Luis Ayala to victory over Aussie Bob Howe and American Darlene Hard.

Coyne (Long) had finished as a runner-up at Roland Garros 5 years earlier when she paired with fellow Aussie Mervyn Rose.[383]

Chapter 10 – Aussies in Grand Slam Mixed Doubles (Amateur Era)

Rod Laver

Rod Laver won his French mixed doubles title in 1961 with American partner Darlene Hard.[384]

Many years later, Laver fondly remembered their partnership: *"They'd start hitting hard shots at her at the net and she would get them all back. Pretty soon, the word was out. You better hit the ball at Laver."*[385]

Owen Davidson

Owen Davidson won the 1967 French mixed doubles title with American Billie Jean Moffitt (King). It was the second leg of his calendar year Grand Slam.

He had won the Australian mixed doubles title with Lesley Turner (Bowrey) earlier in 1967, see the earlier feature box in this chapter.[386]

Aussie Mixed Doubles Runners-Up
French Championships: Amateur Era pre–1968

The following table lists all of the Aussie mixed doubles runners-up in the French Championships of the Amateur Era. Special mention should be made of multiple runners-up Lesley Turner (Bowrey) (3), Fred Stolle (3) and Mervyn Rose (2). Those runner-up performances were as close as they each came to winning the French mixed doubles title.

Where only one player is listed, the Aussie player had an international partner.[387]

Year	Runners-Up
1934	Adrian Quist
1938	Nancye Wynne (Bolton)
1948	Frank Sedgman
1951	Thelma Coyne (Long)/Mervyn Rose
1953	Mervyn Rose
1954	Rex Hartwig
1955	Jenny Staley (Hoad)
1956	Bob Howe
1958	Lorraine Coghlan (Robinson)/Bob Howe
1959	Rod Laver
1960	Roy Emerson
1962	Lesley Turner (Bowrey)/Fred Stolle
1963	Lesley Turner (Bowrey)/Fred Stolle
1964	Lesley Turner (Bowrey)/Fred Stolle
1965	John Newcombe

Aussie Mixed Doubles Champions
Wimbledon: Amateur Era pre-1968

Australia's first mixed doubles success at Wimbledon came in 1920 when pioneer Gerald Patterson partnered with France's Suzanne Lenglen to win the title. He was the first non-Englishman to win the Wimbledon mixed doubles crown.

We had to wait another 38 years before an Australian woman won the Wimbledon mixed doubles title. Lorraine Coghlan (Robinson) joined forces with fellow Aussie Bob Howe to claim victory and become the first Aussie pair to win the mixed doubles at the All England Club.

Let's take a look at our most successful Wimbledon mixed doubles players in the Amateur Era. Once again, the pairings and individuals in the feature boxes in this section are listed in order of the highest number of Wimbledon mixed doubles titles won during this period (including by the most successful of a regular pair in some cases), and where that number is equal, chronologically.[388]

Margaret Smith (Court) and Ken Fletcher (3 titles)

Margaret Smith (Court) and Ken Fletcher's first Wimbledon mixed doubles title was the third leg of their calendar year Grand Slam in 1963. Smith (Court) also became the first Australian woman to win the Wimbledon singles title at the same 1963 event (see Chapter 4).

Smith (Court) and Fletcher won a further 2 Wimbledon mixed doubles titles together in 1965 (beating fellow Aussies Judy Tegart (Dalton) and Tony Roche in the final) and 1966.

They were runners-up to Lesley Turner (Bowrey) and Fred Stolle in 1964.

Fletcher also finished runner-up to fellow Aussie Owen Davidson and his American partner Billie Jean Moffitt (King) in the 1967 Wimbledon mixed doubles final, the last of the Amateur Era.

And as you'll see in Chapter 13, Smith (Court) and Fletcher won their fourth Wimbledon mixed doubles title together in the Open Era, and Smith (Court) went on to win a fifth after Fletcher had retired.[389]

John Bromwich (2 titles)

John Bromwich made 3 consecutive Wimbledon mixed doubles finals with American partner Louise Brough.

They won back-to-back titles in 1947 (beating Aussies Colin Long and Nancye Wynne (Bolton) and 1948 (edging out Frank Sedgman and his American partner Doris Hart), before finishing runners-up in 1949.[390]

Frank Sedgman (2 titles)

Frank Sedgman won back-to-back Wimbledon doubles titles in 1951 and 1952 with his American partner Doris Hart.

The 1952 win gave Sedgman the distinction of becoming the second man to win all 3 Wimbledon titles on offer at the same event – the men's singles, men's doubles (with fellow Aussie Ken McGregor) and mixed doubles. The first was American Bobby Riggs in 1939. No other man has achieved this feat since Sedgman.

Reflecting on the 70-year anniversary of his 1952 "Wimbledon triple", a 94-year-old Sedgman was as humble as ever: *"You know, it was a big day for me because winning Wimbledon and then of course winning the 3 titles in the one year is something special."*[391]

In 1951, Sedgman and Hart beat fellow Aussies Mervyn Rose and Nancye Wynne (Bolton) in the Wimbledon mixed doubles final, while in 1952 they overcame Aussie Thelma Coyne (Long) and her Argentinian partner Enrique Morea.

Early on in their partnership, Sedgman and Hart finished runners-up in the Wimbledon mixed doubles in 1947, beaten by Aussie John Bromwich and his American partner Louise Brough in the final.[392]

Rod Laver (2 titles)

Rod Laver won back-to-back Wimbledon mixed doubles titles in 1959 and 1960 partnering American Darlene Hard.

In 1959, they beat fellow Aussie Neale Fraser and his Brazilian partner Maria Bueno, while in 1960 they beat Aussie Bob Howe and Bueno.[393]

Lesley Turner (Bowrey) and Fred Stolle (2 titles)

Lesley Turner (Bowrey) and Fred Stolle joined forces to win Wimbledon mixed doubles titles in 1961 (beating Aussie Bob Howe and Germany's Edda Buding in the final) and 1964 (when they beat Ken Fletcher and Margaret Smith (Court) to hoist the trophy).

And as you'll see in Chapter 13, Stolle also won a third Wimbledon mixed doubles title in the Open Era.[394]

Gerald Patterson

As mentioned at the start of this section, pioneer Gerald Patterson was the first Australian man (and the first non-Englishman) to win the Wimbledon mixed doubles title.

It happened in 1920 when he partnered Frances's Suzanne Lenglen to win the title.[395]

Pat O'Hara Wood

Just like Gerald Patterson 2 years earlier, pioneer Pat O'Hara Wood partnered with French woman Suzanne Lenglen to win the 1922 Wimbledon mixed doubles title.

They won the final in straight sets.[396]

Jack Crawford

Jack Crawford won the 1930 Wimbledon mixed doubles final partnering America's Elizabeth Ryan. He had finished runner-up a couple of years earlier in 1928 with fellow Aussie pioneer Daphne Akhurst (Cozens) as his partner.[397]

Mervyn Rose

Mervyn Rose won the 1957 Wimbledon mixed doubles title with American Darlene Hard (who was later to partner Rod Laver to his back-to-back mixed titles at the All England Club). Rose and Hard beat fellow Aussie Neale Fraser and America's Althea Gibson.

Rose had finished runner-up with Nancye Wynne (Bolton) earlier in his career in the 1951 Wimbledon mixed doubles event.[398]

Lorraine Coghlan (Robinson) and Bob Howe

As mentioned at the start of this section, Lorraine Coghlan (Robinson) became the first Australian woman when she partnered with Bob Howe to win the 1958 Wimbledon mixed doubles title. They also became the first Aussie mixed pair to win at Wimbledon.

Howe later finished as a runner-up with international partners in Wimbledon mixed doubles finals (in 1960 with Brazilian Maria Bueno and 1961 with German Edda Buding).[399]

Neale Fraser

Neale Fraser won the 1962 Wimbledon mixed doubles final with American partner Margaret duPont, winning the final set 13-11.

Fraser had earlier finished as a runner-up twice (in 1957 when he and American Althea Gibson lost to fellow Aussie Mervyn Rose and American Darlene Hard, and in 1959 when he and Brazilian Maria Beuno were beaten by Rod Laver and American Darlene Hard).[400]

Owen Davidson

Owen Davidson won the 1967 Wimbledon mixed doubles final with American Billie Jean Moffitt (King). It was the third leg of his calendar year Grand Slam. As highlighted earlier in the chapter, he won the 1967 Australian and French titles before arriving at Wimbledon that year, with Lesley Turner (Bowrey) and King respectively.

He and King beat fellow Aussie Ken Fletcher and Brazil's Maria Bueno in the 1967 Wimbledon final. It was the last Wimbledon event of the Amateur Era.

And as you'll see in Chapter 13, Davidson also won another 3 Wimbledon titles in the Open Era with King.[401]

Aussie Mixed Doubles Runners-Up
Wimbledon: Amateur Era pre–1968

The following table lists all of the Aussie mixed doubles runners-up at Wimbledon during the Amateur Era. Special mention should be made of two-time runners-up Harry Hopman and Nancye Wynne (Bolton). Those runner-up performances were as close as they each came to winning the Wimbledon mixed doubles title.

Where only one player is listed, the Aussie player had an international partner.[402]

Year	Runners-Up
1928	Daphne Akhurst (Cozens)/Jack Crawford
1932	Harry Hopman
1935	Nell Hall (Hopman)/Harry Hopman
1946	Geoff Brown
1947	Nancye Wynne (Bolton)/Colin Long
1948	Frank Sedgman
1949	John Bromwich
1950	Geoff Brown
1951	Nancye Wynne (Bolton)/Mervyn Rose
1952	Thelma Coyne (Long)
1954	Ken Rosewall
1957	Neale Fraser
1959	Neale Fraser

Chapter 10 – Aussies in Grand Slam Mixed Doubles (Amateur Era)

Year	Runners-Up
1960	Bob Howe
1961	Bob Howe
1964	Margaret Smith (Court)/Ken Fletcher
1965	Judy Tegart (Dalton)/Tony Roche
1967	Ken Fletcher

Aussie Mixed Doubles Champions
US Championships: Amateur Era pre–1968

Australia's first mixed doubles success at the US Championships came in 1906 when pioneer Edward Dewhurst partnered with American Sarah Coffin to claim the title. He was the first non-Englishman to win the US mixed doubles crown.

We had to wait another 55 years before an Australian woman won the US mixed doubles title. Margaret Smith (Court) joined forces with fellow Aussie Bob Mark to win the US final and become the first Aussie pair to do it.

Let's take a look at our most successful mixed doubles players at the US Championships in the Amateur Era. Once again, the pairings and individuals in the feature boxes in this section are listed in order of the highest number of US mixed doubles titles won during this period (including by the most successful of a regular pair in some cases), and where that number is equal, chronologically.[403]

Margaret Smith (Court) – 5 titles

Margaret Smith (Court) won 5 consecutive US mixed doubles titles between 1961 and 1965 with 4 different Aussie partners.

The 1963 win gave her and partner Ken Fletcher the distinction of being the first players in tennis history to win the mixed doubles calendar year Grand Slam.

As mentioned at the start of this section, Smith (Court) also became the first Aussie woman to win a US mixed

doubles title when she partnered with fellow Aussie Bob Mark to victory in 1961. The following year, she partnered Fred Stolle to win the title and the pair repeated that success in 1965. Smith (Court) also won the US singles title in both of those years.

Following her US mixed doubles win with Fletcher 1963, Smith (Court) teamed up with a 20-year-old John Newcombe to claim the 1964 title.

And as you'll see in Chapter 13, Smith (Court) won a further 3 US mixed doubles titles in the Open Era, as well as finishing runner-up once. [404]

Neale Fraser (3 titles)

Neale Fraser won 3 US mixed doubles titles in a row between 1958 and 1960 with American partner Margaret Osborne (duPont).

Incredibly, he won all 3 men's titles on offer at the 1959 and 1960 US Championships: singles (see Chapter 3), doubles (see Chapter 5) and the mixed doubles. No men's player has achieved the trifecta in a single year at any Grand Slam event since, let alone in consecutive years. [405]

John Hawkes (2 titles)

Victorian pioneer John Hawkes played in 3 US mixed doubles finals, winning in 1925 (with American partner Kittee McKane (Godfree)) and 1928 (when he paired with American Helen Wills (Moody)). [406]

Frank Sedgman (2 titles)

Frank Sedgman won back-to-back US mixed doubles titles in 1951 and 1952 with American Doris Hart. They beat fellow Aussie Mervyn Rose and his American partner Shirley Fry (Irvin).

The 1951 win gave Sedgman and Hart a career Grand Slam in mixed doubles. Sedgman also achieved the rare feat of winning all 3 US men's titles that year (see Chapter 1 for the singles victory and Chapter 8 for the doubles), 8 years before Neale Fraser did the same.

1951 was also the year that Sedgman and Ken McGregor won the calendar year Grand Slam in doubles at the US event, making it a truly memorable tournament for him. Sedgman's 1952 US mixed doubles title also complemented his US singles victory that year (see Chapter 1).

Fred Stolle (2 titles)

Fred Stolle won both of his US mixed doubles titles with Margaret Smith (Court).

In 1962, they beat Lesley Turner (Bowrey) and her American partner Frank Froehling in the final, while in 1965 they overcame Judy Tegart (Dalton) and Froehling.[407]

Owen Davidson (2 titles)

Owen Davidson became the third Aussie (after Margaret Smith (Court) and Ken Fletcher) to claim a calendar year mixed doubles Grand Slam in 1967 when he and Billie Jean Moffitt (King) won the US title, the last of the Amateur Era.

He and Moffitt (King) had won the French and Wimbledon mixed titles together in the lead-up to the 1967 US event, while Davidson had partnered with Lesley Turner (Bowrey) to win the Australian mixed doubles crown earlier that year.

And as you'll see in Chapter 13, Davidson won another 2 US mixed doubles titles in the Open Era with Moffitt (King).[408]

Edward Dewhurst

As mentioned at the start of this section, New South Welshman Edward Dewhurst became the first Aussie to win the US mixed doubles crown in 1906. He and American partner Sarah Coffin won the final in straight sets. Dewhurst had finished runner-up the year before when he paired with American Elizabeth Moore.

Dewhurst had earlier based himself in the United States in 1903 to study dentistry. He remained in the country for the rest of his life and eventually became a US citizen.[409]

Harry Hopman

Harry Hopman won the 1939 US mixed doubles title with American Alice Marble.

His regular partner (and wife) Nell Hall (Hopman) didn't travel to the event to compete, though they had won the Australian mixed title together earlier that year.[410]

Chapter 10 – Aussies in Grand Slam Mixed Doubles (Amateur Era)

John Bromwich

John Bromwich won the 1947 US mixed doubles final with American Louise Brough (Clapp). The win came late in his career, 9 years after he and fellow Aussie Thelma Coyne (Long) finished runners-up at the 1938 event.[411]

Ken McGregor

Ken McGregor won the US 1950 mixed doubles title with American Margaret Osborne (duPont), who was later to partner Neale Fraser to 3 US titles and Ken Rosewall to his sole US mixed victory.

McGregor and Osborne (duPont) beat McGregor's long-time doubles partner Frank Sedgman and his American partner Doris Hart in 3 sets in the 1950 US final.[412]

Ken Rosewall

Ken Rosewall matched Frank Sedgman's feat of winning all 3 men's US titles in the one year at the 1956 US Championships (see Chapters 3 and 5 respectively for the singles and men's doubles wins).

His partner in his 1956 mixed doubles win was American Margaret Osborne (duPont). They beat Rosewall's good friend Lew Hoad and his American partner Darlene Hard.[413]

Bob Mark

As briefly mentioned at the of this section, New South Welshman Bob Mark and Margaret Smith (Court) were the first Aussie pair to win a US mixed doubles title in 1961.

They had a walkover in the final against Darlene Hard and Dennis Ralston because Ralston was suspended from playing the final by the United States Lawn Tennis Association due to his conduct during a Davis Cup match earlier that year (though he was allowed to play the men's double final, which he and his partner won).[414]

Ken Fletcher

Queenslander Ken Fletcher achieved a calendar year mixed doubles Grand Slam along with Margaret Smith (Court) in 1963 when they won the US final.

They beat fellow Aussie Judy Tegart (Dalton) and American Ed Rubinoff in 3 tough sets.[415]

John Newcombe

"Newk" won the only Grand Slam mixed doubles final of his decorated career when he was just 20. He paired with Margaret Smith (Court) to win the 1964 US title in 3 tough sets over fellow Aussie Just Tegart (Dalton) and her American partner Ed Rubinoff.[416]

Aussie Mixed Doubles Runners-Up
US Championships: Amateur Era pre–1968

The following table lists all of the Aussie mixed doubles runners-up at the US Championships during the Amateur Era. Special mention should be made of multiple runners-up Judy Tegart (Dalton) (3) and Thelma Coyne (Long) (2). Those runner-up performances were as close as they each came to winning the US mixed doubles title, and Tegart (Dalton) had a fourth runner-up performance in the Open Era (see Chapter 13).

Where only one player is listed, the Aussie player had an international partner.[417]

Year	Runners-Up
1905	Edward Dewhurst
1923	John Hawkes
1928	Edgar Moon
1938	Thelma Coyne (Long)/John Bromwich
1950	Frank Sedgman
1951	Mervyn Rose
1952	Thelma Coyne (Long)/Lew Hoad
1953	Rex Hartwig
1954	Ken Rosewall
1956	Lew Hoad
1957	Bob Howe
1959	Bob Mark
1962	Lesley Turner (Bowrey)
1963	Judy Tegart (Dalton)
1964	Judy Tegart (Dalton)
1965	Judy Tegart (Dalton)

Part 4
Doubles in the Open Era
(April 1968 onwards)

Chapter 11
Aussies in Grand Slam Men's Doubles
(Open Era)

The Grand Slam Open Era began for both men and women with the renamed French Open in April 1968. Plenty of banned Aussie pros returned to the fold, and Ken Rosewall and Fred Stolle went down in history as the first Grand Slam men's doubles winners.

Let's look at all of our Aussie men's triumphs and near misses in doubles in the Open Era, starting with the French Open. Aussie men who achieved the distinction of winning French Open doubles titles in both the Amateur and Pro Eras were Ken Rosewall, Fred Stolle, John Newcombe and Tony Roche.[418]

Aussie Men's Doubles Champions
French Open: 1968–Present Day

The pairings and individuals in the feature boxes in this section are listed in order of the highest number of French doubles titles won in the Open Era (including by the most successful of a regular pair in some cases), and where that number is equal, chronologically.

John Newcombe (2 titles) and Tony Roche

Long-time partners John Newcombe and Tony Roche won the 1969 French Open doubles final after beating fellow Aussies Roy Emerson and Rod Laver in the final in a 5-set marathon. It was their second French title after they had won the 1967 final in the Amateur Era (see Chapter 8).

Newcombe and Roche are the most successful Grand Slam men's doubles pairing in Australian tennis history with a combined 12 titles across the Amateur and Open Eras.

"Newk" also won another French men's doubles title in 1973 when he and Dutchman Tom Okker won another tough 5-set final.[419]

John Fitzgerald (2 titles)

South Australian John Fitzgerald made 3 French Open men's doubles finals at Roland Garros, winning twice. His first title came in 1986 when he and Czech partner Tomas Smid won a 5-set epic in the final, winning the fifth set 14-12.

"Fitzy" won his second title in 1991 with Swede Anders Jarryd after the pair had finished runners-up in 1988.[420]

Ken Rosewall and Fred Stolle

As mentioned at the start of the chapter, Ken Rosewall and Fred Stolle won the first men's doubles title of the Open Era when they won the 1968 French Open title.

    The win was the second French men's doubles title for both. Rosewall had won 15 years earlier in the Amateur Era, while Stolle had won 3 years prior (see Chapter 8).[421]

Dick Crealy

New South Welshman Dick Crealy won the 1974 French Open doubles title with New Zealand partner Onny Parun. After winning the first 2 sets in the final, they dropped the next 2 before winning in 5.[422]

Mark Edmondson and Kim Warwick

New South Wales' partners Mark Edmondson and Kim Warwick won the 1985 men's doubles title at Roland Garros. Two years earlier, "Eddo" had finished runner-up when he partnered American Sherwood Stewart.[423]

Todd Woodbridge and Mark Woodforde

The "Woodies" are easily Australia's most successful men's doubles pairing of the Open Era, winning 11 Grand Slam titles together. Like John Newcombe and Tony Roche before them, New South Welshman Todd Woodbridge and South Australian Mark Woodforde formed a formidable right-hand/left-hand combination.

They only won a single French Open title in men's doubles during their illustrious partnership, but it was a crucial one in 2000 to give them a career Grand Slam.[424]

Aussie Men's Doubles Runners-Up
French Open: 1968–Present Day

The following table lists all of the Aussie men's doubles runners-up at the French Open during the Open Era. Special mention should be made of two-time runners-up Roy Emerson, Rod Laver and Phil Dent. While Emerson and Laver both won the French doubles title in the Amateur Era (see Chapter 8), the 2 runner-up performances in the Open Era were as close as Dent came.

Where only one player is listed, the Aussie player had an international partner.[425]

Year	Runners-Up
1968	Roy Emerson/Rod Laver
1969	Roy Emerson/Rod Laver
1975	John Alexander/Phil Dent
1979	Ross Case/Phil Dent
1983	Mark Edmondson
1988	John Fitzgerald
1997	Todd Woodbridge/Mark Woodforde
2000	Sandon Stolle

Aussie Men's Doubles Champions
Wimbledon: 1968–Present Day

Aussie men started the Open Era of doubles at Wimbledon with a bang, winning the first 4 events. John Newcombe and Tony Roche won the first 3, giving them the distinction of winning the Wimbledon men's doubles as a pair in both the Amateur and Open Eras. Roy Emerson was the only other Aussie to win Wimbledon men's doubles titles in both Eras.[426]

Once again, the pairings and individuals in the feature boxes in this section are listed in order of the highest number of Wimbledon doubles titles won in the Open Era (including by the most successful of a regular pair in some cases), and where that number is equal, chronologically.

Todd Woodbridge (9 titles) and Mark Woodforde (6 titles)

The "Woodies" had their most Grand Slam success at Wimbledon where they teamed up for an incredible 6 victories. Their first 5 Wimbledon titles were consecutive between 1993 and 1997. Their streak was finally broken when they finished runners-up in 1998 after a tough, 5-set final where they went down 10-8 in the final set.

They bounced back for their sixth and final Wimbledon title together in 2000. Woodbridge went on to win another 3 Wimbledon men's doubles finals in a row with Swede Jonas Björkman in 2002, 2003 and 2004 after Woodforde had retired.[427]

John Newcombe and Tony Roche (4 titles)

"Newk" and Tony Roche won the first 3 Wimbledon men's doubles titles of the Open Era in 1968, 1969 and 1970, and they won a fourth in 1974, giving Newcombe 6 for his overall career and Roche 5 (see Chapter 8 for their Amateur Era victories).

Newcombe also won the Wimbledon men's singles title in 1970 (see Chapter 5) as well as the men's doubles to cap a memorable tournament for him.[428]

Peter McNamara and Paul McNamee (2 titles)

The Victorian "SuperMacs" paired up to win the 1980 and 1982 Wimbledon men's doubles titles, and McNamee also finished as a runner-up in 1985 when he and fellow Aussie Pat Cash lost a 5-set final.[429]

John Fitzgerald (2 titles)

"Fitzy" had 2 runner-up finishes in the Wimbledon men's doubles before he broke through to win 2 titles with Swede Anders Jarryd in 1989 and 1991.

The 1989 win gave him a career Grand Slam in men's doubles, having claimed the French (with Tomas Smid), US (with Tomas Smid) and Australian (with fellow Aussie John Alexander) titles earlier in his career.[430]

Roy Emerson and Rod Laver

"Emmo" and Laver won the 1971 Wimbledon men's doubles title. It was Emerson's third career victory in men's doubles at the All England Club after 2 earlier wins in the Amateur Era (see Chapter 8).[431]

Geoff Masters and Ross Case

Queenslanders Geoff Masters (pictured) and Ross Case made back-to-back Wimbledon men's doubles finals in 1976 and 1977.

They went down in 5 sets in 1976 but bounced back to win in 5 sets themselves in 1977 against fellow Aussies John Alexander and Phil Dent.[432]

Stephen Huss

Victorian Stephen Huss made Wimbledon men's doubles history by becoming part of the first qualifying pair to win the event in 2005 when he partnered South African Wesley Moodie to win the title. They beat 5 seeded pairs on their way through the draw.[433]

Matthew Ebden and Max Purcell

Western Australian Matthew Ebden and New South Welshman Max Purcell won a hard-fought men's double final at Wimbledon in 2022 after they clinched the fifth-set tie-break.

Incredibly, the final was their fifth 5-set victory of the tournament, and they had to stave off 8 match points in earlier rounds. This was the last year that Wimbledon doubles finals were the best of 5 sets.[434]

Aussie Men's Doubles Runners-Up
Wimbledon: 1968–Present Day

The following table lists all of the Aussie men's doubles runners-up at Wimbledon during the Open Era. Special mention should be made of two-time runners-up Ken Rosewall, Fred Stolle and Pat Cash. While Rosewall and Stolle both won the Wimbledon doubles title in the Amateur Era (see Chapter 8), the 2 runner-up performances in the Open Era were as close as Cash came.

Where only one player is listed, the Aussie player had an international partner.[435]

Year	Runners-Up
1968	Ken Rosewall/Fred Stolle
1970	Ken Rosewall/Fred Stolle
1973	John Cooper/Neale Fraser
1976	Ross Case/Geoff Masters
1977	John Alexander/Phil Dent
1984	Pat Cash/Paul McNamee
1985	Pat Cash/John Fitzgerald
1988	John Fitzgerald
1998	Todd Woodbridge/Mark Woodforde
2000	Sandon Stolle
2015	John Peers
2024	Max Purcell/Jordan Thompson

Aussie Men's Doubles Champions
US Open: 1968–Present Day

It only took a year for Aussies to win their first US men's doubles title of the Open Era when Ken Rosewall and Fred Stolle won the 1969 final. Both had already won the US men's doubles title in the Amateur Era with different partners (see Chapter 8). The only other Aussie to achieve that feat was John Newcombe.[436]

Once again, the pairings and individuals in the feature boxes in this section are listed in order of the highest number of US doubles titles won in the Open Era (including by the most successful of a regular pair in some cases), and where that number is equal, chronologically.

Todd Woodbridge (3 titles) and Mark Woodforde (3 titles)

The "Woodies" both won 3 US Open men's doubles titles, but only 2 were with each other.

Mark Woodforde won his first US Open men's doubles title with legendary American and fellow left-hander John McEnroe in 1989, before he and Woodbridge paired up and became a regular duo.[437]

"The Woodies" made 3 consecutive US Open men's doubles finals from 1994 to 1996. They were unsuccessful at their first attempt in 1994 but had back-to-back victories in 1995 and 1996.

Woodbridge then went on to win his third US Open men's doubles title in 2003 with Swede Jonas Björkman after Woodforde had retired.[438]

John Newcombe (2 titles)

"Newk" won 2 US men's doubles titles in the Open Era, but they were both without his long-time partner Tony Roche (who he paired with to win a US title in the Amateur Era —see Chapter 8).

Newcombe's first Open Era US men's doubles title came in 1971 when he and England's Roger Taylor won the final. His second was in 1973 with fellow Aussie Owen Davidson, a year when he also won the US Open men's singles (see Chapter 5).[439]

John Fitzgerald (2 titles)

"Fitzy" won 2 US Open Men's doubles titles, and both were with international partners.

In 1984, he and Czech Tomas Smid won the final in straight sets against Swedish pair Stefan Edberg and Anders Jarryd, while in 1991, he partnered Jarryd to victory when they were the top seeds for the event.[440]

Ken Rosewall and Fred Stolle

As mentioned at the start of this section, Ken Rosewall and Fred Stolle were the first Aussie winners of the US men's double title in the Open Era. When they won the 1969 final.

Both also won the US Open's men's doubles in the Amateur Era with different partners (Stolle twice with Roy Emerson and Rosewall once with Lew Hoad—see Chapter 8).[441]

Chapter 11 – Aussies in Grand Slam Men's Doubles (Open Era)

Owen Davidson

Owen Davidson made back-to-back US Open men's doubles finals in 1972 and 1973 with John Newcombe, winning in 1973 against Rod Laver and Ken Rosewall in an all-Aussie final.

Davidson also won the US mixed doubles title the same year.442

Sandon Stolle

Fred Stolle's son Sandon won the 1998 US Open men's doubles final with Czech partner Cyril Suk. He finished runner-up 3 years earlier to fellow Aussies Todd Woodbridge and Mark Woodforde when they won their first US title together.443

Lleyton Hewitt

Lleyton Hewitt won the 2000 US Open men's doubles title with Belarusian partner Max Mirnyi.

He was just 19 years old at the time and it was to be the only Grand Slam doubles title of his career.444

Max Purcell and Jordan Thompson

New South Wales duo and seventh seeds Max Purcell and Jordan Thompson won the 2024 US Open doubles title with a straight sets victory in the final over German tenth seeds Kevin Krawietz and Tim Pütz. They dispatched the top seeds, Marcel Granollers and Horacio Zeballos, along the way in the quarter-finals. It was Purcell's second grand slam double titles after he'd won the 2022 Wimbledon title with Matthew Ebden, and Thompson's first.

Earlier in 2024, Purcell and Thompson has come agonisingly close to winning the Wimbledon doubles title together, having two match point opportunities before losing in 3 sets to England's Henry Patten and Finland's Harri Heliövaara. All three sets went to tie-breakers.

Aussie Men's Doubles Runners-Up
US Open: 1968–Present Day

The following table lists all of the Aussie men's doubles runners-up at the US Open during the Open Era. Special mention should be made of two-time runner-up Rod Laver. He was also runner-up once in the Amateur Era, and those performances were as close as he would come to winning the US men's doubles title.

Where only one player is listed, the Aussie player had an international partner.[445]

Year	Runners-Up
1970	Roy Emerson/Rod Laver
1972	John Newcombe/Owen Davidson
1973	Rod Laver/Ken Rosewall
1976	Paul Kronk/Cliff Letcher
1981	Peter McNamara
1994	Todd Woodbridge/Mark Woodforde
1995	Sandon Stolle
2015	John Peers
2023	Matthew Ebden

Multiple Aussie Men's Doubles Champions
Australian Open: 1968–Present Day

Not surprisingly, Aussies have had the most men's doubles success in the Open Era at our local major, though as outlined in Chapters 5 and 7, that success hasn't been replicated in men's singles. The doubles success was no doubt helped by the Australian Open struggling to attract the world's top international players in the 1970s and 1980s.

The Aussie men who won our doubles title in both the Amateur and Open Eras were Ken Rosewall, Rod Laver, Roy Emerson, John Newcombe, Tony Roche and Allan Stone.[446]

Once again, the pairings and individuals in the feature boxes in this section are listed in order of the highest number of Aussie doubles titles won in the Open Era (including by the most successful of a regular pair in some cases), and where that number is equal, chronologically.

> ### Mark Edmondson (4 titles) and Kim Warwick (3 titles)
>
> Mark Edmondson and Kim Warwick won back-to-back Australian doubles titles in 1980 and 1981. They beat the defending Australian and reigning Wimbledon champions Peter McNamara and Paul McNamee in the 1980 final when the Australian Open was still played on grass.

Edmondson won 2 more Australian men's doubles titles back-to-back in 1983 (with Paul McNamee) and 1984 (with American Sherwood Stewart).[447]

Before his double success with Edmondson, Warwick had won his first Aussie men's doubles title in 1978 with Poland's Wojtek Fibak.[448]

John Newcombe (3 titles) and Tony Roche (3 titles)

"Newk" and Tony Roche, each won 3 Aussie men's doubles titles in the Open Era, and 2 of those victories were partnering each other (1971 and 1976).

Newcombe also won the 1973 title with Queenslander Mal Anderson, while Roche won the January 1977 event with American Arthur Ashe. Newcombe and Roche paired up to win 2 Aussie men's doubles titles in the Amateur Era (see Chapter 8), giving them 5 each in their careers.[449]

Todd Woodbridge (3 titles) and Mark Woodforde (2 titles)

The "Woodies" won their home Grand Slam men's doubles event twice as partners (1992 and 1997).

Woodbridge went on to win the event for a third time with Swede Jonas Björkman in 2001 after Woodforde had retired.[450]

John Alexander (2 titles)

John Alexander won 2 Australian men's doubles titles. The first was in 1975 when he partnered fellow Aussie Phil Dent to victory after 2 runners-up performances together in earlier years, and the second came in 1982 when he and John Fitzgerald won the final.[451]

Paul McNamee (2 titles)

Paul McNamee's first Aussie men's doubles title was with partner Peter McNamara in 1979. His second victory came in 1983 when he and Mark Edmondson were successful.[452]

All Aussie Men's Doubles Champions
Australian Open: 1969–Present Day

The following table lists all of the Aussie men's doubles winners of our local major during the Open Era. Where only a single player is listed, the player had an international partner. The dominance of Australian winners up to the mid-1980s reflects the lower number of international entrants that the event attracted during those years.[453]

Year	Winner/s
1969	Rod Laver/Roy Emerson
1971	John Newcombe/Tony Roche
1972	Ken Rosewall/Owen Davidson
1973	John Newcombe/Mal Anderson
1974	Ross Case/Geoff Masters
1975	John Alexander/Phil Dent
1976	John Newcombe/Tony Roche
1977 (January)	Tony Roche
1977 (December)	Ray Ruffels/Allan Stone
1978	Kim Warwick
1979	Peter McNamara/Paul McNamee
1980	Mark Edmondson/Kim Warwick
1981	Mark Edmondson/Kim Warwick
1982	John Alexander/John Fitzgerald
1983	Mark Edmondson/Paul McNamee
1984	Mark Edmondson
1992	Todd Woodbridge/Mark Woodforde
1993	Laurie Warder
1997	Todd Woodbridge/Mark Woodforde
1999	Pat Rafter
2001	Todd Woodbridge
2017	John Peers
2022	Nick Kyrgios/Thanasi Kokkinakis

Chapter 11 – Aussies in Grand Slam Men's Doubles (Open Era)

Year	Winner/s
2023	Rinky Hijikata/Jason Kubler
2024	Matthew Ebden

Aussie Men's Doubles Runners-Up
Australian Open: 1969–Present Day

The following table lists all of the Aussie doubles runners-up in our premier tennis event during the Open Era. Again, where only one player is listed, the Aussie player had an international partner, and the number of Australian runners-up through to the mid-1980s reflects the lower number of international entrants that the event attracted during the early Open Era years.[454]

Year	Runners-Up
1969	Ken Rosewall/Fred Stolle
1970	John Alexander/Phil Dent
1972	Ross Case/Geoff Masters
1973	John Alexander/Phil Dent
1974	Syd Ball/Bob Giltinan
1975	Bob Carmichael/Allan Stone
1976	Ross Case/Geoff Masters
1977 (December)	John Alexander/Phil Dent
1978	Paul Kronk/Cliff Letcher
1979	Paul Kronk/Cliff Letcher
1980	Peter McNamara/Paul McNamee
1985	Mark Edmondson/Kim Warwick
1987	Laurie Warder/Peter Doohan
1989	Darren Cahill/Mark Kratzmann
1993	John Fitzgerald
1998	Todd Woodbridge/Mark Woodforde
2000	Andrew Kratzmann
2019	John Peers
2020	Max Purcell/Luke Saville
2022	Matthew Ebden/Max Purcell

Aussie Men's Wheelchair and Quad Doubles at the Majors (2004–Present Day)

As outlined in Chapter 7, wheelchair and quad tennis emerged at the Grand Slams in the early 2000s. The 2 categories reflect the different functional impairments of participants. Wheelchair tennis is for players with the permanent impairment of one or both legs, but who have normal arm function. Quad is for players who have a permanent impairment of one or both legs, plus an impairment of their playing arm that restricts their ability to handle a racquet and move their wheelchair.[455]

There are Grand Slam events for both wheelchair and quad categories for men, and wheelchair only for women. The Australian Open was the first of the majors to introduce the wheelchair men's doubles in 2004 (2 years after wheelchair men's singles was introduced at the event).[456] Wimbledon[457] and the US Open[458] introduced wheelchair men's doubles a year later in 2005, followed by the French Open in 2007.[459] No Australian man has ever won a men's Grand Slam doubles title in wheelchair tennis or finished runner-up in a Grand Slam final.

Quad doubles events were first introduced at the US Open in 2007, followed by the Australian Open in 2008, and finally the French Open and Wimbledon in 2019. Dylan Alcott and Heath Davidson have been the 2 Aussie men to win Grand Slam events in the quad doubles. Let's take a closer look at their achievements.

Dylan Alcott (8 titles) and Heath Davidson (4 titles)

Victorians and long-time friends Dylan Alcott and Heath Davidson won 4 consecutive quad doubles titles at the Australian Open from 2018 to 2021. Alcott also won the Aussie wheelchair singles titles in each of those years as well (see Chapter 7).

Alcott completed a calendar year Grand Slam in quad doubles in 2019 when he won the French Open (with American partner David Wagner), Wimbledon (with England's Andy Lapthorne) and the US Open titles (again with Lapthorne). Alcott went back-to-back in the quad doubles event at the US Open, winning in 2020 as well.[460]

After Alcott retired, Davidson finished runner-up in the quad doubles at both the 2023 French Open and Wimbledon with Canadian partner Robert Shaw.[461]

Top All-Time Aussie Men's Grand Slam Doubles Winners*

Player	Total Number of Grand Slam Men's Doubles Title Wins	Total Number of Amateur Era Grand Slam Men's Doubles Title Wins	Total Number of Open Era Grand Slam Men's Doubles Title Wins
John Newcombe**	17	6	11
Roy Emerson	16	14	2
Todd Woodbridge	16		16
Adrian Quist***	14	14	
John Bromwich***	13	13	
Tony Roche**	13	5	8
Mark Woodforde	12		12
Neale Fraser	11	11	
Fred Stolle	10	8	2
Frank Sedgman****	9	9	
Ken Rosewall*****	9	6	3
Lew Hoad******	8	8	
Dylan Alcott	8		8
Ken McGregor*******	7	7	
John Fitzgerald	7		7
Gerald Patterson	6	6	
Jack Crawford	6	6	
Rod Laver********	6	4	2

* Minimum 6 Grand Slam Men's Doubles title wins. Players listed in order of the number of Grand Slam events won. Where that number is equal, they are listed in chronological order.

** **John Newcombe** and **Tony Roche** were banned from competing in 2 Open Era Grand Slam tournaments in 1972 due to being a part of World Championship Tennis (WCT).

Chapter 11 – Aussies in Grand Slam Men's Doubles (Open Era)

*** **Adrian Quist** and **John Bromwich** missed the opportunity to add to their respective Grand Slam tallies due to 5 Australian, 6 Wimbledon and 1 French Championship/s being cancelled during World War II.

**** **Frank Sedgman** was banned from competing in 52 Grand Slam tournaments between the start of 1953 when he turned pro and the end of 1965 when he retired. However, he briefly returned to play in Grand Slam events in the early years of the Open Era when he was in his early forties.

***** **Ken Rosewall** was banned from competing in 45 Grand Slam tournaments between the start of 1957 when he turned pro and April 1968 when the Open Era commenced. He was also banned from competing in 2 Open Era Grand Slam tournaments in 1972 due to being a part of World Championship Tennis (WCT).

****** **Lew Hoad** was banned from competing in 41 Grand Slam tournaments between mid-1957 when he turned pro and the end of 1967 when he retired. However, he briefly returned to play in Grand Slam events in the early years of the Open Era when he was in his mid-thirties.

******* **Ken McGregor** was banned from competing in 8 Grand Slam tournaments in 1953 and 1954 after he turned pro until he retired.

******** **Rod Laver** was banned from competing in 21 Grand Slam tournaments between the start of 1963 when he turned pro and April 1968 when the Open Era commenced. He was also banned from competing in 2 Open Era Grand Slam tournaments in 1972 due to being a part of World Championship Tennis (WCT).

Australia's Grand Slam Tennis Champions

Top All-Time All-Aussie Men's Grand Slam Doubles Teams*

Player	Total Number of Grand Slam Men's Doubles Title Wins	Total Number of Amateur Era Grand Slam Men's Doubles Title Wins	Total Number of Open Era Grand Slam Men's Doubles Title Wins
John Newcombe/ Tony Roche	12	5	7
Todd Woodbridge/ Mark Woodforde	11		11
John Bromwich/ Adrian Quist	10	10	
Ken McGregor/ Frank Sedgman	7	7	
Roy Emerson/ Neale Fraser	7	7	
Lew Hoad/ Ken Rosewall	6	6	

* Minimum 6 Grand Slam Men's Doubles title wins together. Players listed in order of the number of Grand Slam events won. Where that number is equal, they are listed in chronological order.

Chapter 11 – Aussies in Grand Slam Men's Doubles (Open Era)

Aussie Winners of at least 2 of the 4 Grand Slam Men's Doubles Titles*

Player	Australian Open	French Open	Wimbledon	US Open
Adrian Quist	✓	✓	✓	✓
Frank Sedgman	✓	✓	✓	✓
Ken McGregor	✓	✓	✓	✓
Ken Rosewall	✓	✓	✓	✓
Lew Hoad	✓	✓	✓	✓
Neale Fraser	✓	✓	✓	✓
Roy Emerson	✓	✓	✓	✓
Fred Stolle	✓	✓	✓	✓
John Newcombe	✓	✓	✓	✓
Tony Roche	✓	✓	✓	✓
John Fitzgerald	✓	✓	✓	✓
Mark Woodforde	✓	✓	✓	✓
Todd Woodbridge	✓	✓	✓	✓
Norman Brookes	✓		✓	✓
Jack Crawford	✓	✓	✓	
John Bromwich	✓		✓	✓
Mervyn Rose	✓		✓	✓
Rex Hartwig	✓		✓	✓
Ashley Cooper	✓	✓		✓
Rod Laver	✓	✓	✓	
Pat O'Hara Wood	✓		✓	
Ron Thomas	✓		✓	
James Anderson	✓		✓	
Gerald Patterson	✓			✓
Mal Anderson	✓	✓		
Bob Hewitt**	✓		✓	

Australia's Grand Slam Tennis Champions

Player	Australian Open	French Open	Wimbledon	US Open
Ken Fletcher		✓	✓	
Dick Crealy	✓	✓		
Owen Davidson	✓			✓
Ross Case	✓		✓	
Geoff Masters	✓		✓	
Mark Edmondson	✓	✓		
Kim Warwick	✓	✓		
Peter McNamara	✓		✓	
Paul McNamee	✓		✓	

* Players listed in order of the number of different Grand Slam events won (i.e. 4, 3 or 2). Where that number is equal, they are listed in chronological order.

** Bob Hewitt won all 4 majors in his career but only 2 as an Australian citizen.

Top All-Time Aussie Australian Men's Doubles Winners* [462]

Player	Total Number of Australian Open Men's Doubles Title Wins	Total Number of Amateur Era Australian Open Men's Doubles Title Wins	Total Number of Open Era Australian Open Men's Doubles Title Wins
Adrian Quist	10	10	
John Bromwich	8	8	
Gerald Patterson	5	5	
John Newcombe	5	2	3
Tony Roche	5	2	3
Pat O'Hara Wood	4	4	
Jack Crawford	4	4	
Mark Edmondson	4		4
Rod Laver	4	3	1

Chapter 11 – Aussies in Grand Slam Men's Doubles (Open Era)

Player	Total Number of Australian Open Men's Doubles Title Wins	Total Number of Amateur Era Australian Open Men's Doubles Title Wins	Total Number of Open Era Australian Open Men's Doubles Title Wins
John Hawkes	3	3	
Lew Hoad	3	3	
Ken Rosewall	3	2	1
Neale Fraser	3	3	
Bob Mark	3	3	
Fred Stolle	3	3	
Roy Emerson	3	2	1
Kim Warwick	3		3
Todd Woodbridge	3		3

* Minimum 3 Australian Open Men's Doubles title wins. Players listed in order of the number of titles won. Where that number is equal, they are listed in chronological order.

Top All-Time Aussie French Men's Doubles Winners* [463]

Player	Total Number of French Open Men's Doubles Title Wins	Total Number of Amateur Era French Open Men's Doubles Title Wins	Total Number of Open Era French Open Men's Doubles Title Wins
Roy Emerson	6	6	
Neale Fraser	3	3	
John Newcombe	3	1	2
Frank Sedgman	2	2	
Ken McGregor	2	2	
Ken Rosewall	2	1	1
Ashley Cooper	2	2	
Fred Stolle	2	1	1
Tony Roche	2	1	1
John Fitzgerald	2		2
Jack Crawford	1	1	
Adrian Quist	1	1	
Lew Hoad	1	1	
Don Candy	1	1	
Mal Anderson	1	1	
Rod Laver	1	1	
Ken Fletcher	1	1	
Dick Crealy	1		1
Mark Edmondson	1		1
Kim Warwick	1		1
Todd Woodbridge	1		1
Mark Woodforde	1		1

* Players listed in order of the number of French Men's Doubles titles won. Where that number is equal, they are listed in chronological order.

Chapter 11 – Aussies in Grand Slam Men's Doubles (Open Era)

Top All-Time Aussie Wimbledon Men's Doubles Winners* [464]

Player	Total Number of Wimbledon Men's Doubles Title Wins	Total Number of Amateur Era Wimbledon Men's Doubles Title Wins	Total Number of Open Era Wimbledon Men's Doubles Title Wins
Todd Woodbridge	9		9
John Newcombe	6	2	4
Mark Woodforde	6		6
Tony Roche	5	1	4
Frank Sedgman	3	3	
Lew Hoad	3	3	
Roy Emerson	3	2	1
Norman Brookes	2	2	
Adrian Quist	2	2	
John Bromwich	2	2	
Ken McGregor	2	2	
Ken Rosewall	2	2	
Rex Hartwig	2	2	
Neale Fraser	2	2	
Fred Stolle	2	2	
Bob Hewitt**	2	2	
Peter McNamara	2		2
Paul McNamee	2		2
John Fitzgerald	2		2
Pat O'Hara Wood	1	1	
Ron Thomas	1	1	
James Anderson	1	1	
Jack Crawford	1	1	
Mervyn Rose	1	1	

Player	Total Number of Wimbledon Men's Doubles Title Wins	Total Number of Amateur Era Wimbledon Men's Doubles Title Wins	Total Number of Open Era Wimbledon Men's Doubles Title Wins
Ken Fletcher	1	1	
Rod Laver	1		1
Ross Case	1		1
Geoff Masters	1		1
Stephen Huss	1		1
Matthew Ebden	1		1
Max Purcell	1		1

* Players listed in order of the number of Wimbledon Men's Doubles titles won. Where that number is equal, they are listed in chronological order.

** Bob Hewitt won a further 3 Wimbledon Men's Doubles titles after becoming a South African citizen.

Top All-Time Aussie US Men's Doubles Winners* [465]

Player	Total Number of US Open Men's Doubles Title Wins	Total Number of Amateur Era US Open Men's Doubles Title Wins	Total Number of Open Era US Open Men's Doubles Title Wins
Roy Emerson	4	4	
John Bromwich	3	3	
Neale Fraser	3	3	
Fred Stolle	3	2	1
John Newcombe	3	1	2
Mark Woodforde	3		3
Todd Woodbridge	3		3
Frank Sedgman	2	2	
Mervyn Rose	2	2	

Chapter 11 – Aussies in Grand Slam Men's Doubles (Open Era)

Player	Total Number of US Open Men's Doubles Title Wins	Total Number of Amateur Era US Open Men's Doubles Title Wins	Total Number of Open Era US Open Men's Doubles Title Wins
Ken Rosewall	2	1	1
John Fitzgerald	2	2	
Gerald Patterson	1	1	
Norman Brookes	1	1	
Adrian Quist	1	1	
Bill Sidwell	1	1	
Ken McGregor	1	1	
Rex Hartwig	1	1	
Lew Hoad	1	1	
Ashley Cooper	1	1	
Tony Roche	1	1	
Owen Davidson	1		1
Sandon Stolle	1		1
Lleyton Hewitt	1		1

* Players listed in order of the number of US Open Men's Doubles titles won. Where that number is equal, they are listed in chronological order.

Chapter 12
Aussies in Grand Slam Women's Doubles
(Open Era)

The Grand Slam Open Era began for both men and women with the renamed French Open in April 1968.

Let's look at all of our Aussie women's triumphs and near misses in doubles in the Open Era, starting with the French Open. Margaret Smith (Court) was the only Australian woman who achieved the distinction of winning French Open doubles titles in both the Amateur (see Chapter 9) and Open Eras.[466]

Aussie Women's Doubles Champions
French Open: 1968–Present Day

Margaret Smith (Court)

Margaret Smith (Court) won the 1973 French Open doubles title with England's Virginia Wade to go with the 3 she won as an amateur (see Chapter 9).

Her fourth French doubles crown capped a great tournament for her, as she had earlier won the 1973 singles crown at Roland Garros (her fifth and final French singles title, see Chapter 6).[467]

Wendy Turnbull

Queenslander Wendy Turnbull and her Dutch partner Betty Stove were the 1979 French Open doubles champions.

Turnbull also won the 1979 French mixed title with Australian-born South African Bob Hewitt (see Chapter 13). It could have been a triple celebration for her at Roland Garros in 1979, but she lost the singles final to American Chris Evert (see Chapter 6).[468]

Sam Stosur

Sam Stosur partnered America's Lisa Raymond to a doubles victory at Roland Garros in 2006 in straight sets.

They were the number one seeds after having won the US doubles final the previous year. Their toughest matches came earlier in the tournament when they were pushed to 3 sets in both the third round and the quarter-final.[469]

Alicia Molik

South Australia's Alicia Molik won the 2007 French women's doubles title with Italy's Mara Santangelo. The pair were seeded 17th and survived 3 tough 3-set matches along the way before winning in straight sets in the final.[470]

Aussie Women's Doubles Runners-Up
French Open: 1968–Present Day

The following table lists all of the Aussie women's doubles runners-up at the French Open during the Open Era. Special mention should be made of multiple runners-up Casey Dellacqua (3) and Helen Gourlay (Cawley) (2). Where only one player is listed, the Aussie player had an international partner.[471]

Year	Runners-Up
1969	Margaret Smith (Court)
1971	Helen Gourlay (Cawley)/Kerry Harris
1977	Helen Gourlay (Cawley)
1978	Lesley Turner (Bowrey)
1982	Wendy Turnbull
1988	John Fitzgerald
2002	Rennae Stubbs
2008	Casey Dellacqua
2015	Casey Dellacqua
2017	Casey Dellacqua/Ash Barty

Aussie Women's Doubles Champions
Wimbledon: 1968–Present Day

It only took Aussie women a year to register our first Wimbledon women's doubles title of the Open Era when Margaret Smith (Court) and Judy Tegart (Dalton) won the 1969 final. The win gave Smith (Court) the distinction of winning the title in both the Amateur (see Chapter 9) and Open Eras, a feat only 2 other women accomplished: American partners Billie Jean Moffitt (King) and Rosie Casals.[472]

The pairings and individuals in the feature boxes in this section are listed in order of the highest number of Wimbledon mixed doubles titles won in the Open Era (including by the most successful of a regular pair in some cases), and where that number is equal, chronologically.

Rennae Stubbs (2 titles)

Sydney's Rennae Stubbs is a dual Wimbledon doubles champion, winning her first title with America's Lisa Raymond in 2001 and her second in 2004 with Zimbabwe's Cara Black.

She and fellow Aussie Sam Stosur also finished as runners-up in 2009 to America's Williams' sisters, Serena and Venus.[473]

Margaret Smith (Court) and Judy Tegart (Dalton)

As briefly mentioned at the start of this section, Margaret Smith (Court) and Judy Tegart (Dalton) became the first Aussies to win a Wimbledon women's doubles title in the Open Era when they won the 1969 final.

It was the second title for Smith (Court) after she had won with Lesley Turner (Bowrey) in the Amateur Era (see Chapter 9).[474]

Evonne Goolagong (Cawley)

Evonne Goolagong (Cawley) won the 1974 Wimbledon women's doubles final with American Peggy Michel.

They were unseeded and beat fellow unseeded Aussies Helen Gourlay (Cawley) and Karen Krantzcke in 3 sets in the final. It was the only set they dropped in the entire tournament.[475]

Helen Gourlay (Cawley)

Although Tasmania's Helen Gourlay (Cawley) lost to her unrelated namesake Evonne Goolagong (Cawley) in the 1974 Wimbledon women's doubles final (see the feature box above), she had success 3 years later with American partner

JoAnne Russell. The unseeded pair upset top seeds Martina Navratilova (USA) and Betty Stove (the Netherlands) in straight sets in the final.[476]

Kerry Melville (Reid) and Wendy Turnbull

Kerry Melville (Reid) and Wendy Turnbull paired up to win the 1978 Wimbledon doubles title. The pair were seeded fourth, and they beat 3 seeds along the way to winning a tough 3-set final after dropping the first set. Turnbull would go on to finish runner-up in 4 future Wimbledon women's doubles finals.[477]

Liz Sayers (Smylie)

Western Australian Liz Sayers (Smylie) and her American partner Kathy Jordan won the 1985 Wimbledon doubles crown. They were the event's third seeds and beat top-seeded American pair Martina Navratilova and Pam Shriver in 3 sets in the final. The win ended an incredible streak of 109 consecutive winning matches for Navratilova and Shriver.[478]

Aussie Women's Doubles Runners-Up
Wimbledon: 1968–Present Day

The following table lists all of the Aussie women's doubles runners-up at Wimbledon during the Open Era. Special mention should be made of 3-time runner-up Sam Stosur. Those performances were as close as she would get to winning a Wimbledon women's doubles title, and a win in any of those finals would have given her a career Grand Slam in women's doubles.

Where only one player is listed, the Aussie player had an international partner.[479]

Year	Runners-Up
1971	Margaret Smith (Court) and Evonne Goolagong (Cawley)
1972	Judy Tegart (Dalton)
1974	Helen Gourlay (Cawley)/Karen Krantzcke
1979	Wendy Turnbull
1980	Wendy Turnbull
1983	Wendy Turnbull
1986	Wendy Turnbull
1987	Liz Sayers (Smylie)
1990	Liz Sayers (Smylie)
2008	Sam Stosur
2009	Rennae Stubbs/Sam Stosur
2011	Sam Stosur
2013	Casey Dellacqua/Ash Barty
2023	Storm Sanders (Hunter)

Aussie Women's Doubles Champions
US Open: 1968–Present Day

Margaret Smith (Court) was a partner in the first team to win the US women's doubles in the Open Era, giving her the distinction of being the only Aussie woman to win the event in both the Amateur (see Chapter 9) and Open Eras.[480]

Once again, the pairings and individuals in the feature boxes in this section are listed in order of the highest number of US doubles titles won in the Open Era (including by the most successful of a regular pair in some cases), and where that number is equal, chronologically.

Margaret Smith (Court) – 4 titles

Margaret Smith (Court) won 4 US Open women's doubles titles in the Open Era to add to the one she won in the Amateur Era (see Chapter 9).

She won the first event of the Open Era in 1968 with Brazil's Maria Bueno and followed up with wins in 1970 (with fellow Aussie Judy Tegart (Dalton), 1973 and 1975 (both with England's Virginia Wade).

1970 was an especially memorable US tournament for Smith (Court) as she achieved the rare feat of winning all 3 US women's titles that year: the singles (see Chapter 6) and mixed doubles (with American Marty Riessen, see Chapter 13). She nearly repeated this achievement in 1973, but she and Riessen finished runners-up in the mixed final after she had won the singles and doubles events.[481]

Judy Tegart (Dalton) – 2 titles

Judy Tegart (Dalton) won back-to-back US women's doubles crowns in 1970 and 1971. Her 1970 win with Margaret Smith (Court) gave her a career Grand Slam in women's doubles. She was the third Australian woman to achieve this feat behind Smith (Court) and Lesley Turner (Bowrey).

Tegart (Dalton) successfully defended her US Open doubles title in 1971 with American Rosie Casals as her partner.[482]

Wendy Turnbull – 2 titles

Wendy Turnbull made an incredible 6 US Open women's doubles finals, winning twice. Her first success at the event came in 1979 with Dutch partner Betty Stove (the year they also combined to win the French Open, see earlier feature box in this chapter).

Her second US Open doubles title came in 1982 with American Rosie Casals.[483]

Sam Stosur – 2 titles

Sam Stosur won 2 US women's doubles crowns, and remarkably, her wins were 16 years apart.

In 2005, she and American partner Lisa Raymond took the title after they won a tough 3-set final. In 2021, she and China's Zhang Shuai won another tough 3-set final when Stosur was in the twilight of her long career.[484]

Rennae Stubbs

Rennae Stubbs won her US Open doubles title in 2001 with American Lisa Raymond as her partner. The pair had won Wimbledon together leading into the event (see earlier feature box in this chapter), and they were the top seeds.

Stubbs also won the mixed doubles at the 2001 US Open with fellow Aussie Todd Woodbridge (see Chapter 13).[485]

Ash Barty

Ash Barty won the 2018 US Open women's doubles final with her American partner Coco Vandeweghe in a hard-fought 3-set final.

The pair were seeded 13th and after dropping the first set in the final, they won the next 2 sets in tie-breakers to clinch the title.[486]

Aussie Women's Doubles Runners-Up
US Open: 1968–Present Day

The following table lists all of the Aussie women's doubles runners-up at the US Open during the Open Era. Special mention should be made of two-time runner-up Casey Dellacqua. Those performances were as close as she would come to winning the US women's doubles title. Wendy Turnbull was a 4-time runner-up, but she did win 2 titles.

Where only one player is listed, the Aussie player had an international partner.[487]

Chapter 12 – Aussies in Grand Slam Women's Doubles (Open Era)

Year	Runners-Up
1969	Margaret Smith (Court)
1972	Margaret Smith (Court)
1978	Kerry Melville (Reid)/Wendy Turnbull
1981	Wendy Turnbull
1984	Wendy Turnbull
1986	Wendy Turnbull
1987	Liz Sayers (Smylie)
1995	Rennae Stubbs
2008	Sam Stosur
2013	Casey Dellacqua/Ash Barty
2015	Casey Dellacqua
2019	Ash Barty

Multiple Aussie Women's Doubles Champions
Australian Open: 1968–Present Day

Not surprisingly (and like the men), Aussies have had the most women's doubles success in the Open Era at our local major, though as outlined in Chapters 6 and 7, that success hasn't been replicated in women's singles. Two Aussie women won our doubles title in both the Amateur and Open Eras: Margaret Smith (Court) and Judy Tegart (Dalton).[488]

Once again, the pairings and individuals in the feature boxes in this section are listed in order of the highest number of Aussie women's doubles titles won in the Open Era (including by the most successful of a regular pair in some cases), and where that number is equal, chronologically.

Evonne Goolagong (Cawley) – 5 titles

Evonne Goolagong (Cawley) won 5 Australian Open women's doubles titles with 3 different partners. Her first success came in 1971 with Margaret Smith (Court) when the pair didn't drop a single game in the final.

She then won 3 titles in a row between 1974 and 1976 (back-to-back titles in 1974 and 1975 with American Peggy Michel, followed by a 1976 win with her unrelated namesake and fellow Aussie Helen Gourlay (Cawley). Goolagong (Cawley) also won the women's singles events at the Australian Open between 1974 and 1976.

She and Gourlay (Cawley) shared the 1977 (December) title with fellow Aussie Kerry Melville (Reid) and her American partner Anne Guerrant after the final was washed out. Once again, she also won the women's singles event at that tournament (see Chapter 6).[489]

Margaret Smith (Court) – 4 titles and Judy Tegart (Dalton) – 2 titles

Margaret Smith (Court) and Judy Tegart (Dalton) teamed up to win the first 2 Australian women's doubles titles of the Open Era in 1969 and 1970.

In 1969, Smith (Court) won all 3 Aussie women's titles: the women's singles (see Chapter 6), the mixed doubles (ser Chapter 13) and the women's doubles. In 1970, she won both the women's singles and the doubles events (and no mixed event was played).

Smith (Court) went on to win a further 2 Australian women's doubles titles in 1971 (with Evonne Goolagong (Cawley), a year when she once again won the women's singles) and 1973 (with England's Virginia Wade, when she won the women's singles yet again).

Overall, Smith (Court) won 8 Australian women's doubles titles in her career (4 in the Amateur Era, see Chapter 9, and 4 in the Open Era). Tegart (Dalton) won 4 overall (2 in the Amateur Era, see Chapter 9, and 2 in the Open Era).[490]

Helen Gourlay (Cawley) – 4 titles

Helen Gourlay (Cawley) won 4 women's doubles crowns at the Australian Open, including 3 in a row. Her first success came in 1972 when she partnered Western Australian Kerry Harris.

She then won titles at the 1976, January 1977 and December 1977 events, partnering Evonne Goolagong (Cawley) in 1976 and December 1977, and Dianne

> Fromholtz (Balestrat) in January 1977. As mentioned earlier, the December 1977 final was shared with fellow Aussie Kerry Melville (Reid) and her American partner Anne Guerrant after the final was washed out.[491]

All Aussie Women's Doubles Champions
Australian Open: 1969–Present Day

The following table lists all of the Aussie women's doubles winners of our local major during the Open Era. Where only a single player is listed, the player had an international partner. The dominance of Australian winners in the 1970s reflects the lower number of international entrants that the event attracted during those years.[492]

Year	Winner/s
1969	Margaret Smith (Court)/Judy Tegart (Dalton)
1970	Margaret Smith (Court)/Judy Tegart (Dalton)
1971	Margaret Smith (Court)/Evonne Goolagong (Cawley)
1972	Helen Gourlay (Cawley)/Kerry Harris
1973	Margaret Smith (Court)
1974	Evonne Goolagong (Cawley)
1975	Evonne Goolagong (Cawley)
1976	Evonne Goolagong (Cawley)/Helen Gourlay (Cawley)
1977 (January)	Helen Gourlay (Cawley)/Dianne Fromholtz (Balestrat)
1977 (December)	Evonne Goolagong (Cawley)/Helen Gourlay (Cawley)
1979	Dianne Evers (Brown)
2000	Rennae Stubbs
2005	Alicia Molik
2019	Sam Stosur

Aussie Women's Doubles Runners-Up
Australian Open: 1969–Present Day

The following table lists all of the Aussie doubles runners-up in our premier tennis event during the Open Era. Again, where only one player is listed, the Aussie player had an international partner, and the number of Australian runners-up through to the mid-1980s reflects the lower number of international entrants that the event attracted during the early Open Era years.[493]

Sadly, Wendy Turnbull was a two-time runner-up at her local major, and it was the only Grand Slam women's doubles titles that eluded her in her career. Had she won either of the 1983 or 1988 finals, she would have become only the fourth Australian woman to achieve a career Grand Slam in women's doubles.

Year	Runners-Up
1970	Kerry Melville (Reid)/Karen Krantzcke
1971	Jill Blackman (Emmerson)/Lesley Hunt
1972	Karen Krantzcke/Patricia Coleman
1973	Kerry Melville (Reid)/Kerry Harris
1974	Kerry Melville (Reid)/Kerry Harris
1975	Margaret Smith (Court)
1976	Lesley Turner (Bowrey)
1977 (January)	Kerry Melville (Reid)
1977 (December)	Kerry Melville (Reid)
1978	Pam Whytcross
1979	Leanne Harrison
1983	Wendy Turnbull
1988	Wendy Turnbull
1993	Liz Sayers (Smylie)
2006	Sam Stosur
2013	Casey Dellacqua/Ash Barty

Aussie Women's Wheelchair Doubles at the Majors (2004–Present Day)

As outlined in Chapter 7, wheelchair tennis emerged at the Grand Slams in the early 2000s. There are Grand Slam events for both wheelchair and quad categories for men, and wheelchair only for women.

The Australian Open was the first of the majors to introduce the wheelchair women's doubles in 2004, the same year as the men's doubles event was introduced.[494] The US Open introduced wheelchair women's doubles a year later in 2005,[495] followed by the French Open in 2007[496] and finally Wimbledon in 2009.[497]

Danni Di Toro – Wheelchair Tennis

Danni Di Toro is the only Australian woman to have won a wheelchair doubles title at a Grand Slam event.

She won the 2010 French Open wheelchair women's doubles final with her Dutch partner Aniek van Koot. They beat Dutch wheelchair tennis legend Esther Vergeer and her Dutch partner Korie Homan in the final.[498]

Top All-Time Aussie Women's Grand Slam Doubles Winners*

Player	Total Number of Grand Slam Women's Doubles Title Wins	Total Number of Amateur Era Grand Slam Women's Doubles Title Wins	Total Number of Open Era Grand Slam Women's Doubles Title Wins
Margaret Smith (Court)	19	9	10
Thelma Coyne (Long)**	12	12	
Nancye Wynne (Bolton)**	10	10	
Judy Tegart (Dalton)***	8	3	5
Lesley Turner (Bowrey)	7	7	
Evonne Goolagong (Cawley)	6		6

* Minimum 6 Grand Slam Women's Doubles title wins. Players listed in order of the number of Grand Slam events won. Where that number is equal, they are listed in chronological order.

** **Thelma Coyne (Long)** and **Nancye Wynne (Bolton)** missed the opportunity to add to their respective Grand Slam tallies due to 5 Australian, 6 Wimbledon and 1 French Championship/s being cancelled during World War II.

*** **Judy Tegart (Dalton)** was banned from competing in the 1971 and 1972 Australian Open tournaments due to joining the Virginia Slims breakaway pro tour that later became the modern-day WTA, the governing body of contemporary women's tennis.[499]

Top All-Time All-Aussie Women's Grand Slam Doubles Teams*

Player	Total Number of Grand Slam Women's Doubles Title Wins	Total Number of Amateur Era Grand Slam Women's Doubles Title Wins	Total Number of Open Era Grand Slam Women's Doubles Title Wins
Nancye Wynne (Bolton)/ Thelma Coyne (Long)	10	10	
Margaret Smith (Court)/ Judy Tegart (Dalton)	5	1	4
Margaret Smith (Court)/ Lesley Turner (Bowrey)	4	4	

* Minimum 4 Grand Slam Women's Doubles title wins together. Players listed in order of the number of Grand Slam events won. Where that number is equal, they are listed in chronological order.

Aussie Winners of at least 2 of the 4 Grand Slam Women's Doubles Titles*

Player	Australian Open	French Open	Wimbledon	US Open
Margaret Smith (Court)	✓	✓	✓	✓
Lesley Turner (Bowrey)	✓	✓	✓	✓
Judy Tegart (Dalton)	✓	✓	✓	✓
Wendy Turnbull		✓	✓	✓
Rennae Stubbs	✓		✓	✓
Sam Stosur	✓	✓		✓
Evonne Goolagong (Cawley)	✓		✓	

Chapter 12 – Aussies in Grand Slam Women's Doubles (Open Era)

Player	Australian Open	French Open	Wimbledon	US Open
Helen Gourlay (Cawley)	✓		✓	
Kerry Melville (Reid)	✓		✓	

* Players listed in order of the number of different Grand Slam events won (i.e. 4, 3 or 2). Where that number is equal, they are listed in chronological order.

Top All-Time Aussie Australian Women's Doubles Winners* [500]

Player	Total Number of Australian Open Women's Doubles Title Wins	Total Number of Amateur Era Australian Open Women's Doubles Title Wins	Total Number of Open Era Australian Open Women's Doubles Title Wins
Thelma Coyne (Long)	12	12	
Nancye Wynne (Bolton)	10	10	
Margaret Smith (Court)	8	4	4
Mary Bevis (Hawton)	5	5	
Esna Boyd (Robertson)	4	4	
Daphne Akhurst (Cozens)	4	4	
Judy Tegart (Dalton)	4	2	2

* Minimum 4 Australian Open Women's Doubles title wins. Players listed in order of the number of titles won. Where that number is equal, they are listed in chronological order.

Top All-Time Aussie French Women's Doubles Winners* [501]

Player	Total Number of French Open Women's Doubles Title Wins	Total Number of Amateur Era French Open Women's Doubles Title Wins	Total Number of Open Era French Open Women's Doubles Title Wins
Margaret Smith (Court)	4	3	1
Lesley Turner (Bowrey)	2	2	
Nell Hall (Hopman)	1	1	
Judy Tegart (Dalton)	1	1	
Wendy Turnbull	1		1
Sam Stosur	1		1
Alicia Molik	1		1

* Players listed in order of the number of French Women's Doubles titles won. Where that number is equal, they are listed in chronological order.

Top All-Time Aussie Wimbledon Women's Doubles Winners* [502]

Player	Total Number of Wimbledon Women's Doubles Title Wins	Total Number of Amateur Era Wimbledon Women's Doubles Title Wins	Total Number of Open Era Wimbledon Women's Doubles Title Wins
Margaret Smith (Court)	2	1	1
Rennae Stubbs	2		2
Lesley Turner (Bowrey)	1	1	
Judy Tegart (Dalton)	1		1
Evonne Goolagong (Cawley)	1		1

Chapter 12 – Aussies in Grand Slam Women's Doubles (Open Era)

Player	Total Number of Wimbledon Women's Doubles Title Wins	Total Number of Amateur Era Wimbledon Women's Doubles Title Wins	Total Number of Open Era Wimbledon Women's Doubles Title Wins
Helen Gourlay (Cawley)	1		1
Kerry Melville (Reid)	1		1
Wendy Turnbull	1		1
Liz Sayers (Smylie)	1		1

* Players listed in order of the number of Wimbledon Women's Doubles titles won. Where that number is equal, they are listed in chronological order.

Top All-Time Aussie US Women's Doubles Winners* [503]

Player	Total Number of US Open Women's Doubles Title Wins	Total Number of Amateur Era US Open Women's Doubles Title Wins	Total Number of Open Era US Open Women's Doubles Title Wins
Margaret Smith (Court)	5	1	4
Judy Tegart (Dalton)	2		2
Wendy Turnbull	2		2
Sam Stosur	2		2
Lesley Turner (Bowrey)	1	1	
Robyn Ebbern (Vincenzi)	1	1	
Rennae Stubbs	1		1
Ash Barty			1

* Players listed in order of the number of US Open Women's Doubles titles won. Where that number is equal, they are listed in chronological order.

Chapter 13
Aussies in Grand Slam Mixed Doubles
(Open Era)

The Grand Slam Open Era began for both men and women with the renamed French Open in April 1968.

Let's look at all of our Aussie mixed doubles triumphs and near misses in doubles in the Open Era, starting with the French Open. Margaret Smith (Court) was the only Australian who achieved the distinction of winning French Open mixed doubles titles in both the Amateur (see Chapter 10) and Open Eras.[504]

Aussie Mixed Doubles Champions
French Open: 1968–Present Day

Kim Warwick (2 titles)

New South Welshman Kim Warwick won 2 French mixed doubles titles with different partners. The first was in 1972 with fellow Aussie Evonne Goolagong (Cawley). The second was in 1976 with South African Ilana Kloss.[505]

Wendy Turnbull (2 titles)

Wendy Turnbull won the first of her 2 French mixed doubles titles in 1979 with Australian-born South African Bob Hewitt. It was a year that she made the finals of all 3 women's events at Roland Garros (singles, doubles and mixed doubles), winning all but the singles title.

She won her second French mixed doubles title in 1982 with Englishman John Lloyd.[506]

Margaret Smith (Court)

As mentioned at the start of this chapter, Margaret Smith (Court) was the only Australian to win French mixed doubles titles in both the Amateur and Open Eras. She and American Marty Riessen won the 1969 final to add to her 3 French mixed titles in the Amateur Era.

Smith (Court) also won the 1969 French Open singles final (see Chapter 6).[507]

Evonne Goolagong (Cawley)

Evonne Goolagong (Cawley) won her French Open mixed doubles title with Kim Warwick in 1972.

It was the only Grand Slam mixed doubles title of her career, and she finished runner-up in the singles at Roland Garros in the same year.[508]

Chapter 13 – Aussies in Grand Slam Mixed Doubles (Open Era)

Todd Woodbridge

Todd Woodbridge won the 1992 French mixed doubles title with Spanish partner Arantxa Sanchez Vicario. The pair were the second seeds and it was the second mixed doubles title of his career after he'd won the US mixed title 2 years earlier with Liz Sayers (Smylie), see later feature box in this chapter.

Woodbridge would go on to win a career Grand Slam in mixed doubles, a feat he also later achieved in men's doubles with Mark Woodforde (see Chapter 11).[509]

Mark Woodforde

Left-hander Mark Woodforde's victory in the 1995 French Open mixed doubles final gave him a career Grand Slam. He had won the Australian, Wimbledon and US titles in earlier years with different partners (see later feature boxes in this chapter). He later achieved a career Grand Slam in men's doubles (see Chapter 11).

His partner in the 1995 mixed final at Roland Garros was Latvian right-hander Larisa Savchenko-Neiland, and they won a tight final in straight tie-break sets.[510]

> ### Casey Dellacqua
>
> Western Australian left-hander Casey Dellacqua won the 2011 French Open mixed doubles title with American Scott Lipsky. They were unseeded and beat the top seeds in the final (Slovenia's Katarina Srebotnik and Serbia's Nenad Zimonjic).
>
> It was the only Grand Slam title of Dellacqua's career, but she did reach the final of all 4 Grand Slam events in women's doubles, including the French Open 3 times and the US Open twice.[511]

Aussie Mixed Doubles Runners-Up
French Open: 1968–Present Day

The following table lists all of the Aussie mixed doubles runners-up at the French Open during the Open Era.[512]

Year	Runners-Up
1968	Owen Davidson
1984	Anne Minter (Harris)/Laurie Warder
1986	Mark Edmondson
1990	Nicole Provis (Bradtke)
2000	Rennae Stubbs/Todd Woodbridge

Aussie Mixed Doubles Champions
Wimbledon: 1968–Present Day

Aussies Margaret Smith (Court) and Ken Fletcher won the first Wimbledon mixed doubles title of the Open Era in 1968. The win gave them the distinction of winning the title in both the Amateur (see Chapter 10) and Open Eras, a feat only achieved by one other team: fellow Aussie Owen Davidson and his American partner Billie Jean Moffitt (King).[513]

Chapter 13 – Aussies in Grand Slam Mixed Doubles (Open Era)

The pairings and individuals in the feature boxes in this section are listed in order of the highest number of Wimbledon mixed doubles titles won in the Open Era (including by the most successful of a regular pair in some cases), and where that number is equal, chronologically.

Margaret Smith (Court) – (2 titles) and Ken Fletcher

Margaret Smith (Court) and Ken Fletcher won the 1968 Wimbledon mixed doubles final to give them their fourth title together at the All England Club after their 3 wins in the Amateur Era (see Chapter 10).

It was the last Grand Slam event that they won together and they remain the most successful mixed doubles pairing in tennis history with 10 Grand Slam titles.

Smith (Court) went on to win a second Open Era Wimbledon mixed doubles title in 1975 with American Marty Riessen. It was the last Grand Slam win in mixed doubles of her career, and she remains the most successful mixed doubles player in tennis history with 21 Grand Slam titles overall, as well as being the most successful women's singles player in history (see Chapter 7).[514]

Wendy Turnbull (2 titles)

Wendy Turnbull made 3 consecutive Wimbledon mixed doubles finals with England's John Lloyd, winning back-to-back titles in 1983 and 1984.

Their first title in 1983 came after a tough 3-set final. They were seeded second and came back after losing the first set in a tie-break to win the next 2 sets 7-6, 7-5 against American's Billie Jean Moffitt (King) and Steve Denton, the top seeds.[515]

Sam Stosur (2 titles)

Sam Stosur's 2 Wimbledon mixed doubles titles came with different international partners.

The first was in 2008 with American Bob Bryan. They were unseeded but beat the top seeds (Bryan's twin brother Mike and his Slovenian partner Katarina Srebotnik) in straight sets in the final.

Stosur's second Wimbledon mixed doubles title came in 2014 with Serbian Nenad Zimonjic.[516]

Fred Stolle

Fred Stolle won the 1969 Wimbledon mixed doubles final with England's Ann Jones. They beat Aussies Tony Roche and Judy Tegart (Dalton) in the final.

The win gave Stolle 3 Wimbledon mixed doubles titles for his career, after he had won 2 in the Amateur Era with fellow Aussie Lesley Turner (Bowrey), see Chapter 10.[517]

Owen Davidson

Owen Davidson won 3 Wimbledon mixed doubles titles in the Open Era with his long-time partner, American Billie Jean Moffitt (King), giving them 4 overall after they had won the last event of the Amateur Era in 1967 (see Chapter 10).

Their 1971 final win came after an epic battle with Margaret Smith (Court) and American Marty Riessen. They dropped the first set, won the second and then won a marathon third set 15-13 to take the match.[518]

Tony Roche

Tony Roche won the 1976 Wimbledon mixed doubles crown with French partner 'Frankie' Dürr. The pair were unseeded but paved their way to the title with an upset win over third seeds, Czech-born American Martina Navratilova and American Marty Riessen, in the second round.[519]

Paul McNamee

Victorian Paul McNamee partnered Czech-born American Martina Navratilova to victory in the 1985 Wimbledon mixed doubles final. They were the number 2 seeds and beat seventh seeds, Aussies John Fitzgerald and Liz Sayers (Smylie), in 3 sets in the final.[520]

Liz Sayers (Smylie) and John Fitzgerald

It was a case of third time lucky for Western Australian Liz Sayers (Smylie) and South Australian John Fitzgerald (pictured) when they won the 1991 Wimbledon mixed doubles final. The pair had finished runner-up in 1985 (to fellow Aussie Paul McNamee and Martina Navratilova, see feature box above), and in 1990.

In 1991 they were the second seeds for the event and they beat the top seeds, Belarusan Natasha Zvereva and American Bill Pugh, in straight sets in the final.[521]

Mark Woodforde

Mark Woodforde won his Wimbledon mixed doubles title with Czech-born American and fellow left-hander Martina Navratilova in 1993.

He and Todd Woodbridge also won the first of their 6 Wimbledon men's doubles titles that same year (see Chapter 11).[522]

Todd Woodbridge

Todd Woodbridge won his Wimbledon mixed doubles title with Czechoslovakia's Helena Sukova in 1994 to give him a career Grand Slam.

He had previously won the Australian and French mixed doubles titles with Arantxa Sanchez Vicario, and the US crown with fellow Aussie Liz Sayers (Smylie), see later feature box in this chapter.[523]

Aussie Mixed Doubles Runners-Up
Wimbledon: 1968–Present Day

The following table lists all of the Aussie mixed doubles runners-up at Wimbledon during the Open Era. Special mention should be made of two-time runner-up Alicia Molik. Those performances were as close as she would get to winning a Wimbledon mixed doubles title.

Where only one player is listed, the Aussie player had an international partner.[524]

Year	Runners-Up
1969	Judy Tegart (Dalton)/Tony Roche
1971	Margaret Smith (Court)
1972	Evonne Goolagong (Cawley)/Kim Warwick
1975	Allan Stone
1978	Ray Ruffels
1980	Dianne Fromholtz (Balestrat)/Mark Edmondson
1982	Wendy Turnbull
1985	Liz Sayers (Smylie)/John Fitzgerald
1987	Nicole Provis (Bradtke)/Todd Woodbridge
1989	Jenny Byrne/Mark Kratzmann
1990	Liz Sayers (Smylie)/John Fitzgerald
1996	Mark Woodforde
2000	Lleyton Hewitt
2004	Alicia Molik/Todd Woodbridge
2005	Paul Hanley
2007	Alicia Molik
2022	Sam Stosur/Matthew Ebden

Aussie Mixed Doubles Champions
US Open: 1968–Present Day

Margaret Smith (Court) was the first Aussie to win a mixed doubles title in the Open Era in 1969 when she partnered American Marty Riessen to win the title. Once again, the win gave her the distinction of winning the US mixed doubles title in both the Amateur (see Chapter 10) and Open Eras, a feat that was only achieved by fellow Aussie Owen Davidson and his American partner Billie Jean Moffitt (King).[525]

The pairings and individuals in the feature boxes in this section are again listed in order of the highest number of US mixed doubles titles won in the Open Era (including by the most successful of a regular pair in some cases), and where that number is equal, chronologically.

Margaret Smith (Court) – 3 titles

Margaret Smith (Court) won 3 US mixed doubles titles in the Open Era (1969, 1970 and 1972), adding to the 5 she won in the Amateur Era (see Chapter 10).

All 3 of her Open Era titles came with US partner Marty Riessen, including a 1970 finals' victory over fellow Aussie Judy Tegart (Dalton) and her South African partner Frew McMillan. She won all women's titles on offer at the US Open that year–singles (see Chapter 6), doubles (see Chapter 12) and the mixed doubles.

It was a feat she almost achieved a year earlier in 1969 when she won both the US women's singles and mixed doubles events, but she finished runner-up in the doubles.[526]

Todd Woodbridge (3 titles)

Todd Woodbridge won 3 US Open mixed doubles titles with 3 different partners across 11 years. His first win came in 1990 when he was just 19 and he partnered fellow Aussie Liz Sayers (Smylie) to victory. They were the number 8 seeds and beat the top seeds (Belarusan Natasha Zvereva and American Jim Pugh) in straight sets in the final.

In 1993, he and Czech partner Helena Sukova beat his men's doubles partner Mark Woodforde and Marina Navratilova in straight sets to clinch the title. In 2001, Woodbridge won his third US mixed doubles title with fellow Aussie Rennae Stubbs (see later feature box in this section).[527]

Owen Davidson (2 titles)

Owen Davidson won 2 US mixed doubles crowns in the Open Era with long-time American partner Billie Jean Moffitt (King), matching the 2 that they won together in the Amateur Era (see Chapter 10).

Their Open Era wins came in 1971 and 1973, and they beat fellow Aussie Margaret Smith (Court) and her American partner Marty Riessen in a tie-breaker in the third and deciding set of the 1973 final.[528]

Liz Sayers (Smylie) – 2 titles and John Fitzgerald

Liz Sayers (Smylie) and John Fitzgerald (pictured) made 3 consecutive US Open mixed doubles finals between 1983 and 1985.

They were unseeded in the 1983 event and cleared their path to the final by upsetting American second seeds Kathy Jordan and Eliot Teltscher in straight sets in the second round. They then beat American top seeds Barbara Potter and Ferdi Taygan in 3 sets in the final after dropping the first set. They finished runners-up in 1984 and 1985.

Sayers (Smylie) later clinched a second US mixed doubles title in 1990 with fellow Aussie Todd Woodbridge (see earlier feature box in this section).[529]

Geoff Masters

Queenslander Geoff Masters and his American partner Pam Teeguarden were unseeded at the 1973 US Open. But they upset top seeds Billie Jean Moffitt (King) and Owen Davidson in straight sets in the semi-finals, before doing the same against the third-seeded Americans Chris Evert and Jimmy Connors in the final to clinch the title.[530]

Phil Dent

New South Welshman Phil Dent won his US Open mixed doubles title with American Billie Jean Moffitt (King) in 1976, after her long-term Aussie partner Owen Davidson had retired. The pair were seeded third for the 1976 event.[531]

Wendy Turnbull

Wendy Turnbull won the 1980 US mixed doubles crown with American Marty Riessen, after his long-time Aussie partner Margaret Smith (Court) had retired.

The pair were the top seeds for the 1980 tournament, and they won the final in straight sets.[532]

Nicole Provis (Bradtke) and Mark Woodforde

Victorian right-hander Nicole Provis (Bradtke) and left-hander Mark Woodforde (pictured) won the 1992 US open mixed doubles title.

The pair had won the Australian mixed doubles final earlier that year (see later feature box in this chapter).[533]

Rennae Stubbs

Rennae Stubbs paired up with Todd Woodbridge to win the mixed doubles at the 2001 US Open. They were the top seeds and they beat the second seeds (American Lisa Raymond and Indian Leander Paes) in the final.

Stubbs also won the US women's doubles event in the same year (see Chapter 12).[534]

Storm Sanders (Hunter) and John Peers

Queensland left-hander Storm Sanders (Hunter) and Victorian right-hander John Peers won the 2022 US mixed doubles title. It was the first time the pair had played together in a tournament, and it paid immediate dividends.[535]

Aussie Mixed Doubles Runners-Up
US Open: 1968–Present Day

The following table lists all of the Aussie mixed doubles runners-up at the US Open during the Open Era. Where only one player is listed, the Aussie player had an international partner.[536]

Year	Runners-Up
1970	Judy Tegart (Dalton)
1973	Margaret Smith (Court)
1975	Fred Stolle
1978	Ray Ruffels
1984	Liz Sayers (Smylie)/John Fitzgerald
1985	Liz Sayers (Smylie)/John Fitzgerald
1988	Liz Sayers (Smylie)
1993	Mark Woodforde

Year	Runners-Up
1994	Todd Woodbridge
2004	Alicia Molik/Todd Woodbridge

Multiple Aussie Mixed Doubles Champions
Australian Open: 1968–Present Day

The Aussie mixed doubles event was played at the first Australian event of the Open Era in 1969, and then not played again until 1987. The Australian Open struggled to attract the world's top international players in the 1970s and 1980s, especially male players. It also struggled to attract decent prizemoney compared to the other Grand Slam events during the early years of the Open Era.

Sadly, the decision not to play the mixed doubles event for more than a decade at the Australian Open probably cost Wendy Turnbull the chance to achieve a career Grand Slam. She won the mixed doubles at every other Grand Slam event in her career. It also arguably cost Margaret Smith (Court) the opportunity to add to her all-time record of 21 Grand Slam titles in mixed doubles.[537]

Only one Aussie has won multiple mixed doubles titles at our local Grand Slam event – Mark Woodforde.

Mark Woodforde – 2 titles

Mark Woodforde won his first Australian Open mixed doubles title in 1992 with Nicole Provis (Bradtke). They were the number 3 seeds and beat his doubles partner Todd Woodbridge and his Spanish partner Arantxa Sanchez-Vicario (the top seeds) in an epic final where they won the deciding third set, 11-9. The Woodies had earlier combined to win the first of their 11 Grand Slam men's doubles titles at the 1992 Australian Open.

Woodforde's second Australian title came in 1996 when he and Latvian right-hander Larisa Savchenko-Neiland were the top seeds.[538]

All Aussie Mixed Doubles Champions
Australian Open: 1969–Present Day

The following table lists all of the Aussie mixed doubles winners of our local major during the Open Era. Where only a single player is listed, the player had an international partner.[539]

Year	Winner/s
1969	Margaret Smith (Court) and Fred Stolle*
1992	Nicole Provis (Bradtke)/Mark Woodforde
1993	Todd Woodbridge
1996	Mark Woodforde
2000	Rennae Stubbs
2005	Sam Stosur/Scott Draper
2013	Jarmila Gajdošová (Wolfe)/Matthew Ebden

* Smith (Court) and Fred Stolle had international partners and were due to meet in the final. It was washed out, so the title was shared.

Aussie Mixed Doubles Runners-Up
Australian Open: 1969–Present Day

The following table lists all of the Aussie mixed doubles runners-up in our premier tennis event during the Open Era. Again, where only one player is listed, the Aussie player had an international partner.[540]

Year	Runners-Up
1992	Todd Woodbridge
1994	Todd Woodbridge
2000	Todd Woodbridge
2001	Josh Eagle
2003	Todd Woodbridge
2011	Paul Hanley
2019	Astra Sharma/John-Patrick Smith

Chapter 13 – Aussies in Grand Slam Mixed Doubles (Open Era)

Year	Runners-Up
2021	Sam Stosur/Matthew Ebden
2022	Jaimee Fourlis/Jason Kubler

Top All-Time Aussie Grand Slam Mixed Doubles Winners*

Player	Total Number of Grand Slam Mixed Doubles Title Wins	Total Number of Amateur Era Grand Slam Mixed Doubles Title Wins	Total Number of Open Era Grand Slam Mixed Doubles Title Wins
Margaret Smith (Court)	21	14	7
Owen Davidson	11	6	5
Ken Fletcher	10	9	1
Frank Sedgman**	8	8	
Fred Stolle	7	5	2
Todd Woodbridge	6		6

* Minimum 6 Grand Slam Mixed Doubles title wins. Players listed in order of the number of Grand Slam events won. Where that number is equal, they are listed in chronological order.

** **Frank Sedgman** was banned from competing in 52 Grand Slam tournaments between the start of 1953 when he turned pro and the end of 1965 when he retired. However, he briefly returned to play in Grand Slam events in the early years of the Open Era when he was in his early forties.

Australia's Grand Slam Tennis Champions

Top All-Time All-Aussie Grand Slam Mixed Doubles Teams*

Player	Total Number of Grand Slam Mixed Doubles Title Wins	Total Number of Amateur Era Grand Slam Mixed Doubles Title Wins	Total Number of Open Era Grand Slam Mixed Doubles Title Wins
Margaret Smith (Court)/ Ken Fletcher	10	9	1
Nell Hall (Hopman)/ Harry Hopman	4	4	
Nancye Wynne (Bolton)/ Colin Long	4	4	

* Minimum 4 Grand Slam Mixed Doubles title wins together. Players listed in order of the number of events won. Where that number is equal, they are listed in chronological order.

Aussie Winners of at least 2 of the 4 Grand Slam Mixed Doubles Titles*

Player	Australian Open	French Open	Wimbledon	US Open
Frank Sedgman	✓	✓	✓	✓
Margaret Smith (Court)	✓	✓	✓	✓
Ken Fletcher	✓	✓	✓	✓
Owen Davidson	✓	✓	✓	✓
Todd Woodbridge	✓	✓	✓	✓
Mark Woodforde	✓	✓	✓	✓
Wendy Turnbull		✓	✓	✓
Fred Stolle	✓		✓	
Liz Sayers (Smylie)			✓	✓
John Fitzgerald			✓	✓

Chapter 13 – Aussies in Grand Slam Mixed Doubles (Open Era)

Player	Australian Open	French Open	Wimbledon	US Open
Nicole Provis (Bradtke)	✓			✓
Rennae Stubbs	✓			✓
Sam Stosur	✓		✓	

* Players listed in order of the number of different Grand Slam events won (i.e. 4, 3 or 2). Where that number is equal, they are listed in chronological order.

Top All-Time Aussie Australian Mixed Doubles Winners* [541]

Player	Total Number of Australian Open Mixed Doubles Title Wins	Total Number of Amateur Era Australian Open Mixed Doubles Title Wins	Total Number of Open Era Australian Open Mixed Doubles Title Wins
Daphne Akhurst (Cozens)	4	4	
Nell Hall (Hopman)	4	4	
Harry Hopman	4	4	
Nancye Wynne (Bolton)	4	4	
Colin Long	4	4	
Thelma Coyne (Long)	4	4	
Margaret Smith (Court)	4	3	1

* Minimum 4 Australian Open Mixed Doubles title wins. Players listed in order of the number of titles won. Where that number is equal, they are listed in chronological order.

Top All-Time Aussie French Mixed Doubles Winners* [542]

Player	Total Number of French Open Mixed Doubles Title Wins	Total Number of Amateur Era French Open Mixed Doubles Title Wins	Total Number of Open Era French Open Mixed Doubles Title Wins
Margaret Smith (Court)	4	3	1
Ken Fletcher	3	3	
Frank Sedgman	2	2	
Bob Howe	2	2	
Kim Warwick	2		2
Wendy Turnbull			2
Jack Crawford	1	1	
Lew Hoad	1	1	
Thelma Coyne (Long)	1	1	
Rod Laver	1	1	
Owen Davidson	1	1	
Evonne Goolagong (Cawley)	1		1
Todd Woodbridge	1		1
Mark Woodforde	1		1
Casey Dellacqua	1		1

* Players listed in order of the number of French Mixed Doubles titles won. Where that number is equal, they are listed in chronological order.

Top All-Time Aussie Wimbledon Mixed Doubles Winners* 543

Player	Total Number of Wimbledon Mixed Doubles Title Wins	Total Number of Amateur Era Wimbledon Mixed Doubles Title Wins	Total Number of Open Era Wimbledon Mixed Doubles Title Wins
Margaret Smith (Court)	5	3	2
Ken Fletcher	4	3	1
Owen Davidson	4	1	3
Fred Stolle	3	2	1
Wendy Turnbull	2		2
Sam Stosur	2		2
Tony Roche	1		1
Paul McNamee	1		1
Liz Sayers (Smylie)	1		1
John Fitzgerald	1		1
Todd Woodbridge	1		1
Mark Woodforde			1

* Players listed in order of the number of Wimbledon Mixed Doubles titles won. Where that number is equal, they are listed in chronological order.

Top All-Time Aussie US Mixed Doubles Winners* 544

Player	Total Number of US Open Mixed Doubles Title Wins	Total Number of Amateur Era US Open Mixed Doubles Title Wins	Total Number of Open Era US Open Mixed Doubles Title Wins
Margaret Smith (Court)	8	5	3
Owen Davidson	4	2	2
Neale Fraser	3	3	

Australia's Grand Slam Tennis Champions

Player	Total Number of US Open Mixed Doubles Title Wins	Total Number of Amateur Era US Open Mixed Doubles Title Wins	Total Number of Open Era US Open Mixed Doubles Title Wins
Todd Woodbridge	3		3
John Hawkes	2	2	
Frank Sedgman	2	2	
Fred Stolle	2	2	
Liz Sayers (Smylie)	2		2
Edward Dewhurst	1	1	
Harry Hopman	1	1	
John Bromwich	1	1	
Ken McGregor	1	1	
Ken Rosewall	1	1	
Bob Mark	1	1	
Ken Fletcher	1	1	
John Newcombe	1	1	
John Fitzgerald	1		1
Geoff Masters	1		1
Phil Dent	1		1
Wendy Turnbull	1		1
Nicole Provis (Bradtke)	1		1
Mark Woodforde	1		1
Rennae Stubbs	1		1
Storm Sanders (Hunter)	1		1
John Peers	1		1

* Players listed in order of the number of US Open Mixed Doubles titles won. Where that number is equal, they are listed in chronological order.

Chapter 14
The Greatest Aussie Grand Slam Winners of All Time

There's an old saying in sport that you can't compare different eras. It's certainly the case in tennis where there has been massive changes since the first Grand Slam events were played more than 100 years ago. Over that time, we've seen massive changes in racquets, balls, court surfaces, player eligibility and the ability of players to travel across the globe to compete in the 4 Grand Slam events. We've also seen the change from players being amateurs to full-time professionals competing for massive prizemoney, as well as specialising in singles or doubles rather than playing multiple events.

Despite the impracticality of comparing different eras, it's still an interesting exercise that's sure to generate debate. If you go strictly by the number of Grand Slam career titles won by Australian players in each event (singles, doubles and mixed doubles), then the following is the list of the greatest Aussie Grand Slam winners of all time (with a minimum of 15 career Grand Slam titles). Where the total number of career Grand Slam titles is equal, the players are listed in chronological order.

With modern players tending to focus exclusively on singles or doubles, it's hard to imagine both the Australian and world record of Margaret Smith (Court) ever being broken.

Australia's Grand Slam Tennis Champions

Player	Total Career Grand Slam Titles	Total Grand Slam Singles Titles	Total Grand Slam Men's/Women's Doubles Titles	Total Grand Slam Mixed Doubles Titles
Margaret Smith (Court)	64	24	19	21
Roy Emerson	28	12	16	
John Newcombe*	26	7	17	2
Dylan Alcott	23	15	8	
Frank Sedgman**	22	5	9	8
Todd Woodbridge	22		16	6
Nancye Wynne*** (Bolton)	20	6	10	4
Rod Laver****	20	11	6	3
John Bromwich***	19	2	13	4
Thelma Coyne (Long) ***	19	2	12	5
Neale Fraser	19	3	11	5
Fred Stolle	19	2	10	7
Ken Rosewall *****	18	8	9	1
Jack Crawford	17	6	6	5
Adrian Quist***	17	3	14	
Mark Woodforde	17		12	5
Tony Roche*	16	1	13	2

The career Grand Slam totals of the following players could arguably have been higher:

* **John Newcombe** and **Tony Roche** were banned from competing in 2 Open Era Grand Slam tournaments in 1972 due to being a part of World Championship Tennis (WCT).

** **Frank Sedgman** was banned from competing in 52 Grand Slam tournaments between the start of 1953 when he turned pro and the end of 1965 when he retired. However, he briefly returned to play in Grand Slam events in the early years of the Open Era when he was in his early forties.

*** **Nancye Wynne (Bolton), John Bromwich, Adrian Quist** and **Thelma Coyne (Long)** missed the opportunity to add to their respective Grand Slam tallies due to 5 Australian, 6 Wimbledon and 1 French Championship/s being cancelled during World War II.

**** **Rod Laver** was banned from competing in 21 Grand Slam tournaments between the start of 1963 when he turned pro and April 1968 when the Open Era commenced. He was also banned from competing in 2 Open Era Grand Slam tournaments in 1972 due to being a part of World Championship Tennis (WCT).

***** **Ken Rosewall** was banned from competing in 45 Grand Slam tournaments between the start of 1957 when he turned pro and April 1968 when the Open Era commenced. He was also banned from competing in 2 Open Era Grand Slam tournaments in 1972 due to being a part of World Championship Tennis (WCT).[545]

Image Credits

Jack Crawford – Public Domain, National Library of Australia
James Anderson – Public Domain, Bain News Service, The Library of Congress
Adrian Quist – Public Domain
Pat O'Hara Wood – Public Domain, National Library of France
John Bromwich – Public Domain, State Library of Queensland
Frank Sedgman – Public Domain, State Library of Victoria
Harry Hopman – Public Domain, National Library of Australia
Horace Rice – Public Domain, National Library of France
Gerald Patterson – Public Domain, Sport & General Press Agency Ltd.
Ken McGregor – Public Domain, State Library of Victoria
Norman Brookes – Public Domain, National Library of France
Nancye Wynne (Bolton) – Public Domain, National Portrait Gallery
Joan Hartigan (Bathurst) – Public Domain, National Portrait Gallery
Coral McInnes (Buttsworth) – Public Domain, Tennis Australia
Thelma Coyne (Long) – Creative Commons, National Library of Australia
Esna Boyd (Robertson) – Public Domain, National Portrait Gallery
Sylvia Lance (Harper) – Public Domain, Tennis Australia
Nell Hall (Hopman) – Public Domain, National Portrait Gallery
Roy Emerson – Creative Commons, Hugo van Gelderen/Anefo
Rod Laver – Public Domain, Joost Evers/Anefo
Ken Rosewall – Public Domain, State Library of Victoria
Ashley Cooper – Creative Commons, Joop van Bilsen/Anefo, Dutch National Archives
Neale Fraser – Keystone Press, licensed via Alamy
Fred Stolle – Keystone Press, licensed via Alamy
Lew Hoad – Public Domain, Ern McQuillan, National Library of Australia
Mervyn Rose – Creative Commons, Ern McQuillan, National Library of Australia
Tony Roche – Creative Commons, Eric Koch/Anefo

John Newcombe – Keystone Press, licensed via Alamy
Mal Anderson – Creative Commons, Hans Peters/Anefo
Rex Hartwig – Creative Commons, National Library of Australia
Margaret Smith (Court) – Creative Commons, Eric Koch/Anefo
Lesley Turner (Bowrey) – Creative Commons, Eric Koch/Anefo
Evonne Goolagong (Cawley) – Creative Commons, W. Punt/Anefo
Wendy Turnbull – Trinity Mirror/Mirrorpix, licensed via Alamy
Judy Tegart (Dalton) – CSU Archives/Everett Collection, licensed via Alamy
Kerry Melville (Reid) – Creative Commons, Bert Verhoeff (Anefo)
Ash Barty – Creative Commons, Carine06/Flickr
Pat Cash – Trinity Mirror/Mirrorpix, licensed via Alamy
Lleyton Hewitt – Creative Commons, si.robi/Flickr
Sam Stosur – Creative Commons, Carine06/Flickr
Pat Rafter – PA Images/Jon Buckle, licensed via Alamy
Mark Philippoussis – Allstar Picture Library, licensed via Alamy
Nick Kyrgios – Creative Commons, si.robi/Flickr
David Hall – Creative Commons, Australian Paralympic Committee
Dylan Alcott – Creative Commons, Australian Paralympic Committee
Danni Di Toro – Creative Commons, Australian Paralympic Committee
Bob Mark – Creative Commons, Joop van Bilsen/Anefo
Ken Fletcher – Keystone Press, licensed via Alamy
Marjorie Cox (Crawford) – Public Domain, National Library of Australia
Edgar Moon – Public Domain, National Library of Australia
Owen Davidson – Keystone Press, licensed via Alamy
John Fitzgerald – Colaimages, licensed via Alamy
Dick Crealy – Public Domain, National Archives of Australia
Todd Woodbridge – Allstar Picture Library, licensed via Alamy
Mark Woodforde – Reuters, licensed via Alamy
Geoff Masters – Creative Commons, Bert Verhoeff (Anefo)
Matthew Ebden – Creative Commons, si.robi/Flickr
Max Purcell – Creative Commons, si.robi/Flickr
Jordan Thompson – Creative Commons, si.robi/Flickr
Heath Davidson – Creative Commons, Australian Paralympic Committee
Rennae Stubbs – Creative Commons, Robbie Mendelson, Flickr
Storm Sanders (Hunter) – Creative Commons, si.robi/Flickr
John Peers – Creative Commons, si.robi/Flickr

Endnotes

1. https://www.grandslamhistory.com/grand-slam/australian-open
2. https://ausopen.com/history/honour-roll/mens-singles
3. https://web.archive.org/web/20131204221219/
http://www.ausopen.com/en_AU/event_guide/history/draws/1905_MS_1.html
4. https://web.archive.org/web/20150119104354/
http://www.ausopen.com/en_AU/event_guide/history/draws/1924_MS_1.html
5. https://www.tennisfame.com/hall-of-famers/inductees/jack-crawford
6. https://www.tennisfame.com/hall-of-famers/inductees/james-anderson
7. https://www.tennisfame.com/hall-of-famers/inductees/adrian-quist
8. https://ausopen.com/history/honour-roll/mens-singles
9. Ibid.
10. https://peopleaustralia.anu.edu.au/biography/ohara-wood-arthur-holroyd-24295
11. https://www.awm.gov.au/collection/R1520730
12. https://www.tennisfame.com/hall-of-famers/inductees/don-budge
13. https://www.tennisfame.com/hall-of-famers/inductees/john-bromwich
14. https://ausopen.com/history/hall-fame/frank-sedgman#:
15. https://ausopen.com/history/honour-roll/mens-singles
16. Ibid.
17. https://www.tennisfame.com/hall-of-famers/inductees/harry-hopman
18. https://ausopen.com/history/honour-roll/mens-singles
19. https://adb.anu.edu.au/biography/patterson-gerald-leighton-7982#:~:
20. https://ausopen.com/history/honour-roll/mens-singles
21. https://adelaideaz.com/articles/world-tennis-doubles-champ-ken-mcgregor-in-1950s-quite-tennis-to-add-to-family-football-fame-in-adelaide
22. https://www.rolandgarros.com/en-us/palmares
23. https://www.tennisfame.com/hall-of-famers/inductees/henri-cochet
24. https://www.rolandgarros.com/en-us/palmares
25. Ibid.
26. https://www.tennisfame.com/hall-of-famers/inductees/major-walter-clopton-wingfield

27	https://www.britannica.com/sports/Wimbledon-Championships
28	https://trove.nla.gov.au/newspaper/article/139213478
29	https://adb.anu.edu.au/biography/brookes-sir-norman-everard-5373
30	https://www.tennisfame.com/hall-of-famers/inductees/sir-norman-brookes
31	https://www.tennisfame.com/hall-of-famers/inductees/gerald-patterson
32	https://www.tennisfame.com/hall-of-famers/inductees/jack-crawford
33	https://www.youtube.com/watch?v=JlEQDhUNZ1c
34	https://www.wimbledon.com/en_GB/draws_archive/champions/gentlemenssingles.html
35	https://www.tennisfame.com/hall-of-famers/inductees/john-bromwich
36	https://www.tennisfame.com/hall-of-famers/inductees/ken-mcgregor
37	https://www.usopen.org/en_US/visit/history.html
38	https://www.britannica.com/sports/US-Open-tennis
39	Ibid.
40	https://www.usopen.org/en_US/visit/history/mschamps.html
41	Ibid.
42	https://www.wimbledon.com/en_GB/draws_archive/champions/ladiessingles.html
43	https://ausopen.com/history/honour-roll/womens-singles
44	Ibid.
45	https://www.tennisfame.com/hall-of-famers/inductees/nancye-wynne-bolton
46	https://ausopen.com/history/great-champions/daphne-akhurst
47	https://www.tennis.com.au/news/2022/01/04/joan-hartigan-a-pioneering-champion
48	https://adb.anu.edu.au/biography/molesworth-maud-margaret-mall-14985
49	https://www.tennis.com.au/news/2021/12/29/margaret-molesworth-honouring-an-inaugural-champion
50	https://trove.nla.gov.au/newspaper/article/128303503
51	https://trove.nla.gov.au/newspaper/article/50121566
52	https://www.tennisfame.com/hall-of-famers/inductees/thelma-coyne-long
53	https://www.tennis.com.au/news/2021/02/17/mary-carter-reitano-joins-the-australian-tennis-hall-of-fame
54	https://ausopen.com/history/honour-roll/womens-singles
55	https://ausopen.com/history/honour-roll/womens-singles
56	Ibid.
57	Ibid.
58	https://www.tennisfame.com/hall-of-famers/inductees/nancye-wynne-bolton
59	https://tenniscompanion.org/open-era-in-tennis/#:~:
60	https://ausopen.com/history/honour-roll/mens-singles
61	Ibid.

Endnotes

62	McCauley, Joe (2000). The History of Professional Tennis. Windsor: The Short Run Book Company Limited. p. 136.
63	https://www.tennisfame.com/hall-of-famers/inductees/roy-emerson
64	https://www.tennisfame.com/hall-of-famers/inductees/ken-rosewall
65	https://www.tennisfame.com/hall-of-famers/inductees/rod-laver
66	https://www.tennisfame.com/hall-of-famers/inductees/ashley-cooper
67	https://ausopen.com/history/honour-roll/mens-singles
68	https://www.tennis.com.au/player-profiles/neale-fraser
69	https://www.tennisfame.com/hall-of-famers/inductees/fred-stolle
70	https://www.rolandgarros.com/en-us/palmares
71	Ibid.
72	https://www.tennisfame.com/hall-of-famers/inductees/ken-rosewall
73	https://www.itftennis.com/en/about-us/organisation/history-of-the-itf/
74	https://www.tennisfame.com/hall-of-famers/inductees/rod-laver
75	https://www.tennisfame.com/hall-of-famers/inductees/lew-hoad
76	https://www.tennisfame.com/hall-of-famers/inductees/mervyn-rose
77	https://www.tennisfame.com/hall-of-famers/inductees/fred-stolle
78	https://www.tennisfame.com/hall-of-famers/inductees/tony-roche
79	https://www.tennis.com.au/news/2020/02/01/roche-celebrated-at-australian-open
80	https://www.wimbledon.com/en_GB/draws_archive/champions/gentlemenssingles.html
81	https://www.tennisfame.com/hall-of-famers/inductees/rod-laver
82	https://www.tennisfame.com/hall-of-famers/inductees/lew-hoad
83	https://www.wimbledon.com/en_GB/draws_archive/champions/champions.html
84	https://www.wimbledon.com/en_GB/news/articles/2016-09-20/from_the_archive_ashley_cooper_wimbledons_original_marathon_man.html
85	https://www.tennis.com.au/player-profiles/neale-fraser
86	https://www.tennisfame.com/hall-of-famers/inductees/john-newcombe
87	https://www.tennisfame.com/hall-of-famers/inductees/ken-rosewall
88	https://www.tennisfame.com/hall-of-famers/inductees/fred-stolle
89	https://www.wimbledon.com/en_GB/draws_archive/champions/gentlemenssingles.html
90	https://www.usopen.org/en_US/visit/year_by_year.html
91	https://www.tennisfame.com/hall-of-famers/inductees/neale-fraser
92	https://www.tennisfame.com/hall-of-famers/inductees/roy-emerson
93	https://www.tennisfame.com/hall-of-famers/inductees/ken-rosewall
94	https://www.tennisfame.com/hall-of-famers/inductees/rod-laver
95	https://www.tennisfame.com/hall-of-famers/inductees/john-newcombe

96	https://www.tennisfame.com/hall-of-famers/inductees/mal-anderson
97	https://www.tennisfame.com/hall-of-famers/inductees/ashley-cooper
98	https://sahof.org.au/hall-of-fame-member/fred-stolle/
99	https://www.tennis.com.au/player-profiles/rex-hartwig
100	https://www.canberratimes.com.au/story/6139099/gang-gang-fifty-seven-years-ago-lew-turns-pro/
101	https://www.tennisfame.com/hall-of-famers/inductees/lew-hoad
102	https://www.sbs.com.au/news/article/laver-says-turning-pro-made-him-twice-as-good/md7a9ma2n
103	https://www.tennis.com.au/news/2012/11/22/rosewall-reflects-on-pro-struggles
104	https://www.tennisfame.com/hall-of-famers/inductees/margaret-smith-court#:~:
105	https://ausopen.com/history/honour-roll/womens-singles
106	https://www.tennisfame.com/hall-of-famers/inductees/margaret-smith-court#:~:
107	https://www.tennis.com.au/player-profiles/jan-lehane-oneill
108	https://www.tennisfame.com/hall-of-famers/inductees/lesley-turner-bowrey
109	https://www.tennis.com.au/news/2012/05/12/aussies-at-roland-garros-%E2%80%93-margaret-smith-1962
110	https://www.tennisfame.com/hall-of-famers/inductees/margaret-smith-court
111	https://www.tennisfame.com/hall-of-famers/inductees/lesley-turner-bowrey
112	https://www.tennisfame.com/hall-of-famers/inductees/margaret-smith-court
113	Ibid.
114	https://www.youtube.com/watch?v=QNVPbcv_hwk
115	https://www.itftennis.com/en/about-us/organisation/history-of-the-itf/
116	https://ausopen.com/history/honour-roll/mens-singles
117	https://www.wimbledon.com/en_GB/draws_archive/champions/gentlemenssingles.html
118	https://www.usopen.org/en_US/visit/year_by_year.html
119	https://www.rolandgarros.com/en-us/palmares
120	https://www.wimbledon.com/en_GB/news/articles/2016-12-14/from_the_archive_stan_smith_the_man_beyond_the_shoe.html
121	Ibid.
122	https://www.tennis.com.au/news/2012/05/19/aussies-at-roland-garros-%E2%80%93-ken-rosewall-1968
123	https://www.rolandgarros.com/en-us/article/richey-recalls-roland-garros-triumph-1968
124	https://www.tennisfame.com/rod-laver-grand-slam-anniversary-celebration
125	https://www.wimbledon.com/en_GB/about_wimbledon/prize_money_and_finance.html

Endnotes

126	https://www.tennisfame.com/hall-of-famers/inductees/rod-laver
127	https://www.tennis.com/news/articles/the-career-centerpiece-john-newcombe-s-halcyon-wimbledon-days
128	https://vault.si.com/vault/1972/02/21/lose-a-battle-and-a-war
129	https://www.tennis.com/news/articles/the-career-centerpiece-john-newcombe-s-halcyon-wimbledon-days
130	https://www.tennisfame.com/hall-of-famers/inductees/tony-roche
131	https://www.tennisfame.com/hall-of-famers/inductees/ken-rosewall
132	https://www.britannica.com/sports/US-Open-tennis
133	Rod Laver: A Memoir (Pan Macmillan Australia, 2013).
134	https://tennis-buzz.com/1969-us-open-rod-laver-completes-his-second-grand-slam/
135	https://www.tennisfame.com/rod-laver-grand-slam-anniversary-celebration
136	https://www.tennisfame.com/hall-of-famers/inductees/rod-laver
137	https://www.usopen.org/en_US/news/articles/2020-09-02/the_us_open_introduced_the_tiebreak_set_50_years_ago_today.html
138	https://www.tennisworldusa.org/tennis/news/Blast_From_the_Past/60150/us-open-1974-jimmy-connors-thumps-ken-rosewall-for-maiden-us-open-crown/
139	https://www.usopen.org/en_US/visit/year_by_year.html
140	https://www.nytimes.com/1973/09/10/archives/newcombe-wins-us-tennis-title-newcombe-defeats-kodes-for-us-tennis.html
141	https://www.tennisfame.com/hall-of-famers/inductees/john-newcombe
142	https://ausopen.com/history/honour-roll/mens-singles
143	https://www.tennisfame.com/hall-of-famers/inductees/ken-rosewall
144	https://www.tennisfame.com/hall-of-famers/inductees/john-newcombe
145	https://www.tennisfame.com/hall-of-famers/inductees/rod-laver
146	https://edition.cnn.com/videos/sports/2016/01/25/spc-open-court-mark-edmondson.cnn
147	https://www.tennis.com.au/player-profiles/mark-edmondson
148	https://www.tennisfame.com/hall-of-famers/inductees/margaret-smith-court
149	https://www.tennisfame.com/hall-of-famers/inductees/evonne-goolagong
150	https://www.tennis.com.au/news/2012/05/21/aussies-at-roland-garros-%E2%80%93-margaret-court-1970
151	https://www.tennisfame.com/hall-of-famers/inductees/margaret-smith-court
152	https://www.tennisfame.com/hall-of-famers/inductees/evonne-goolagong
153	https://www.tennisfame.com/hall-of-famers/inductees/billie-jean-king
154	https://www.rolandgarros.com/en-us/article/rg2021-50-year-rewind-goolagong-cawley-relives-breakthrough-major-title
155	https://www.wtatennis.com/news/2015724/legacy-spotlight-helen-gourlay

156	https://www.rolandgarros.com/en-us/article/rg2021-50-year-rewind-goolagong-cawley-relives-breakthrough-major-title
157	https://www.tennis.com.au/player-profiles/wendy-turnbull
158	https://www.tennis.com.au/news/2021/07/03/a-wimbledon-dream-goolagong-cawley-and-newcombe-look-back
159	https://www.wtatennis.com/news/1701157/-it-s-not-that-easy-after-children-goolagong-on-1980-wimbledon-win
160	https://bleacherreport.com/articles/1679890-the-most-memorable-matches-in-wimbledon-history
161	https://www.foxsports.com.au/tennis/tennis-makes-major-change-to-scoring-system-at-grand-slams/news-story/39e8834124f6ab926c481fc0927c34b3
162	https://www.tennisfame.com/hall-of-famers/inductees/margaret-smith-court
163	https://www.tennis.com.au/player-profiles/judy-tegart-dalton
164	https://tennismash.com/2018/04/22/australians-original-9-dalton-reid/
165	https://www.espn.com/tennis/story/_/id/24599816/us-open-follow-money-how-pay-gap-grand-slam-tennis-closed
166	https://www.tennisfame.com/hall-of-famers/inductees/margaret-smith-court
167	https://www.cbssports.com/tennis/news/tennis-legend-margaret-court-says-serena-williams-media-have-never-admired-her/
168	https://www.tennisfame.com/hall-of-famers/inductees/evonne-goolagong
169	https://www.tennis.com.au/player-profiles/kerry-melville-reid
170	https://tennismash.com/2018/04/22/australians-original-9-dalton-reid/
171	https://www.tennis.com.au/player-profiles/wendy-turnbull
172	https://ausopen.club/history/
173	https://ausopen.com/history/honour-roll/womens-singles
174	https://www.wtatennis.com/photos/1406226/maternal-glow-mothers-who-have-won-slams
175	https://www.tennisfame.com/hall-of-famers/inductees/margaret-smith-court
176	https://www.tennisfame.com/hall-of-famers/inductees/evonne-goolagong
177	https://www.tennis.com.au/player-profiles/kerry-melville-reid
178	https://www.tennis.com.au/player-profiles/chris-o%E2%80%99neil
179	https://ausopen.club/history/
180	https://www.espn.com/tennis/story/_/id/24599816/us-open-follow-money-how-pay-gap-grand-slam-tennis-closed
181	https://ausopen.com/history/honour-roll/womens-singles
182	https://ausopen.com/history/honour-roll
183	https://www.tennis.com.au/player-profiles/ashleigh-barty
184	https://ausopen.com/articles/news/ash-barty-retires-ive-given-absolutely-everything

Endnotes

185 https://www.amazon.com/Uncovered-Autobiography-Pat-Cash/dp/1903267080
186 https://www.daviscup.com/en/draws-results/tie.aspx?id=M-DC-1986-WG-M-AUS-SWE-01
187 https://www.tennis.com.au/player-profiles/pat-cash
188 https://www.tennis.com.au/player-profiles/lleyton-hewitt
189 https://www.espn.com/tennis/story/_/id/24599816/us-open-follow-money-how-pay-gap-grand-slam-tennis-closed
190 https://www.rolandgarros.com/en-us/palmares
191 https://wwos.nine.com.au/tennis/ash-barty/ff8bcbe1-2636-4671-9d41-3430f81cd841
192 https://www.wimbledon.com/en_GB/draws_archive/index.html
193 https://www.espn.com/tennis/story/_/id/24599816/us-open-follow-money-how-pay-gap-grand-slam-tennis-closed
194 https://www.atptour.com/en/news/atp-heritage-cash-1987-wimbledon
195 https://www.thesportsman.com/articles/winning-the-title-is-an-amazing-feeling-lleyton-hewitt-on-his-2002-wimbledon-glory
196 https://www.nma.gov.au/explore/blog/ash-barty-wimbledon-2021-outfit
197 https://www.abc.net.au/news/2021-07-11/how-ash-barty-sealed-her-wimbledon-dream-win/100283646
198 https://www.atptour.com/en/news/flashback-agassi-rafter-wimbledon-rivalry
199 https://www.tennis.com/news/articles/pete-sampras-no-1-achievement-wasn-t-his-14-grand-slam-titles
200 https://www.atptour.com/en/news/wimbledon-best-wild-card-runs
201 https://www.daviscup.com/en/news/317229.aspx
202 https://www.tennis.com.au/player-profiles/mark-philippoussis
203 https://www.tennis.com.au/news/2022/07/11/nick-kyrgios-beaten-in-wimbledon-2022-singles-final
204 https://www.tennis.com/news/articles/novak-djokovic-wins-record-breaking-23rd-career-grand-slam-title-roland-garros
205 https://www.usopen.org/en_US/visit/history/mschamps.html
206 https://www.espn.com/tennis/story/_/id/24599816/us-open-follow-money-how-pay-gap-grand-slam-tennis-closed
207 https://www.foxsports.com.au/tennis/us-open/from-good-bloke-to-tennis-great-marking-20-years-since-pat-rafters-breakthrough-major-win-at-1997-us-open/news-story/41eccf9af89ab6e13caad440da0625d9
208 https://archive.nytimes.com/www.nytimes.com/library/sports/090897ten-us-open-men.html
209 https://www.tennis.com.au/news/2020/09/11/flashback-friday-rafter-beats-philippoussis-in-us-open-1998-final

210	https://bleacherreport.com/articles/319283-history-repeats-what-sampras-rafter-can-teach-us-about-nadal-soderling
211	https://www.tennis.com.au/news/2020/09/04/flashback-friday-lleyton-hewitt-wins-2001-us-open-title
212	https://bleacherreport.com/articles/2556450-ranking-the-most-disappointing-losses-in-us-open-history
213	https://www.tennisworldusa.org/tennis/news/ATP_Tennis/47269/september-12-2004-roger-federer-destroys-hewitt-to-clinch-first-us-open/
214	https://www.foxsports.com.au/tennis/stosur-fights-for-epic-win/news-story/f452c5842767839140762cc912972514
215	https://archive.nytimes.com/straightsets.blogs.nytimes.com/2011/09/04/stosur-outlasts-kirilenko/?scp=2&sq=Stosur%2520longest&st=cse
216	https://www.foxsports.com.au/tennis/slammin-sam-shows-petulant-serena-how-to-act-like-a-lady-s-grace-and-humility-triumph-in-final/news-story/9da122054e199a7ba9d0b826d23390b7
217	https://www.tennis.com.au/news/2020/09/11/flashback-friday-rafter-beats-philippoussis-in-us-open-1998-final
218	https://www.foxsports.com.au/tennis/walk-on-the-wild-side/news-story/b17ed61742ef6ebf37ca8aefaf951510
219	https://www.paralympic.org/wheelchair-tennis/classification#:~
220	https://www.theguardian.com/sport/2016/jul/06/wimbledon-first-wheelchair-tennis-singles-tournament
221	https://www.tennis.com.au/news/2019/07/13/dylan-alcott-wins-wimbledon-quad-singles-title
222	https://ausopen.com/history/honour-roll/mens-wheelchair-singles
223	https://www.paralympic.org.au/david-hall-oam/
224	https://www.tennisfame.com/hall-of-famers/inductees/david-hall
225	https://ausopen.com/history/honour-roll/mens-quad-wheelchair-singles
226	https://www.tennis.com.au/news/2019/06/08/alcott-wins-french-open-quad-title
227	https://www.abc.net.au/news/2020-10-11/superb-dylan-alcott-wins-french-open-take-11th-grand-slam-title/12752122
228	https://www.foxsports.com.au/tennis/french-open/french-open-2021-results-dylan-alcott-mens-wheelchair-singles-winner-rafael-nadal-record-roland-garros/news-story/e1aa9bedfa68c1303b590820519f4b3e
229	https://www.foxsports.com.au/tennis/wimbledon/australian-no1-dylan-alcott-wins-inaugural-quad-wheelchair-singles-final-at-wimbledon/news-story/6b6908de06d260ae65798345702f90d3
230	https://www.wimbledon.com/en_GB/news/articles/2020-04-01/cancellation_of_the_

Endnotes

championships_2020.html
231 https://www.tennis.com.au/news/2021/07/10/dylan-alcott-crowned-wimbledon-champion
232 https://www.abc.net.au/news/2015-09-14/dylan-alcott-wins-epic-us-open-wheelchair-quad-final/6773660
233 https://www.usopen.org/en_US/news/articles/2018-01-29/2018_us_open_spotlight_dylan_alcott.html
234 https://www.paralympic.org/news/us-open-2019-andy-lapthorne-leads-grand-slam-winners
235 https://www.tennis.com.au/news/2021/09/13/dylan-alcott-completes-golden-slam
236 https://www.theguardian.com/australia-news/2022/jan/25/i-am-so-lucky-five-things-to-know-about-2022-australian-of-the-year-dylan-alcott
237 https://www.tennis.com.au/player-profiles/dylan-alcott
238 https://ausopen.com/articles/news/congratulations-dylan-alcott-2022-australian-year#:~:
239 https://www.paralympic.org.au/athlete/dylan-alcott/#:~:
240 https://www.tennis.com.au/player-profiles/daniela-di-toro
241 https://engagingwomen.com.au/stories/paralympian-daniella-di-toro/
242 https://www.abc.net.au/news/2016-05-27/daniela-di-toro-on-positivity-and-playing-for-fun/7449940
243 https://www.paralympic.org.au/athlete/danni-di-toro/
244 https://www.smh.com.au/sport/tennis/why-dylan-alcott-and-heath-davidson-are-the-best-mates-worth-cheering-for-20210831-p58nh1.html
245 https://ausopen.com/history/honour-roll
246 https://www.rolandgarros.com/en-us/palmares
247 https://www.wimbledon.com/en_GB/draws_archive/champions/champions.html
248 https://www.usopen.org/en_US/visit/year_by_year.html
249 https://www.britannica.com/sports/US-Open-tennis
250 https://ausopen.com/history/honour-roll/mens-doubles
251 https://www.wimbledon.com/en_GB/draws_archive/index.html
252 https://www.britannica.com/sports/French-Open
253 https://www.tennisfame.com/hall-of-famers/inductees/adrian-quist
254 https://www.tennisfame.com/hall-of-famers/inductees/john-bromwich
255 https://www.tennisfame.com/hall-of-famers/inductees/gerald-patterson
256 https://adb.anu.edu.au/biography/ohara-wood-hector-pat-7895
257 https://www.tennisfame.com/hall-of-famers/inductees/harry-hopman
258 https://www.tennisfame.com/hall-of-famers/inductees/jack-crawford
259 https://www.tennisfame.com/hall-of-famers/inductees/lew-hoad

260	https://www.tennisfame.com/hall-of-famers/inductees/ken-rosewall
261	https://www.tennisfame.com/hall-of-famers/inductees/neale-fraser
262	https://www.tennisfame.com/hall-of-famers/inductees/rod-laver
263	https://www.tennisfame.com/hall-of-famers/inductees/fred-stolle
264	https://www.tennis.com.au/player-profiles/rodney-heath
265	https://wais.org.au/hallofchampions/ernest-parker/
266	https://ausopen.com/history/honour-roll/mens-doubles
267	https://www.tennisfame.com/hall-of-famers/inductees/frank-sedgman
268	https://www.tennisfame.com/hall-of-famers/inductees/ken-mcgregor
269	https://www.tennisfame.com/hall-of-famers/inductees/roy-emerson
270	https://www.tennisfame.com/hall-of-famers/inductees/john-newcombe
271	https://ausopen.com/history/honour-roll/mens-doubles
272	Ibid.
273	https://www.infosportsworld.com/french-open-doubles-champions-list/
274	https://www.tennisfame.com/hall-of-famers/inductees/roy-emerson
275	https://www.tennisfame.com/hall-of-famers/inductees/neale-fraser
276	https://www.tennisfame.com/hall-of-famers/inductees/frank-sedgman
277	https://www.tennisfame.com/hall-of-famers/inductees/ashley-cooper
278	https://www.tennisfame.com/hall-of-famers/inductees/jack-crawford
279	https://www.tennisfame.com/hall-of-famers/inductees/adrian-quist
280	https://www.tennisfame.com/hall-of-famers/inductees/lew-hoad
281	https://www.tennisfame.com/hall-of-famers/inductees/ken-rosewall
282	https://www.britannica.com/sports/French-Open
283	https://www.tennisfame.com/hall-of-famers/inductees/mal-anderson
284	https://www.tennisfame.com/hall-of-famers/inductees/rod-laver
285	https://www.tennis.com.au/player-profiles/ken-fletcher
286	https://www.tennisfame.com/hall-of-famers/inductees/fred-stolle
287	https://www.tennisfame.com/hall-of-famers/inductees/john-newcombe
288	https://www.britannica.com/sports/French-Open
289	https://www.wimbledon.com/en_GB/draws_archive/index.html
290	https://www.tennisfame.com/hall-of-famers/inductees/frank-sedgman
291	https://www.tennisfame.com/hall-of-famers/inductees/lew-hoad
292	https://www.tennisfame.com/hall-of-famers/inductees/ken-rosewall
293	https://www.tennisfame.com/hall-of-famers/inductees/sir-norman-brookes
294	https://www.tennisfame.com/hall-of-famers/inductees/anthony-wilding
295	https://www.tennisfame.com/hall-of-famers/inductees/adrian-quist
296	https://www.tennisfame.com/hall-of-famers/inductees/john-bromwich#:~:
297	https://www.tennis.com.au/player-profiles/rex-hartwig

Endnotes

298	https://www.tennisfame.com/hall-of-famers/inductees/roy-emerson
299	https://www.tennisfame.com/hall-of-famers/inductees/neale-fraser
300	https://www.tennisfame.com/hall-of-famers/inductees/fred-stolle
301	https://www.wimbledon.com/en_GB/draws_archive/index.html
302	https://www.tennisfame.com/hall-of-famers/inductees/john-newcombe
303	https://www.wimbledon.com/en_GB/draws_archive/index.html
304	https://www.tennisfame.com/hall-of-famers/inductees/james-anderson
305	https://www.tennisfame.com/hall-of-famers/inductees/jack-crawford
306	https://www.tennisfame.com/hall-of-famers/inductees/mervyn-rose
307	https://www.tennis.com.au/player-profiles/ken-fletcher
308	https://www.wimbledon.com/en_GB/draws_archive/index.html
309	https://www.usopen.org/en_US/visit/year_by_year.html
310	https://www.tennisfame.com/hall-of-famers/inductees/roy-emerson
311	https://www.tennisfame.com/hall-of-famers/inductees/john-bromwich
312	https://www.tennisfame.com/hall-of-famers/inductees/neale-fraser
313	https://www.tennisfame.com/hall-of-famers/inductees/frank-sedgman
314	https://www.tennisfame.com/hall-of-famers/inductees/mervyn-rose
315	https://www.tennisfame.com/hall-of-famers/inductees/fred-stolle
316	https://www.tennisfame.com/hall-of-famers/inductees/gerald-patterson
317	https://www.tennisfame.com/hall-of-famers/inductees/adrian-quist
318	https://tributes.smh.com.au/obituaries/418115/oswald-william-thomas-sidwell/?r= https://tributes.smh.com.au/obituaries/smh-au/
319	https://www.tennis.com.au/news/2022/12/31/tribute-remembering-rex-hartwig
320	https://www.tennisfame.com/hall-of-famers/inductees/ken-rosewall
321	https://www.tennisfame.com/hall-of-famers/inductees/ashley-cooper
322	https://www.tennisfame.com/hall-of-famers/inductees/john-newcombe
323	https://www.usopen.org/en_US/visit/year_by_year.html
324	https://ausopen.com/history/honour-roll/womens-doubles
325	https://www.britannica.com/sports/French-Open
326	https://www.wimbledon.com/en_GB/draws_archive/index.html
327	https://www.britannica.com/sports/US-Open-tennis
328	https://www.tennisfame.com/hall-of-famers/inductees/nancye-wynne-bolton
329	https://www.tennisfame.com/hall-of-famers/inductees/thelma-coyne-long
330	https://ausopen.com/history/honour-roll/womens-doubles
331	Ibid.
332	https://www.tennisfame.com/hall-of-famers/inductees/daphne-akhurst
333	https://www.tennisfame.com/hall-of-famers/inductees/margaret-smith-court
334	https://ausopen.com/history/honour-roll/womens-doubles

335	https://adb.anu.edu.au/biography/molesworth-maud-margaret-mall-14985
336	https://ausopen.com/history/honour-roll/womens-doubles
337	https://www.tennisfame.com/hall-of-famers/inductees/lesley-turner-bowrey
338	https://ausopen.com/history/honour-roll/womens-doubles
339	Ibid.
340	https://www.tennis.com.au/player-profiles/beryl-penrose-collier
341	https://ausopen.com/history/honour-roll/womens-doubles
342	https://www.tennis.com.au/player-profiles/judy-tegart-dalton
343	https://ausopen.com/history/honour-roll/womens-doubles
344	Ibid.
345	https://www.britannica.com/sports/French-Open
346	https://www.tennisfame.com/hall-of-famers/inductees/margaret-smith-court
347	https://adb.anu.edu.au/biography/hopman-eleanor-mary-nell-10543
348	https://www.tennis.com.au/player-profiles/judy-tegart-dalton
349	https://www.britannica.com/sports/French-Open
350	https://www.wimbledon.com/en_GB/draws_archive/index.html
351	https://www.tennisfame.com/hall-of-famers/inductees/lesley-turner-bowrey
352	https://www.tennisfame.com/hall-of-famers/inductees/margaret-smith-court
353	https://www.wimbledon.com/en_GB/draws_archive/index.html
354	https://www.usopen.org/en_US/visit/year_by_year.html
355	https://www.tennisfame.com/hall-of-famers/inductees/lesley-turner-bowrey
356	https://www.tennisfame.com/hall-of-famers/inductees/margaret-smith-court
357	https://www.usopen.org/en_US/visit/year_by_year.html
358	https://ausopen.com/history/honour-roll/mixed-doubles
359	https://www.britannica.com/sports/French-Open
360	https://www.wimbledon.com/en_GB/draws_archive/index.html
361	https://www.britannica.com/sports/US-Open-tennis
362	https://www.tennisfame.com/hall-of-famers/inductees/daphne-akhurst
363	https://adb.anu.edu.au/biography/hopman-eleanor-mary-nell-10543
364	https://www.tennisfame.com/hall-of-famers/inductees/nancye-wynne-bolton
365	https://ausopen.com/history/honour-roll/
366	https://www.tennisfame.com/hall-of-famers/inductees/jack-crawford
367	https://bleacherreport.com/articles/302534-queens-of-the-court-the-queen-of-them-all-margaret-court
368	https://ausopen.com/history/honour-roll/mixed-doubles
369	Ibid.
370	https://www.tennisfame.com/hall-of-famers/inductees/frank-sedgman
371	https://www.tennis.com.au/news/2022/12/31/tribute-remembering-rex-hartwig

Endnotes

372	https://www.tennis.com.au/player-profiles/jan-lehane-oneill
373	https://www.tennisfame.com/hall-of-famers/inductees/lesley-turner-bowrey
374	https://www.tennisfame.com/hall-of-famers/inductees/owen-davidson
375	https://ausopen.com/history/honour-roll/mixed-doubles
376	Ibid.
377	https://www.britannica.com/sports/French-Open
378	https://www.tennisfame.com/hall-of-famers/inductees/margaret-smith-court
379	https://www.tennisfame.com/hall-of-famers/inductees/frank-sedgman
380	https://www.britannica.com/sports/French-Open
381	https://www.tennisfame.com/hall-of-famers/inductees/jack-crawford
382	https://www.tennisfame.com/hall-of-famers/inductees/lew-hoad
383	https://www.tennisfame.com/hall-of-famers/inductees/thelma-coyne-long
384	https://www.tennisfame.com/hall-of-famers/inductees/rod-laver
385	https://www.latimes.com/sports/story/2021-12-04/appreciation-the-quiet-extraordinary-life-of-tennis-champ-darlene-hard-aka-darlene-in-publications
386	https://www.tennisfame.com/hall-of-famers/inductees/owen-davidson
387	https://www.britannica.com/sports/French-Open
388	https://www.wimbledon.com/en_GB/draws_archive/index.html
389	https://www.tennisfame.com/hall-of-famers/inductees/margaret-smith-court
390	https://www.tennisfame.com/hall-of-famers/inductees/john-bromwich
391	https://www.wimbledon.com/en_GB/news/articles/2022-07-05/sedgman_marks_70_years_since_his_wimbledon_triple_feat.html
392	https://www.tennisfame.com/hall-of-famers/inductees/frank-sedgman
393	https://www.tennisfame.com/hall-of-famers/inductees/rod-laver
394	https://www.tennisfame.com/hall-of-famers/inductees/fred-stolle
395	https://www.tennisfame.com/hall-of-famers/inductees/gerald-patterson
396	https://adb.anu.edu.au/biography/ohara-wood-hector-pat-7895
397	https://www.tennisfame.com/hall-of-famers/inductees/jack-crawford
398	https://www.tennisfame.com/hall-of-famers/inductees/mervyn-rose
399	https://www.wimbledon.com/en_GB/draws_archive/index.html
400	https://www.tennisfame.com/hall-of-famers/inductees/neale-fraser
401	https://www.tennisfame.com/hall-of-famers/inductees/owen-davidson
402	https://www.wimbledon.com/en_GB/draws_archive/index.html
403	https://www.usopen.org/en_US/visit/year_by_year.html
404	https://www.tennisfame.com/hall-of-famers/inductees/margaret-smith-court
405	https://sahof.org.au/hall-of-fame-member/neale-fraser/
406	https://www.usopen.org/en_US/visit/year_by_year.html
407	https://www.tennisfame.com/hall-of-famers/inductees/fred-stolle

408	https://www.tennisfame.com/hall-of-famers/inductees/owen-davidson
409	https://www.amazon.com/Science-Lawn-Tennis-Edward-Dewhurst/dp/1010575856
410	https://www.tennisfame.com/hall-of-famers/inductees/harry-hopman
411	https://www.usopen.org/en_US/visit/year_by_year.html
412	https://www.tennisfame.com/hall-of-famers/inductees/ken-mcgregor
413	https://www.tennisfame.com/hall-of-famers/inductees/ken-rosewall
414	https://www.usopen.org/en_US/visit/year_by_year.html
415	https://www.tennis.com.au/player-profiles/ken-fletcher
416	https://www.tennisfame.com/hall-of-famers/inductees/john-newcombe
417	https://www.usopen.org/en_US/visit/year_by_year.html
418	https://www.britannica.com/sports/French-Open
419	https://www.tennisfame.com/hall-of-famers/inductees/john-newcombe
420	https://www.britannica.com/sports/French-Open
421	https://www.tennisfame.com/hall-of-famers/inductees/ken-rosewall
422	https://www.tennis.com.au/player-profiles/dick-crealy
423	https://www.tennis.com.au/player-profiles/mark-edmondson
424	https://www.tennisfame.com/hall-of-famers/inductees/todd-woodbridge
425	https://www.britannica.com/sports/French-Open
426	https://www.wimbledon.com/en_GB/draws_archive/index.html
427	https://www.tennisfame.com/hall-of-famers/inductees/todd-woodbridge
428	https://www.tennisfame.com/hall-of-famers/inductees/john-newcombe
429	https://www.tennis.com.au/player-profiles/peter-mcnamara
430	https://www.tennis.com.au/player-profiles/john-fitzgerald
431	https://www.tennisfame.com/hall-of-famers/inductees/roy-emerson
432	https://www.tennis.com.au/player-profiles/geoff-masters
433	https://www.tennis.com.au/player-profiles/stephen-huss
434	https://www.tennis.com.au/player-profiles/matt-ebden
435	https://www.wimbledon.com/en_GB/draws_archive/index.html
436	https://www.usopen.org/en_US/visit/year_by_year.html
437	https://www.tennisfame.com/hall-of-famers/inductees/mark-woodforde
438	https://www.tennisfame.com/hall-of-famers/inductees/todd-woodbridge
439	https://www.tennisfame.com/hall-of-famers/inductees/john-newcombe
440	https://www.tennis.com.au/player-profiles/john-fitzgerald
441	https://www.tennisfame.com/hall-of-famers/inductees/fred-stolle
442	https://www.tennisfame.com/hall-of-famers/inductees/owen-davidson
443	https://www.usopen.org/en_US/visit/year_by_year.html
444	https://www.tennis.com.au/player-profiles/lleyton-hewitt
445	https://www.usopen.org/en_US/visit/year_by_year.html

Endnotes

446	https://ausopen.com/history/honour-roll/mens-doubles
447	https://ausopen.com/history/hall-fame/mark-edmondson
448	https://ausopen.com/history/honour-roll/mens-doubles
449	Ibid.
450	Ibid.
451	Ibid.
452	Ibid.
453	https://ausopen.com/history/honour-roll/mens-doubles
454	Ibid.
455	https://www.paralympic.org/wheelchair-tennis/classification#:~
456	https://ausopen.com/history/honour-roll/mens-wheelchair-doubles
457	https://www.wimbledon.com/en_GB/draws_archive/events.html
458	https://www.usopen.org/en_US/visit/year_by_year.html
459	https://www.britannica.com/sports/French-Open
460	https://www.paralympic.org.au/athlete/dylan-alcott/
461	https://www.tennis.com.au/news/2023/06/10/davidson-and-shaw-beaten-in-roland-garros-doubles-final
462	https://ausopen.com/history/honour-roll
463	https://www.rolandgarros.com/en-us/palmares
464	https://www.wimbledon.com/en_GB/draws_archive/champions/champions.html
465	https://www.usopen.org/en_US/visit/year_by_year.html
466	https://www.britannica.com/sports/French-Open
467	https://www.tennisfame.com/hall-of-famers/inductees/margaret-smith-court
468	https://www.tennis.com.au/player-profiles/wendy-turnbull
469	https://www.tennis.com.au/player-profiles/sam-stosur
470	https://www.tennis.com.au/player-profiles/alicia-molik
471	https://www.britannica.com/sports/French-Open
472	https://www.wimbledon.com/en_GB/draws_archive/index.html
473	https://www.tennis.com.au/player-profiles/rennae-stubbs
474	https://www.tennisfame.com/hall-of-famers/inductees/margaret-smith-court
475	https://www.tennisfame.com/hall-of-famers/inductees/evonne-goolagong
476	https://www.wimbledon.com/en_GB/draws_archive/events.html
477	https://www.tennis.com.au/player-profiles/kerry-melville-reid
478	https://www.tennis.com.au/player-profiles/elizabeth-sayers-smylie
479	https://www.wimbledon.com/en_GB/draws_archive/index.html
480	https://www.usopen.org/en_US/visit/year_by_year.html
481	https://www.tennisfame.com/hall-of-famers/inductees/margaret-smith-court
482	https://www.tennis.com.au/player-profiles/judy-tegart-dalton

483	https://www.tennis.com.au/player-profiles/wendy-turnbull
484	https://www.tennis.com.au/player-profiles/sam-stosur
485	https://www.tennis.com.au/player-profiles/rennae-stubbs
486	https://www.tennis.com.au/player-profiles/ashleigh-barty
487	https://www.usopen.org/en_US/visit/year_by_year.html
488	https://ausopen.com/history/honour-roll/womens-doubles
489	https://www.tennisfame.com/hall-of-famers/inductees/evonne-goolagong
490	https://www.tennisfame.com/hall-of-famers/inductees/margaret-smith-court
491	https://ausopen.com/history/honour-roll/womens-doubles
492	Ibid.
493	Ibid.
494	https://ausopen.com/history/honour-roll/womens-wheelchair-doubles
495	https://www.usopen.org/en_US/visit/year_by_year.html
496	https://www.britannica.com/sports/French-Open
497	https://www.wimbledon.com/en_GB/draws_archive/events.html
498	https://www.rolandgarros.com/en-us/palmares
499	https://ausopen.com/articles/news/dalton-reid-aussie-original-9-members-who-helped-found-womens-pro-tennis
500	https://ausopen.com/history/honour-roll
501	https://www.rolandgarros.com/en-us/palmares
502	https://www.wimbledon.com/en_GB/draws_archive/champions/champions.html
503	https://www.usopen.org/en_US/visit/year_by_year.html
504	https://www.britannica.com/sports/French-Open
505	Ibid.
506	https://www.tennis.com.au/player-profiles/wendy-turnbull
507	https://www.tennisfame.com/hall-of-famers/inductees/margaret-smith-court
508	https://www.tennisfame.com/hall-of-famers/inductees/evonne-goolagong
509	https://www.tennisfame.com/hall-of-famers/inductees/todd-woodbridge
510	https://www.tennisfame.com/hall-of-famers/inductees/mark-woodforde
511	https://www.tennis.com.au/player-profiles/casey-dellacqua
512	https://www.britannica.com/sports/French-Open
513	https://www.wimbledon.com/en_GB/draws_archive/index.html
514	https://www.tennisfame.com/hall-of-famers/inductees/margaret-smith-court
515	https://www.tennis.com.au/player-profiles/wendy-turnbull
516	https://www.tennis.com.au/player-profiles/sam-stosur
517	https://www.tennisfame.com/hall-of-famers/inductees/fred-stolle
518	https://www.tennisfame.com/hall-of-famers/inductees/owen-davidson
519	https://www.tennisfame.com/hall-of-famers/inductees/tony-roche

Endnotes

520	https://www.wimbledon.com/en_GB/draws_archive/index.html
521	https://www.tennis.com.au/player-profiles/john-fitzgerald
522	https://www.tennisfame.com/hall-of-famers/inductees/mark-woodforde
523	https://www.tennisfame.com/hall-of-famers/inductees/todd-woodbridge
524	https://www.wimbledon.com/en_GB/draws_archive/index.html
525	https://www.usopen.org/en_US/visit/year_by_year.html
526	https://www.tennisfame.com/hall-of-famers/inductees/margaret-smith-court
527	https://www.tennisfame.com/hall-of-famers/inductees/todd-woodbridge
528	https://www.tennisfame.com/hall-of-famers/inductees/owen-davidson
529	https://www.tennis.com.au/player-profiles/elizabeth-sayers-smylie
530	https://www.tennis.com.au/player-profiles/geoff-masters
531	https://www.tennis.com.au/player-profiles/phil-dent
532	https://www.tennis.com.au/player-profiles/wendy-turnbull
533	https://www.tennis.com.au/player-profiles/nicole-provis-bradtke
534	https://www.tennis.com.au/player-profiles/rennae-stubbs
535	https://www.tennis.com.au/player-profiles/storm-sanders
536	https://www.usopen.org/en_US/visit/year_by_year.html
537	https://ausopen.com/history/honour-roll/mixed-doubles
538	https://www.tennisfame.com/hall-of-famers/inductees/mark-woodforde
539	https://ausopen.com/history/honour-roll/mixed-doubles
540	Ibid.
541	https://ausopen.com/history/honour-roll
542	https://www.rolandgarros.com/en-us/palmares
543	https://www.wimbledon.com/en_GB/draws_archive/champions/champions.html
544	https://www.usopen.org/en_US/visit/year_by_year.html
545	https://www.grandslamhistory.com/stats/grand-slam/all

www.ingramcontent.com/pod-product-compliance
Lightning Source LLC
Chambersburg PA
CBHW060526010526
44107CB00059B/2612